How to Become
a Master
Sales Builder

HOW TO BECOME A MASTER SALES BUILDER:
Personal Selling Power's Blueprint for Success

Gerhard Gschwandtner

Prentice-Hall, Inc.
Englewood Cliffs, New Jersey 07632

Prentice-Hall International, Inc., *London*
Prentice-Hall of Australia, Pty. Ltd., *Sydney*
Prentice-Hall Canada, Inc., *Toronto*
Prentice-Hall of India Private Ltd., *New Delhi*
Prentice-Hall of Japan, Inc., *Tokyo*
Prentice-Hall of Southeast Asia Pte. Ltd., *Singapore*
Whitehall Books, Ltd., Wellington, *New Zealand*
Editora Prentice-Hall do Brasil Ltda., *Rio de Janeiro*
Prentice-Hall Hispanoamericana, S.A., *Mexico*

© 1987 *by*

PRENTICE-HALL, INC.

Englewood Cliffs, N.J.

Library of Congress Cataloging-in-Publication Data

Gschwandtner, Gerhard.
   How to become a master sales builder.

   1. Selling.   I. Title.
HF5438.25.G78   1987   658.8′5   86-17037

ISBN 0-13-396177-X

Printed in the United States of America.

DEDICATION

To the professional salesperson
who strives for excellence

Do You Want to Become a Professional Salesperson?

There are over ten million salespeople in this country. However, in the eyes of some of the leading sales experts, like Larry Wilson and Zig Ziglar, only very few can be considered professionals—perhaps only one in ten.

Although amateurs and professionals may look alike in appearance and grooming, they are significantly different in the way they deal with a customer.

Where amateurs talk *at* the prospect, the professional listens to the person *behind* the prospect. Where amateurs are preoccupied with *price* and *discounts,* the professional focuses on customer *needs* and *benefits.* While amateurs leave loose ends *untied* the professional *follows up.* In essence, the professional salesperson uses knowledge and skills for the sole purpose of helping other people, thus creating a true win/win situation. While amateurs haggle over who will get a bigger slice of the pie, the professional helps create more pies for everyone!

As a result, the nine million amateur salespeople in this country pay the price of mediocrity while the one million professional salespeople earn a good living and the respect of their customers.

By now you're probably asking yourself, "How can I transcend the amateur status?" You can begin with a *commitment* to professionalism. Only *you* can make this decision. And once you've decided to commit your energies to developing professional skills and knowledge, you will begin to avoid the problems amateurs create through a lack of commitment.

Many amateurs keep themselves from becoming professionals because their real career interests lie elsewhere. This one really wants to be a teacher, another one has dreams of running a vineyard and another one has frustrated ambitions of becoming a writer. The sad truth is that none of them is a professional at selling—or at anything else.

People always confuse the term occupation with profession. It doesn't matter what the occupation; if you don't approach it with a professional attitude, you cannot expect to be successful.

You cannot reach success in any field without first reaching the stage of professionalism.

Acknowledgments

This book would not be possible without the expert contributions of the nation's most respected sales professionals. Their support of *Personal Selling Power,* and this project, is invaluable. We have added a special reference section at the end of the book that includes their names and addresses so that you can obtain further information on specific topics.

We would also like to thank Laura B Gschwandtner for her help with layout and visuals, and the staff of *Personal Selling Power* for their cooperation when we monopolized their typewriters and the copy machine for "just one more article."

Gerhard Gschwandtner

How This Book
Will Help You Build Sales

During the past four years, PERSONAL SELLING POWER, the country's leading sales education/motivation publication, has selected some of the best sales building articles written by the nation's leading sales experts. The authors are all top sales professionals and noted seminar leaders with extensive experience in selling and sales management.

This unique collection of "ready-to-use" sales building ideas will help you sell more, sell better and sell faster. Sales success is the result of three essential factors: knowledge, skills and motivation. This book will cover all three.

You'll increase your sales knowledge by reviewing the many realistic selling situations and practical solutions. You'll also find all the essential selling skills you need from call preparation, planning your approach, analyzing customer needs, making effective presentations, handling objections as well as many different closing techniques. There is even an in-depth review of telephone sales techniques and a self-test to cure your telephone hang-ups.

In the increasingly competitive field of selling, the winners don't depend on the tried and true alone, nor do they wait for their luck to improve. They continuously work on sharpening their skills because with improved skills comes improved confidence. With improved confidence, you'll work smarter, not harder. You'll earn more money and more respect from your customers. But what's more important, improved skills will raise you to the level of a professional—an individual who achieves *consistent sales results* no matter what market conditions prevail.

The skills building ideas in this book have been tested and proven. Their on-the-job application has resulted in many additional subscriptions for *Personal Selling Power*. It is not uncommon to hear sales executives say: "I've been reading this new closing tip in your latest issue. I've used this idea to handle a very difficult sale this afternoon and got the order!" No wonder *Personal Selling Power* now has over 75,000 enthusiastic readers worldwide.

The final section of this book will unlock the secrets of motivation for you. A master sales builder is a master motivator. And mastering motivation begins with becoming the master of oneself. You will find a collection of the best ideas from leading motivators to inspire you to make the biggest sale you'll ever make: to sell yourself on yourself. That's the first sale we all need to make every day if we want to reach our full potential. For motivation to be effective, it must become an ongoing process. You can never graduate in self-motivation.

The main objective of this book is to assist you in becoming a winner. We believe that you can become a master sales builder by following the blueprints of the country's leading sales experts— listen to their advice, learn from their experience, benefit from their enormous wealth of ideas. They have paid their dues to lower the price of your sales success.

Read this book *several* times and use it as your guidebook for growth. If you follow this advice, you'll expand your vision, sharpen your skills, increase your motivation and inevitably, you'll increase your earnings.

A final word of caution: Don't try to set reading records but selling records. Don't speedread, skim, or just jump from one idea to the next. Focus on one idea at a time. Visualize the action steps. Practice them with a colleague. Make the new idea a part of you. Take one step at a time and you'll soon become a master sales builder.

Contents

Part III SELF-MOTIVATION   203

Sales Classics 261

Reference 281

How to Become
a Master
Sales Builder

Part I
<u>SELLING SKILLS</u>

You can increase your sales success by planning every phase of the sales call. In Part I of *How To Become A Master Sales Builder*, each section gives you a variety of ideas for developing new approaches and refining your skills.

Prospecting and call preparation are the blueprint for a successful sale. Openings can anchor a client/seller relationship or create a shaky foundation for business. Presentation skills are the steel girders that keep your call strong and secure. When objections surface, a solid reinforcement job will put you back on track—but the best way to deal with objections, like fires, is to prevent them. Your close will put the finishing touches on your sales building. And follow-up visits are your best insurance for continued success as a Master Sales Builder.

Prospecting and Call Preparation

Whether you're a veteran salesperson or a new recruit, there's no substitute for effective prospecting and thorough call preparation. Before you're face to face with clients, you'll want to be sure that they are likely buyers. This step is a sales building necessity. It saves you time and money on fruitless cold calls. Once you have located suitable prospects, be sure you'll meet their individual needs by preparing yourself with information that will get you the sale.

The following articles will help you organize your prospecting and planning so that you get the most out of every sales call. They include tips on generating and using leads, combining your social and prospecting talents, and broadening your business horizons. These articles will provide the foundation for a solid buyer/seller relationship. There's even a three-minute course in overcoming procrastination so that you can put the information to use right away.

Eleven Winning Prospecting Techniques

by Homer Smith

Are you satisfied with the number of sales you are making? If you are not, there is only one thing standing in the way. You are just not seeing enough of the right kind of prospects in the right way.

That might seem like a pretty rough statement, but think about it. Every sale you did make came about because you located a prospect who bought from you after listening to your proposition. Right? Your prospect, your presentation, and your timing were just right to create the sale.

Sales Start with Prospects

No salesperson will argue with the observation that before you can make a sale you must have a prospect.

In today's recession, industrial salespeople have different prospecting problems from salespeople in consumer markets. But every salesperson must sharpen his or her skills in finding and qualifying prospects for both immediate survival and future growth in selling. In some lines of selling, it has been estimated that prospecting skills account for 80 percent of the salesperson's success.

Where to Find Prospects

Studies made on why salespeople have difficulty in getting good prospects show that the poorer salespeople have one or more of these three deficiencies:

1. They don't recognize good prospects.
2. They don't know where to find them.
3. They are too lazy to look for them.

Let's consider the first two problems. (There is not much we can do about the third one here!)

Even the professional sales representative will pass by good prospects every day without recognizing them. A new company comes to town or a new family moves into an apartment. A small company grows without the salesperson's knowing it and now could use his or her products which they had no use for before. A change in management occurs and the new authorities might be more receptive to the same offer which was turned down previously. Existing customers have additional needs that could be filled by the salesperson if he were just aware of what was going on in other departments.

Certainly, everyone is going to miss some opportunities to some degree. But in today's economy, the sales professional takes nothing for granted. He or she does more checking, more prodding, more observing to find prospects. Let's look at some of the sources salespeople have for locating prospects.

Eleven Ways to Recognize and Find New Prospects

1. *Existing Customers.* Salespeople naturally expect to get re-orders from their regular customers. But every present customer is also a prospect for goods or services he or she is not presently buying from the salesperson. Too often a seller discovers that one of his good customers has purchased something from a competitor which the salesperson could have sold the customer had he known the customer was in the market for it. In most of these cases, the customer didn't realize that he could have obtained the product from the first sales rep. The other salesperson just happened to be there at the right time with the right suggestion.

Existing customers are the best kind of prospects. They are easier to sell than a new account because they are already satisfied with you and your firm.

2. *The Prospect Chain.* Use your present satisfied customers to forge an endless chain of prospects. Most customers are flattered to be asked to supply the names of friends who might be in the market for your product or service. Your request for prospect leads is particularly timely just after you have completed a sale and the customer is happy with the result.

To get an idea of the tremendous possibilities of the endless chain idea for getting prospects from existing customers, suppose you select just one of your customers and get enough leads from him or her to end up with two more customers. Get leads from these two additional customers in the same way and you end up with four more customers. Repeat this process with equal success just a dozen times, and on the twelfth round alone you would add over 8,000 customers as a result of the two leads you got from the first one.

Obviously, the system doesn't work as well in practice as it does on paper. Even if it did, no salesperson could physically handle such results. But would you settle for just 800 new customers from one? How about 80?

3. *Inactive Customers.* If you have been selling for a reasonable length of time, you have lost your share of customers. How much would your sales be improved if most of your old customers, or the customers of the salespeople who preceded you in the territory, were back on the list? When you are looking for prospects check the inactive accounts in your area.

Weed out the impossible ones. Consider the rest of them as prospects. Call on them to find out why they quit buying. Correct any misunderstandings that may come out in the interview. Find out what it would take to get them buying again. There may have been some changes since you or another salesperson called on them that could now make them customers again.

4. *Same Market Segment.* Whenever you sell to one type of business or market segment, use the sale as a testimonial to sell the same product or service to a similar business. If your product or service made one bank's recordkeeping easier, another bank would be glad to hear about it.

Try to get the personal assistance of the customer in these cases, as we suggested before; but failing that, make your own list of prospects in similar businesses or markets in similar situations.

5. *Advertising Leads.* Most business firms will advertise their merchandise or services to get leads for their sales force or to persuade prospects to visit the store or showroom. When the leads from the advertising involve making a call on the prospect, they should be followed up quickly. The advertising investment is wasted if the follow-up is delayed too long. If a competitor happens to contact your prospect first, you risk losing the sale.

6. *Business Directories.* Every community has published lists of people and business firms from which the professional salesperson can collect prospects. The classified telephone directory is perhaps the most used printed source for prospects. Owning a telephone doesn't tell much about the quality of a prospect, but the classified directory does break down the firms and professional people by types of business or trades.

Libraries and government offices will have other directories that are helpful in searching out specific types of prospects. Government records on taxes, licenses, building permits, births, deaths, and similar data will give specific types of prospects.

Often two salespeople will exchange prospect lists when their products or services are not competitive but their customers can use the services of both.

7. *Newspapers.* Get prospect leads from the news stories carried by the local newspapers. Real estate transactions, weddings, obituaries, promotions of executives, and business reports are favorite prospecting events for salespeople with products or services related to the persons or firms involved. Industrial sales reps watch for newspaper stories on new businesses in town, reorganizations, staff changes, new branches, expanded production, big contracts awarded, new owners, moves to new locations. One good approach used by many is to congratulate the prospect on the good news, or sympathize on the bad news, then offer the services to help solve any resulting problems.

8. *Bird Dogs.* Like the hunter who uses a trained dog to run before him to spot the game and flush it out, many firms use people other than salesmen to locate and check out prospects. These prospects are turned over to the experienced salesperson for follow-up and sales presentations. Frequently, sales trainees are used for this purpose because it gives them valuable experience which they can use to great advantage when they are assigned to sales territories of their own. Service and repair personnel, and other people whose jobs involve meeting the public, make good prospect spotters.

9. *Centers of Influence.* Certain persons are in a position that gives them influence over other people who have the final authority to buy the seller's goods or services. They may influence this person sufficiently to cause the sale to go through, or they may give the salesperson important information he or she can use to help persuade the key executive to buy. Examples of these centers of influence are lower level executives, secretaries, wives, teachers, bankers, politicians, and building managers. They may offer their influence out of pure friendship, or expect to gain from the sale themselves.

10. *Listening.* You can pick up prospect leads merely by listening for them. Conversation with friends and acquaintances, or even just listening to others talk, can frequently result in getting the names of actual prospects or ideas for locating them. Go to clubs and social gatherings. The people there are potential prospects or represent firms who might be. When you tune your ears and your

mind to recognize leads, you're more apt to recognize them. Be particularly careful not to betray a confidence.

11. *Cold Canvassing*. The cold canvass is not last on your list because it is considered least important. Actually, this method produces the most prospects in many areas of selling. In most selling, it uncovers leads which cannot be found in any other way.

Every professional salesperson will agree that that's why the salesperson also finds the least competition there. But intelligent, selective canvassing can produce a high rate of profitable returns. Knocking on doors may not be as profitable as following up selected leads, but when the prospect list starts to get low, you will find that there are few substitutes for smart canvassing.

Prospects Protect Your Selling Career

Your good customers of today, no matter how satisfactory their volume of sales, may be lost tomorrow for one reason or another.

If you expect to grow in sales potential and earning power, you must get the growth either from existing customers or from prospects you can convert into better customers than the ones you have. Many salespeople feel that they must have as many prospects on their list as they have customers to guarantee their current volume and to provide for reasonable growth.

Through intelligent prospecting, careful qualification and cultivation, you can assure your future success in selling.

Prospecting is your best recession insurance.

Prospecting Pays

Everyone in his company told Peter never to prospect at parties. He was new at selling, so he followed their advice—for a while.

Then one evening, while attending a friend's birthday party, he was asked by a young lady "What do you do?"

Trying to avoid "talking business," Peter replied vaguely "Oh, I'm in banking."

"Really? What's your job?" she persisted.

"Retirement accounts" said Peter, hoping to quickly change the subject.

"Gee, I've been thinking about opening an IRA. Can you tell me about the different types of accounts? I'd love to get some inside information! By the way, my name is Shelly."

Peter finally realized that Shelly really did want to hear about his work, and his bank. He informally described the differences in retirement accounts, their benefits, and restrictions.

Shelly was very impressed with Peter's knowledge about IRA's, and his friendly, nonpushy attitude—so impressed that she looked him up at work the next week, and set up an account within the month. She even referred her friends to Peter when they needed information on banking and retirement accounts.

Now Peter doesn't avoid discussing his profession, or his services, at parties. He's realized that "talking business" doesn't necessarily bore people, and sometimes it's even helpful to them. What do the other people in Peter's department think? They just shake their heads and wonder why so many customers walk in and ask for Peter. Why not use your social contacts to the fullest, for their benefit as well as your own? No matter what you sell.

Generate Leads
to Eliminate Cold Calls

Ms. Gail M. Chrystal, president of her own direct marketing group, in Arlington Heights, IL, says that companies can avoid cold calls, and still make profits. "The trick is not to find out who is interested, but to find out who isn't. Eliminate people who would be a total waste of time," states Chrystal.

A comprehensive lead-generation program will use the same basic target group of prospects as a cold call list but the unlikely prospects are already weeded out. "If a salesperson can only make six calls during a day," Chrystal remarks, "Why shouldn't they be to the most qualified prospects?" Best of all, the technique can be used to sell everything from copy machines to Lincoln Continentals, and can work for any company with a sales force.

Chrystal states that "a lead must be followed up quickly, in 24-48 hours, to be most effective." Incentive programs can motivate a sales force to follow up on leads, and remembering that turnover in a position may provide a prospect who is ready to buy can also increase the number of contacts salespeople make.

The steps to developing a well-planned, successful lead-generation program include:

- Decide on the product to be promoted, determine its unique selling points, cost differential, and benefits to purchasers.
- Define the target audience for the product.
- Develop a program using as many of the following elements as your budget allows: a space advertising and direct mail lead-generation campaign, a comprehensive sales follow-up program including mail, telemarketing and personal contact, and strong incentive program to motivate the sales force to follow up on leads.
- Pinpoint the best lists and media available for the target audience.
- Set up a call-report program to record results of follow-ups to leads.
- Be creative.

"I've even recommended sending videotapes to prospects in the case of high-ticket items," says Chrystal.

Some suggested techniques to use in developing the creative approach are:

- Personalization—obviously the more personalized the mailing, the better. If you're going after the top executive, the campaign must be extremely compelling, have an expensive look and be very personalized.

- Toys—sweepstakes houses use this technique often, with pieces that have to be punched out, stuck on or peeled off. These "toys" require a recipient to go through the entire package.

- Premiums—a free offer nets good response, but a less qualified one. Companies should never offer their own products as a premium, unless it is an attempt at a cross-sell.

Another key ingredient to success in direct mailing is a compelling cover letter. In general, the fewer pieces in a mailing, the longer the letter should be. "Recipients tend to think a longer letter has an important message about a product," notes Chrystal.

Targeting the mailing, or selecting lists, is also critical. "People always think they have to send their package to the company president. They discount the influence the actual product user can have," Chrystal emphasizes. "A mailing to secretaries about typewriters is more effective than a mailing to the person who writes the check. Multiple mailings appealing to the motivations of several different titles with purchasing influence is the most effective method of targeting," she concludes.

When a lead-generation program fails, it is usually due to a lack of sales follow-up:

- Many companies obtain lead cards weeks or months after the prospects have responded to the initial probe.

- The sales force lacks motivation because they doubt that the generated leads really are qualified.

- There is only one contact with the prospect.

While lead-generation programs are proven, they often meet with resistance. "I never read junk mail" is a common objection. "My answer to that," says Chrystal, "is that Direct Marketers are like accountants. We're always looking at the bottom line. Unlike other forms of promotion, you know exactly how much money you make from any given ad, mailing, or lead in direct response. This is an $87 billion business—it works!"

With all these suggestions, your sales force should be in for some toasty profits, instead of cold feet.

Call Preparation: Back to Basics

**by Tony Alessandra
and Jim Cathcart**

If you rely solely on your instincts during a sales call, you're cheating yourself. Even the most experienced salesperson can't "wing it" without preparing a solid base of information—and that takes research. With prior preparation, you can customize your call by understanding:

1. the prospect
2. the prospect's needs
3. who makes the decisions
4. your own reason for the call

Researching the Buyer

Nothing impresses a buyer more than your knowledge of his or her business. First, do your homework and research the buyer's business, then ask specific questions to check your information:

1. To check a general overview of the company from your client's point of view you could ask: "Tell me a bit about your business."

2. To obtain more specific information to help to tailor your presentation, you may probe: "I've read that your company is branching out into semiconductor production. Could you tell me more about this?"

3. To identify specific problems and opportunities for helping your client, you could ask: "Could you tell me about any special problems with your present product or service?" Remember that knowledge breeds trust. The more your client believes that you understand the business, the more trust he or she will place in you.

Researching Needs

Part of your call preparation should be devoted to uncovering the reasons why your product will suit your prospect's needs. These needs will vary depending upon the position your prospect holds. The chief executive, for instance, will be interested in the long-term goals of the company and in overall sales and profits. Middle managers, however, will base opinions on cost effectiveness. First-line supervisors will be concerned with installation and operation.

Once you have determined your prospect's individual needs, you can probe a "needs gap." When the client's expectations are not being met, there is a needs gap. The greater the needs gap, the greater and more immediate is the need for change, and a need for your product or service. When you know in advance what these needs are, you can prepare yourself with words and visual proof of how your product or service will meet these needs.

Researching Decisions

In order to make the most of your call, you must have an accurate picture of the decision maker and the decision-making process. Learn all you can about the prospect, company, and industry. Add these questions to your call preparations routine:

1. What are the prospect's personal style, idiosyncracies, and temperament?
2. Family interests, hobbies, sports?
3. Does he or she buy on opinion or fact; friendship or reciprocity?
4. What is the present product usage?
5. What does your competition look like for this account?
6. What is the volume of business?
7. What trends in the industry might affect the purchase decision?

The more questions you can answer, the better prepared you'll be for your sales interview. Also, be sure to talk with the right person—the decision maker. Remember, some company structures require the completion of a long chain of events before a decision can be made. If this is the case, ask your prospect "Would you give me an idea of your company's decision-making process for a purchase such as this?" If the process involves more than one person, you can try to arrange your presentation for everyone at once.

Putting It All Together

After you've done your basic research, begin to formulate your approach. Every sales call must have a reason. Is this an initial call? Are you giving a presentation? Will you close a deal that has been prepared during a previous call? Knowing what you are shooting for will narrow your focus and allow you to emphasize your main points. Ideally, each call will produce tangible evidence that you are making progress with the prospect.

Another part involves developing a questioning strategy. Use the information you have gathered on the buyer, his or her needs, and the decision-making process to decide what questions you will need to ask to gain any data you have not been able to obtain on your own. Organize your questions in a logical order and combine them with the information you are going to give the prospect about your product or service and its benefits. A long string of questions can be annoying. Insightful questions asked at appropriate times will make an excellent impression.

Next, prepare your "proofs." Do you have testimonials from people the prospect knows and trusts? Are there reports or statistics that will back up your key benefit statements? Is there something about you that is unique—that gives you an advantage over other companies and salespeople? You might say, "In addition to the product, you also get me. I'll be here to make sure that everything runs smoothly and that you realize the full benefits of the product." You can be your own proof of reliable service after the sale.

Finally, decide on your concluding actions. At the end of the call do you want: more information, a referral, permission to give a demonstration, the order? Knowing how to end the call will give you the confidence to conclude assertively.

The Selling Power of Planning

by J. Donald Staunton

Forty percent of failure in selling is due to poor organization and planning.

Seven additional reasons account for the other 60 percent. Three of the seven reasons (or 38 percent) are indirect results of poor planning.

The above figures are based on a survey conducted several years ago. The study concluded that 78 percent of failure in selling is either directly or indirectly due to poor planning.

Peter Drucker once said, *"Planning* and *doing* are separate parts of the same job. There is no work that can be performed effectively unless it contains elements of both."

While it is true that involving your customer is just as important as planning, it is also true that planning precedes any sales action if consequences of the action are to be considered.

A question many sales people ask is, "Can't you overplan with the risk of rigidity and lack of flexibility?" Efficient planning is a lot different from overplanning. A total estimate of the sales situation will always give you more options for flexibility, not rigidity. The more options (alternate directions) you have, the more appropriate will be your strategy. Another fact of the selling life is that in industrial selling, 65 percent of calls made are on the wrong person—a direct result of poor planning and call preparation. The "No Plan" approach is unprofessional and is easily recognized as such by customers. Just as "plan your work—work your plan" is the essence of management by objectives—it is also the essence of selling by objectives. A true professional will plan to work the territory with intelligence and defined purpose, then proceed to work the plan with discipline, skill and personal impact.

There are eight questions that will help you increase your planning skills:

1. What do you want done?

2. Where do you want to go or be?

3. Whom do you plan to see?

4. What are you going to say?

5. What do you plan to sell?

6. How much do you expect to sell?

7. What period of time do you expect to invest?

8. How will you follow through?

Take the time now to write these eight planning questions on the back of your business card and carry this card in your wallet. If you use these questions consistently prior to every sales call, you'll be able to cut your failure rate in selling by 78 percent.

Peter Drucker made a valuable distinction between efficiency and effectiveness. People with an aversion to planning identify efficiency with planning and then "cop out," saying, "I'd rather be effective than efficient."

This is absurd. The difference between effectiveness and efficiency is prioritizing—working efficiently on the most valuable things.

"Reaction" people tend to respond to the next immediate stimulus they are exposed to and thereby become "LIFO" oriented (Last In, First Out). Unless you prioritize your "reactions," you will be doomed to working on low-priority items most of the time (80 percent) and never have time to work on the most valuable items. You may develop a high degree of efficiency working on low-value items, but this kind of efficiency will prove to have a very low effectiveness.

It has been said that most salespeople are "reactors," but the ones that survive become professionals by becoming "directors"—the directors of their own sales success.

Steps to Sales Success

by James F. Evered, CSP

A sale doesn't just happen. A sale is the result of the learning, planning, and execution of a salesperson's knowledge and skill. The sale is where his or her self-discipline pays off.

You have often been told of the importance of learning product knowledge, product features, and ways of translating features into benefits, of knowing as much about the customer as possible. You have likewise been trained to develop personal characteristics that help create a professional atmosphere that customers will like and respect.

All these things must be brought together to develop a logical, intelligent presentation that will reach the desired goal—the sale. A plan must be developed to tilt the scales of value in the right direction. We need to develop a plan of how to reach the objective, how to influence the customer, how to make the sale.

There are many ways of dividing a sale into a series of steps necessary for its completion. First, we need to recognize the psychological stages in mental attitude of a customer making a purchase. Once we know the steps a customer goes through in making a purchase, we can plan a selling purchase that will help him take those steps.

These are the things a salesperson must create, appeal to, bring about, amplify, and use in order to close a sale. Determining how to take a prospect through these steps requires understanding and planning.

A customer will never purchase anything unless it attracts his attention. Getting the customer's attention is the purpose of advertising, merchandising, and displaying. It is unlikely that a prospect's attention will be retained unless the product will satisfy a need for him. Perhaps the product itself will make him aware of a need. Once the prospect's attention is called to a product, it must portray benefits or he will move on.

When the prospect begins to see ways he would benefit from

purchasing the product, a desire for ownership begins to kindle. Unless further benefits are given, the flame will quickly die. However, if sufficient benefits are offered to satisfy the prospect, he becomes convinced of his desire for the product. At this point he may still put off making a decision to buy unless someone helps him make a favorable decision.

Recognizing the psychological steps of buying makes it possible to plan the logical steps of selling. *Each step must be carefully planned and executed before moving to the next. It must be in sequence; like moving from one room to another—close the door before moving to the next.*

A salesperson would do well to forget that his or her objective is the sale, and concentrate instead on one objective at a time. Each objective must be met before the next one becomes a target. Failure to meet one makes the next one more difficult or sometimes impossible. Meet one objective head on, achieve it, then move on to the next one. If done professionally and naturally, the ultimate sale will be the final objective achieved.

If each step is not achieved in sequence, the result will be a barrier of resistance at closing time. The salesperson will not have earned the right to the sale because he or she did not lay the proper groundwork to get there.

In the planning stage of every sales presentation, the salesperson should ask these questions:

"How can I get the customer's favorable attention?"

"What am I going to do to generate a high degree of interest in my customer?"

"How am I going to get him or her to really want to buy?"

"How do I convince the prospect that he or she needs the product?"

"How do I plan to ask for the business?"

"What will I do to be certain that he or she is satisfied with the purchase after the sale?"

If you can't answer each of these questions, don't waste the customer's or your own time.

Strategies for Overcoming Fear
of Rejection

by Ron Willingham

In my opinion, the number one plague that devastates salespeople is call reluctance—fear of rejection. Because we fear rejection—are uptight about how we'll be accepted by people—we resort to self-destructive actions.

What kind of self-destructive actions? Things like not making enough calls. Not asking for commitments or decisions. Spending our time on tension-relieving activities, instead of on result-producing activities.

Like my friend Jerry Little, an American General Life Insurance Agency manager for 25 years, once said: "Most young life insurance agents soon learn how to deal with fear of rejection!"

"How?" I demanded, wanting to hear the secret of ages brought out into the open.

"They quit making calls!" he answered.

He's right! Most salespeople who fail, fail because they quit making calls. They quit making calls because they give in to their fears. They fear rejection.

How well I understand the problem! My experience has shown me that most people do fear rejection.

Most of us care what others think of us. We want to be liked, accepted, welcomed.

I could write a whole book titled *Call Reluctance I Have Had!*

I can remember as an office equipment salesman in the 50's driving round and round an office building—hoping I couldn't find a parking spot. Then when I did—hoping that it was too small for my 1954 Chevy.

Then for six years I owned a retail furniture store. I felt comfortable with people who came into my store. But I had a horror of telephone follow-ups.

I'm sure I missed many sales because of this fear.

I remember when I first began working with Dr. Maxwell

Maltz in 1969. The first two or three times I visited him I was nervous and uptight—intimidated by his office, his world acclaim and his quick manner.

Then one day as I was waiting in his reception room for him to finish his last appointments of the day, his wife, Ann, came in and sat down.

After exchanging pleasantries for a couple minutes, she said, "Isn't it a beautiful spring day in New York?"

"Yes, it is," I answered.

"It's so beautiful," she went on, "that I hung Maxie's long johns out on the terrace to sun and air out!"

As she said this, I just died laughing. The thought of this world famous person running around in long johns that needed airing out was hilarious. I visualized him making his hospital rounds wearing woolly long johns.

The more I mentally pictured that sight, the less intimidated I was.

From then on, the fear of approaching him was gone and I learned a valuable lesson.

After that I started viewing all my customers running around in long johns that needed airing out—the trap door flapping in the breeze!

It put a different perspective on my calls!

How about you? Stop a moment and think about a customer or prospect who intimidates you. Someone who's difficult to call on.

Visualize that person in his or her usual setting . . . but instead of wearing normal clothes, see 'em wearing long johns! Woolly ones that have been worn all winter and need airing out!

Replay that scene several times and see if you don't lose some of your awe of them.

Try it . . . and see! See if this strategy doesn't help you lose some of your fear of rejection!

The Magic of Rapport: Bridging Differences

It's inevitable that you'll encounter clients who's wealth, education, race, culture, or sex are unlike your own. Feeling uncomfortable will put you at a severe disadvantage. Your client is likely to assume the worst from your tension—that you're stupid, or a bigot, or a chauvinist or a feminist. So invest a few minutes to think through your approach and responses to those who are "different" from you. You'll be more relaxed, and better prepared to avoid communicating any negative emotions you may have.

Differences in Wealth and Education

Many salespeople tend to express signs of tension when dealing with a "richer" or "better-educated" prospect. This tension can lead either to a high-pressured sales presentation or increased confusion and loss of confidence.

It may help to keep in mind that the purpose of the call is not to measure the differences between the client and yourself, but to get the order. Check your own tension level during the call. Remember that the relaxed salesperson is always perceived as superior.

Differences in Race and Culture

The color of the skin is communicated nonverbally. Culture is communicated through tone of voice (foreign accent). Beware of your own negative feelings and attitudes about blacks, whites, foreigners! Try harder to understand the differences and to bridge the gaps.

Studies have shown that black people have greater "reading skills" in the field of nonverbal communication. However, many black people tend to express tension signals and decreased eye contact during selling situations with white people. People from Latin America tend to have less frequent eye contact when dealing with the non-Latin client.

How can you bridge the gap? Rehearse increased eye contact.

Use relaxation techniques prior to the call. Visualize. (The charisma of Sidney Poitier lies in slower movements and increased eye contact!) If you are white and calling on a black prospect, use open and relaxed postures. Observe all communication channels (face, arms, hands, legs, body angle). Try to accept and understand any differences and then focus on your selling task.

Differences in Sex

In male/female selling situations, it is advisable to avoid communicating nonverbal expressions that hint at seduction or aggressiveness.

The professional salesperson has to make a clear commitment to the initial task, while maintaining a friendly relationship.

Women should avoid "preening" gestures (e.g., arranging hair, palms facing male). Men should avoid aggressive postures such as hands on hips, moving too close, or staring at breasts.

Use creative imagery prior to the call. Become aware of any negative fantasies (or distracting thoughts) or anxieties about the call. Anticipate your own confident and purposeful attitude throughout the call. Try to assume a firm and friendly attitude. The key to success is to balance these qualities. (If you are too firm, you'll meet resistance and won't reach your goal; if you are too friendly, you pursue the wrong goals—ending up without a sale.)

How to Bridge
the Generation Gap
between You
and Your Client

Did you know that your chances for making a sale decrease proportionally to the age difference between you and your prospect? A recent study among insurance salespeople revealed that if the age difference is less than nine years, the average insurance salesperson sells to one out of three prospects. If the age difference is over nine years, the closing ratio is reduced to one in four. Our own studies revealed that age differences of more than ten years can create an increasing number of tension signals (expressed by the younger person) and withdrawal signals (expressed by the older person). You can bridge the generation gap to the older prospect by "tuning down" your own nonverbal expressions during the call. This means to show increasingly relaxed postures and movements, as well as poised behavior. Avoid "echoing" the older client's posture. Avoid exaggerated and sudden switches from "slower" to "faster" movements. Imagine how you would act, feel and think at your prospect's age. Visualize yourself prior to the call being 10, 20 or 30 years older.

You can bridge the generation gap to the younger client by "tuning up" your own nonverbal expressions. This means to show increased enthusiasm, mental readiness and flexibility. Avoid becoming increasingly excited. Try to be complementary. Imagine how you acted, felt and thought at the younger prospect's age. If you are able to bridge the generation gap, you will be able to increase your sales by 10 to 12 percent!

The Sincere Smile:
How to Get It
and Keep It

Smiling requires training. Your customer can easily distinguish between a "phony" smile and a sincere smile. *The sincere smile flashes repeatedly and appears at appropriate times;* the "phony" smile fades quickly and is used to cover internal anxiety or hostility.

We've found a practice exercise that any salesperson can use. It's simple and takes only 21 seconds. Put on a smile, hold it for 21 seconds. Watch how your own mood changes. At first you may feel odd about this, then you may feel like smiling at yourself. By the time you reach 21 seconds (use watch and mirror, if available), you are ready to smile sincerely. Try this before you see your next prospect!

A Three-Minute Course
in Overcoming Procrastination

Have you ever heard the old saying: *Unfinished business tends to be remembered longer?*

Take a sheet of paper right now and list all tasks you intend to do today. Then identify how many unfinished items you've got on your list.

An unfinished business item is a job or task that you've intended to do for several days, but for one reason or another you've put it off. For example, you may have been meaning to call a difficult prospect for several days to find out if he's made a decision on your offer. Or you've figured that you would turn in your expense report on Monday morning (but today is Wednesday). Got it?

Now, add up the total number of all tasks you intend to do today. In addition, add the number of unfinished tasks. If your total number of tasks is 12 and you've got six that have been put off previously, you know that your share of procrastination is 50 percent. (If you've got three unfinished, your share would be 25 percent.)

Procrastination is a warning signal. A high number of put-off tasks creates high internal stress.

What's worse, if you're a procrastinator, you're likely to find it more difficult to deal with a procrastinating prospect. (That can hurt in the pocketbook.)

Think about what you're telling yourself when you put off that task. Do you realize that you trick yourself by transforming a short-term discomfort (like doing your expense report now) into a long-term frustration (you can't remember what you spent, you're thinking about that bloody paperwork when you eat supper, finish watching TV or before you go to bed ... .)?

Want to try a new antiprocrastinating exercise and reduce your internal stress? The first step is to develop a list of tasks for each business day. At the end of the day write next to the task you didn't complete (but meant to):

a) The negative thoughts you've had about this task during the day.

b) The worries or anxieties you may have experienced which are related to the task.

Ex.: Call Kaiser Enterprise today.—Didn't call; I don't think they will be able to afford our high price; I am afraid they will say no.

The writing process will expose your source of discomfort (fear of rejection) and the *real reasons* for procrastinating. No time management technique in the world will get you to call Kaiser tomorrow. But the second step of this antiprocrastination exercise will:

Reappraise your negative (and unrealistic) thoughts like this:

a) *"I don't think they will be able to afford our high price."* "That's unrealistic! How do I know what they think? I need to stop mind reading!"

b) *"I am afraid they will say no!"* "So what! That doesn't mean the end of the world. I'll get a chance to find out why and I'll create an opportunity to learn more about their true needs."

Once you've exposed your irrational thoughts, you've eliminated your "reasons" for procrastinating.

Procrastination is a painful road to travel. It hurts a little less than failing, but it hurts all the time. It interferes with your life and affects your performance. But what's worse, it doesn't protect you from failing. The little procrastination barriers that you build inside become giant roadblocks in the pursuit of your goals.

Change your self concept today. Change it from:

Procrastinators put off learning how to overcome procrastination forever.

to:

It's easy for me to use the antiprocrastination exercise every day.

Become a "Do It Now" Salesperson!

Become a Better Listener

I once heard a saying that "Your customers don't care how much you know until they know how much you care." And listening is caring. A professional salesperson is a problem solver—you can't find real problems unless you know how to listen.

Dr. Lyman Steil, a worldwide expert on listening, says that we all make at least one major listening mistake per day, and that can be quite expensive. A study done by Xerox Learning Systems found that the most successful salespeople are the ones who are able to uncover more needs than their less successful colleagues.

There are really five obstacles or barriers to successful listening. The first one is that many sales people think that selling is primarily a job of persuading and persuading means talking. They tend to forget that nobody ever listened himself out of a sale.

The second is that we all tend to overprepare for what we're going to say and tend to use the listening time in waiting for our turn. Many times, while we wait our turn, we miss vital information we could use later when we close the sale.

The third barrier is that we all have emotional filters that prevent us from hearing what we don't want to hear. And sometimes we are so busy with ourselves that we don't hear at all. Sigmund Freud once said, "A man with a toothache cannot be in love." Now I'm saying that a salesperson with emotional filters cannot sell successfully. So by developing increased emotional fitness, you will improve your listening effectiveness.

The fourth barrier is that we tend to speak at a rate of about 180 wpm but we have the ability to listen at a rate of about 300-500 wpm. The passive listener uses the time lag for carrying on some internal dialogue—daydreaming. The active listener uses the extra time to achieve better understanding, evaluate the information, think ahead and review and summarize the content.

Now—I'd like to ask you—do you remember the first four obstacles to listening that I just mentioned? The reason you don't remember them all is that we tend to assume that listening is a passive process and we don't always assume the responsibility for active listening. When you ask people, "Who takes the main responsibility for the success in a communication—is it the sender or the listener?" most people say it's the sender.

Now, in selling, the responsibility for the success of the communication depends 80 percent on the salesperson and 20 percent on the prospect. If you, as a salesperson, accept this responsibility, the obstacles to listening will become stepping stones to better communication and to more sales.

Eight Ways to Get
More Attention

Some customers have shorter attention spans than others, so you need to prepare some "grabbers" that will appeal to a number of personality types. You can usually determine whether your customer is shy or outgoing, interested in prestige or concrete results, analytical or impulsive, a story lover or a fact fanatic. If you've listened carefully to what the client said and how he said it, you can choose from the following attention getters:

Analogies

Create vivid mental pictures by comparing your product/service or customer problem to a common experience.

Example: "Think of your present faulty equipment as a single weed (put up one finger) in a garden. The longer it's there, the more ground it takes over (spread hands apart), and the more money and time it takes to remove it (open palms to client)."

Drama and Action

Feed the prospect's ego by telling the person how impressed everyone will be when your product/service is a success.

Example: "I can see you in a few months (tilt head and nod). Your secretarial pool is putting out *twice* (emphasis with voice and move hands to indicate a large stack of papers) as much work and *enjoying* (smile) it. Everyone's saying what a terrific decision you made on this equipment."

Confront the Opposition

Acknowledge a problem and turn it into a benefit.

Example: "I agree that our price appears higher than the average (direct eye contact), but when you figure in the longer product life (open hands gesture) and reduced maintenance costs (bring hands closer together), you're actually saving money (raise hands, palms toward client)."

Immediacy

Convince the client that now is the time to buy.

Example: "I'll have to increase the cost of this item (shake head slightly, look of concern) when the new price list comes in, and it was due yesterday (direct eye contact, hand to chest)."

Prestige

Offer the prospect a better reputation for himself and his company.

Example: "This product will increase (open arms, palms out toward client) your productivity by 15 percent (emphasize 15 percent with hand gestures and voice) within just four (use fingers) months, pulling you well in front of the competition."

Convenience

Assure the customer of readily available assistance.

Example: "Our service technicians are on call 24 hours a day (emphasize 24 hours a day with nod of head and voice)."

Similarity

Show your understanding of the client's needs by mentioning your own or another customer's experience with the product.

Example: "I've got one of these at home (point to sample, brochure), and even my kids (raise eyebrows, emphasize with voice) have figured out how it works."

Caring

Demonstrate that you're concerned about your client's reputation.

Example: "One of our customers had a key component fail during a peak production period (direct eye contact). Our service department had it fixed within three (use fingers) hours of her call to us, and the warranty covered all the costs (sweeping hand motion)."

These attention getters don't just perk up your customer's interest. They give you the opportunity to 1) vary the tone of your voice because they are not cut and dried facts, 2) use a broader range of gestures for emphasis, and 3) put you on a friendlier, more relaxed level with your client than a "formal" presentation allows. Matching your attention getters to the personalities of your clients

will also let them know that you are tuned in to their individual
needs—a plus in any sales situation.

Helping Your Customer
Hear What You Say

Prospects don't always listen. You can't teach them better listening skills but you can make sure they hear your important points. The three keys to helping your customers hear what you say are: (1) eliminating distractions, (2) avoiding overload and (3) summarizing benefits.

Eliminating distractions will help your prospect's concentration. Ask if you can close the door. If noises from the hall are bothering you, they're probably disturbing your client, too. Phone calls also detract from clear communication. Explain that your meeting will be much shorter and more helpful if incoming calls are held until the discussion is completed. Although you can't *directly* stop a client's noisy, nervous habits (foot tapping, pen clicking, finger picking, etc.) you can reduce tension indirectly by maintaining an open, relaxed posture and avoiding all sound-making and self-touching gestures yourself.

Next, don't overload your client with information. People's brains are like computers—when the memory is filled up, something gets dumped. When you give your clients too much detail, or discuss topics that don't deal with their individual needs, they simply stop paying attention to you. A look of preoccupation is a warning that says, "I can't absorb more." The best you can do is to refocus on your prospect's dominant needs and to ask feedback questions that allow the client to verbalize his or her understanding of your product or services.

Summarize the benefits, not the features, of your product. A customer's hearing improves dramatically when you point out what's in it for him or her. Explain how other customers rave about your product today. Make sure they hear your reasons for buying by concluding each topic with a benefit summary. What seems obvious to you may be completely new to the client. Pull together the essence of your complete presentation into a single benefit statement that reflects your individual prospect's needs.

Help your customers to hear your message. You'll increase their desire for your product, which will increase your potential for more and bigger sales.

Openings

What you say in the first few minutes of a sales call will set the pace for the entire relationship. Your opening can motivate your prospect to hear more about your product or service, or it can bring the sale to a screeching halt.

To gain the necessary momentum for carrying the sale beyond the opening, we have selected a number of ideas for improving your opening statements and lead questions. Don't let a few carelessly placed supports bring down your sales call. Learn how to make a terrific first impression by using proper dress, relaxation techniques, enthusiasm, well-planned questions, positive body language, listening skills, and a caring attitude.

First Impressions Count!

We're all taught that appearances shouldn't determine our reactions to people—it's what's inside that counts. But your customer's primary aim is not to become friends. He or she needs to decide, in a short amount of time, whether you are reliable, truthful, and *professional*. Even before you greet a client, your dress, posture, and bearing indicate how you feel about your job. So here are a few tips for creating a positive first impression that can make what you *say* much more effective.

1. *Dress conservatively.* Each profession has a uniform, whether it's Wall Street pin stripe or Record Store khakis and sport coat. Outlandish fashions may catch the client's attention, but will leave a *negative* impression.

2. *Colors create an image.* Solid suits of gray, beige, and navy blue, with white or blue shirts for men, and two-piece dresses with a jacket or a suit in similar colors for women are basics. You should avoid aggressive colors of orange or turquoise, and any color that doesn't suit your hair, eyes, and skin color.

3. *Neatness counts.* Attention to the details of your clothing, such as a well-pressed shirt and polished shoes, tell the customer that you're conscientious. A disheveled appearance gives the impression of disorganization and carelessness.

4. *Quality is the key.* No matter what the price of your suit or dress, get a good tailoring job, and never skimp on accessories. Ties, jewelry, and attaché cases that are tacky can ruin your overall image.

5. *Stand tall.* Good posture and a confident stride say you are happy and *capable.* Slouching, or a shuffling gait can convey an "I don't care about what I'm doing" attitude, and will make a well-tailored outfit hang poorly.

When you realize that the deciding factor for a sale could rest on your client's first impression of you, doesn't it make sense to project the very best image possible? A basic, conservative wardrobe, attention to the details of your appearance, and a confident stance can add up to improved self-confidence and increased sales.

How to Win Customers
with a Successful Opening Strategy

Make no mistake about this: how you handle the first few minutes of a sales call can make or break a sale.

Here are a few suggestions that can help you enter your prospect's mind and heart with high chances for success:

Open Up and Cheer Up

... before you see your prospect! Doug Roberts, a sales rep working for a small industrial dealer, has this advice: "You have to separate yourself from the effects of everyday stress before the appointment. As I park my car, I relax my body, loosen my neck, my arms and legs. As I approach the prospect's place of business, I try to breathe deeply. The moment I open the front door, I put on a smile and hold it until I receive positive feedback from the people I run into. By the time I reach the receptionist, people start to smile back at me."

Stop Observing Yourself
as You Wait!

Continue to be relaxed. A sales rep of a midwestern chemical company reported that longer waiting periods used to increase his self-awareness to a point that made it difficult for him to control his feelings of frustration. Now he has learned how to occupy his mind by reading a copy of a business magazine which he keeps in his briefcase just for this purpose. In addition, he works on maintaining a pleasant and relaxed appearance.

State Your Purpose

Explain your reason for calling. For example: "The reason for my call is to help you with your ... needs." Or: "I'd like to show you a way in which you could increase your productivity by 23 percent." By giving your prospect a reason for investing his time, you will make it easy for him to shift his attention to your presentation.

Show That You Did Not
Come to Intrude

Your relaxed and open postures will do wonders in reducing your prospect's initial apprehension. Avoid moving too close. Allow your prospect to size you up first. Avoid up and down hand gestures during this phase (they can increase his apprehensions). Instead use subtle hand gestures with your palms open.

Involve the Prospect
with an Open Question

Give your prospect a chance to communicate. Your questions should be designed to reflect your genuine interest in his specific needs.

Kathy West, a bank marketing executive, suggests: "It's counterproductive to continue the call by showing off your knowledge and skills. After you've stated the purpose of your call, prospects do not really care how much you know, until they've realized how much you care. For this reason, I ask them to help me by describing their specific needs. As they reply, I tilt my head slightly to one side, a move that expresses genuine interest. This way I can get my prospects to loosen up and increase their confidence and trust in me."

Communicate Your Understanding
of Your Prospect's Needs

Prospects will show increased confidence in you when you demonstrate that you've truly understood their needs. Here are some examples:

Thank you, Mr. Williams, for sharing this information with me. As I can see from your comments, your needs call for ... (review needs) ... Have I got that right?

Mrs. McGee, it appears that you not only need increased production, but also need to reduce maintenance time. I'm glad you told me about this; now we can both review how our new product can help you to solve both problems.

Friendly, Not Forceful, Gets the Sale

In an article entitled "Gaining Rapport, the Key to Friendly Bargaining," David Richardson, a motivational speaker, consultant, and author, shared these tips on gaining your client's confidence *before* you make a presentation.

Dave says that if you can get your client comfortably yet firmly within the "buyer's box" during your opening discussions, you will both be in the best frame of mind for friendly bargaining, and a successful sale. The buyer's box consists of four sides: 1) Attitude—show lots of *enthusiasm,* and focus your mind on *achievement,* not money. 2) Sincerity—*warm up* the selling relationship by creating an atmosphere of mutual help and *listen* to how he answers your questions. 3) Competence—prove through your *statements and questions* that you're a consultant and an educator, not just a product pusher. 4) Establishment of needs and goals—pinpoint exactly what the client needs, wants, and expects, so that you can tailor your presentation to him personally. If you have matched your tone and tempo to your prospect's voice, and mirrored his posture during these steps, your client will be at ease and ready for a friendly bargaining session.

The Art of Asking Questions

by Dr. Milt Grassell

As a consultant, speaker, and seminar leader, I have used the fine art of asking questions to get into an excellent position for giving a tailored presentation. I have successfully used this art to sell products and services to business, industry, institutions, and government agencies.

Don't look for prospects who fit your presentation—be flexible with the prospects who come along. Ask questions that allow your prospects to tell you what they want to know.

First, even before making an appointment for a sales call, find out if your prospect has the authority to buy. An indirect question like, "May I ask who will be making the final decision on this?" will get the answer you need.

Next, when you meet your prospect, give him the bare necessities—your name, company, and product or service—then ask permission to probe. This way you will seem less like a rapid-fire investigative reporter and it gives you a psychological edge—the prospect's agreement to give you information.

While in the probing stage, remember reasons for asking questions and use them to give direction and focus to your presentation.

1. To make sales presentations prospect oriented: "What seems to be the problem?"
2. To get quick yes or no answers: "Can you let me know today?"
3. To get quick short answers: "When can you let me know?"
4. To get the prospect to talk about a problem of his choice: "What opportunities do you see in the future in your business?"
5. To get the prospect to talk about a topic of your choice: "Just suppose you decided to put in our economy line. What level of productivity would you expect?"
6. To redirect the prospect back to the point: "Let's get back to cost effectiveness. Can we make sure that I understand your point?"

7. To get the prospect to expand on something he has already said: "I like your second point. Would you expand on that please?"

8. To bridge differences of opinion: "Could the real problem be the machinery you are now using?"

Finally, don't give your presentation until the prospect is really ready to hear it. You may give it on the spot, using the answers he has given you to decide which areas to highlight and which to omit. You may set up a future date for presenting the exact information you now know he'll be interested in getting. Either way, you will have improved your chances for success by tailoring your presentation to the prospect's needs. Your interest in him is sure to make a favorable impression and get you the sale.

Dirty Stories

by V. H. Godkin

This article, originally published in 1928, is particularly appropriate in today's sales world, where the seller or the buyer is just as likely to be a woman as a man.

I had been traveling for the B _____ Company for about a year, making a fair success. But a salesman for my chief competitor always seemed to me to be selling rings around me. He dressed better, acted more confident and prosperous, and had a manner that, to me, seemed to bring all the choice orders his way.

Determined to find out the reason for his apparent success, I studied him every chance I got; and this was often, as we crossed each other's trail several times a week. Sometimes, I would walk into a store just as he was writing an order in his book. Again, he would come in just as I was leaving.

Finally, one day he came in just as I finished writing up an order for a merchant, and making the excuse that I had a little time to kill before my train was due, I hung around within earshot to listen to his canvass. Within a few minutes I thought I had found out the key to his success.

Greeting the buyer affably, he almost immediately launched into a new "story" that he had recently heard. It was a rather smutty one, but he laughed loudly at its conclusion, and the buyer appeared to enjoy it, too.

"Here," I thought, "is his secret. He tells them stories and gets them in good humor, then it is an easy matter to write up their orders."

To make sure of my discovery I watched him again at the first opportunity, and he repeated the process, using another "off-color" story, and getting a good-sized order.

"If that's what gets the business, then I'm going after it too," thought I. And immediately I proceeded to learn a couple of good (?) stories. I spent an evening practicing them in my room, and the next morning went forth to knock 'em cold.

My first prospect was a big general merchant in a small town. I had always secured an order from him with comparative ease, for as soon as he was at liberty he handed me his want book, and I copied down the items he needed.

It was a rather cool morning, and a group of loungers was gathered around the big stove in the rear, so I went back and joined in the general conversation while the merchant waited on a customer. But in a few minutes he came back by the stove, and I launched into one of my stories.

At its conclusion the group laughed loud and long. I felt quite pleased with myself, and immediately told the second story. This one brought forth more laughter than the first one from the group, and I felt I had made a hit. I could turn the trick just as well as my competitor.

Glancing around to where I thought the merchant had been standing, I was surprised to find him missing from the group. However, a second look showed him marking some goods at the rear, so I confidently approached and greeted him affably.

Mr. Merchant returned my greeting courteously, but without enthusiasm, and quickly informed me that he was not in need of anything today.

I could hardly believe my ears, for I had always secured some kind of an order from him, and confidently felt that after my display of funny stories he would do even better by me.

It happened that I went into the house the next morning, and you can imagine my surprise when the boss informed me that this same merchant had telephoned in an order the night before.

"Weren't you up there yesterday?" the boss inquired.

Of course I told him that I was, and suggested that the merchant had not discovered that he needed anything till after I had left. I tried to console myself with the same thought, but when I called on this merchant the next week, he again politely informed me that he needed nothing.

Convinced that something was wrong, I went outside and walked around for a half hour, trying to locate the trouble. Then, a thought occurred to me, and I made a beeline back to the store.

"Mr. Henry," I began, as soon as I had cornered him alone, "I want to ask you a question, and I'd like to have you be perfectly frank with me in answering."

He gave me a searching look, but told me to shoot.

"Last week you refused to give me an order, but phoned it in to the house after I had left. Today you again turned me down." I paused a moment and looked him squarely in the eye.

"Now, here's what I would like to know. Did you turn me down because of those stories I told here last week?"

He eyed me narrowly for a minute, then nodded his head.

"Yes," was the short answer.

I had guessed right.

During the next five minutes I did some of the tallest talking I've ever indulged in. I took him completely into my confidence, and told him just how I came to tell the stories, ending up with the statement: "That was the first and only time I have done a thing of that sort, and believe me it's going to be the last, if I never sell another cent's worth of goods."

All during my recital he had watched me closely, and when I finished he grasped my hand and shook it warmly. "Boy, I believe you. Just stick to that resolution—for a clean salesman always gets further than a dirty one. Now, get out your order book and start writing."

He gave me the largest order I had ever written, and in the bargain told me, from his years of observation and experience, just why some men were better salesmen than others, and how I could improve my methods.

And the best part of it was that he had the right dope on it. By following his suggestions I became one of the high men for our company, and was soon outselling my story-telling competitor, while he hit the down grade and finally lost his job.

Since then I have never resorted to dirty stories. I hesitate to think what the result might have been had I not right-about-faced when I did.

Traffic Signals
to the Buyer's Mind:
How to Read
Your Prospect's Body Language

How many times has your sales prospect invited you to sit when you entered his office, and you wondered with a tinge of hesitancy which of several chairs to choose? The one directly opposite his desk? The chair beside it? Does it matter?

Or how about the vague uneasiness you've felt when, even though the prospect is smiling, there's something tense in the air that suggests your pitch is running off track? Is it just your imagination, or is something going wrong?

If you chose the most advantageous chair—the one beside the desk—you'd actually be in a much better position to know what's concealed behind the prospect's smile. But what's more important, you would know whether your presentation really is on track and what you can do if it isn't.

Unfortunately, most salespeople aren't trained in nonverbal communication, so they miss precious opportunities to make a sale.

In fact, scientific research suggests that people communicate just seven percent of their feelings and attitudes with words, thirty-eight percent with their tone of voice, and a whopping fifty-five percent through nonverbal signals.

Salespeople who are sensitive to nonverbal cues can read those signals almost like a traffic light.

"Green signals" tell them that the prospect is open and to proceed with the pace and direction of the presentation.

"Yellow signals" indicate the seller is losing the prospect, and that it's time to re-engage him with questions about his interest and needs.

"Red signals" warn the seller to stop and redirect the approach because the buyer has just about been lost.

Those "traffic signals" also indicate how the salesperson must

Classic green light: full speed ahead.

Classic yellow: guarded and reserved.

Red light: It might be too late to recover.

act to be sure he isn't communicating negative nonverbal messages ("yellow" or "red") to the buyer.

Read beyond the Smile

Although the face is the most obvious channel of nonverbal communication, research has found that many buyers can hide their true feelings behind a friendly face.

To identify the buyer's true attitude, the seller must examine additional nonverbal channels such as hands, legs, arms, body angle and eye contact. For that reason, the chair beside the desk is the best choice, so the buyer cannot hide negative nonverbal cues and the seller can respond effectively to the buyer's true feelings.

Only a few buyers can hide their feelings or attitudes in their hand gestures. Open and relaxed hands, for example, are a valuable green signal indicating that the sale is progressing well. Open and relaxed arms, uncrossed legs and a body angle directed toward the salesperson are also important green signals.

Green signals between seller and buyer tend to reinforce each other, putting both at ease, and move the discussion toward a successful close.

But what if the buyer's hands, for example, don't match the openness implied by a friendly facial expression, and instead are clasped or closed?

Tension signals yellow, and time for open questions.

That's a common yellow signal, as is a closed posture or a body angle turned away from the salesperson. Inattentiveness to yellow signals puts obvious obstacles in the way of the sale. What's worse, they can negatively influence the salesperson's attitude, thus reinforcing the buyer's negative feelings. Charging ahead, as if yellow signals were green, risks pushing the buyer to communicate red and may result in losing the sale. Indeed, yellow signals indicate the most critical part of a sales presentation. They appear, for example, when the buyer is wary, aggressive, frustrated, tense or doubtful. Those feelings can be communicated in many different ways and each prospect adds his individual character to them.

The causes and meanings behind those negative attitudes may in fact be quite different, depending on the situation and the customer's personality. That is why there's little value gained by attempting to psychoanalyze the meaning of what the buyer expresses behind thousands of individual gestures. (There are more than 5,000 hand gestures alone!) The salesperson need only know that the buyer has posted a warning and is signaling an obstacle preventing open communication.

If the warning is ignored, the buyer may soon express a red signal and it may be too late to recover.

Recovery Tactics

Hence, the salesperson must respond to yellow signals early and turn them back to green. No matter what the specific reason behind the yellow signal, the seller's best move is to relax and express green signals. Certainly, the salesperson must avoid giving out negative signals which imply "don't buy from me."

Meeting the buyer's yellow signals with openness.

In addition, the salesperson must use "open questions" to draw out the buyer's real feelings. Like the underwater part of an iceberg, they hide beneath nonverbal expressions. One might ask the buyer, for example, "I'd like to get your objective opinion on this; how do you think our product will help you with your production?"

Open questions give the buyer a chance to open up and express his concern. The salesperson's open posture, a green signal, combined with the open question can bring the presentation quickly on track.

If, however, the buyer slips into red signals, the salesperson must stop and redirect the presentation. Salespeople can recognize red signals by observing the buyer's increased aggressiveness or progressive withdrawal.

The first recovery step is to communicate understanding of the buyer's negative attitude. The prospect must hear and see that the seller is fully aware of the red signal.

The second step is to redirect attention to the main advantages of the sales proposal. Again, green signals from the salesperson will positively influence the buyer.

Of course, the best way to handle red is prevention at the yellow stage. The seller's strategy must be to constantly monitor the buyer's face, hands, arms, legs and overall body posture—all non-verbal communication channels—throughout the call.

Going on the Green

The buyer must be influenced to express green signals, because only then can the actual product presentation meet a receptive mind. Indeed, the buyer may not start by showing green signals at the beginning of a call. That means the salesperson's first tactic is to use open questions designed to elicit the buyer's real feelings long before the actual product presentation begins.

During the early stage of the sales call it is especially important to scan the buyer's nonverbal expressions. Once the traffic light turns green, the product can be presented. As long as it stays green, the sale can move toward a successful close.

Special Yellows

Many salespeople seem to forget that their failure to maintain eye contact at strategic moments of the call can amount to self-defeating communication. For example, when describing the technical characteristics of the product, seller and buyer both naturally direct their eyes to the product itself, a brochure, specification sheet, or similar object.

But in stressing the benefit—what the product means to the customer—eye contact is essential. Without it, the negative message conveyed neutralizes the benefit and the prospect may conclude that the salesperson is not quite convinced of his own presentation.

Similarly averted eyes, distracted behavior or other yellow signals from the salesperson in response to the prospect's verbal objections imply that the prospect has hit upon the seller's weakness, catching him flatfooted. Sadly, the thousands of selling situations we've studied on videotape indicate that most salespeople reveal negative nonverbal reactions when prospects raise objections. The yellow signals so produced outweigh even the most unperturbed verbal reply.

Some yellow signals on the part of the salesperson are simply the product of oversight. But others may be caused by fundamental differences between buyer and seller. Oversights such as poor appearance, poor call preparation or other negative nonverbal expressions, can be easily corrected. Interestingly, even the salesperson's briefcase, if incorrectly handled, can arouse a buyer's negative reaction. The best place for a salesperson to put it is on the floor. Holding it expresses insecurity and the need for protection. Placing it on the next chair could be interpreted by the buyer as invasion of his turf.

Understanding the traffic signals of nonverbal expressions can facilitate the selling task tremendously. By paying close attention to the buyer's nonverbal communication channels one can quickly sense a negative undercurrent and counteract with green signals and open questions—before the buyer's attitude hardens and the sale is lost. Once salespeople become aware that it's their own ability to communicate green signals to the buyer which will lead to the order, they'll have a more positive attitude toward their jobs and themselves.

Four Little Words
Equal One Big Difference

by Dottie M. Walters, CSP

In a sales interview, four little words can make the difference between catching the customer's interest and losing it. These words have nothing to do with a particular product or a set sales pitch. They're not bold or clever. You use them all the time with friends and family, when they have a problem or a decision to make. The catch is this—they require refocusing from inward to outward, from selfish to *serve-ish*.

They require your concentrating on what the *customer's* problems and needs are—not *your* wares and services. When the client hints at what his concerns are, be sincere, be interested, and say—*Tell me about it!*

I Don't Sell,
I Develop Relationships

by Ron Willingham

He's gone now, but one of the great legends of professional selling was Elmer Leterman. In the years when only a small percentage of life insurance agents sold one million a year, Elmer sold $250 million a year for many years.

I first met Elmer one morning in the late '60s in the Plaza Hotel in New York. I was in the gift shop browsing through the book racks. I spotted a book on selling by Elmer Leterman.

I'd heard of him but had never met him. As I picked up the book and flipped through it, a voice behind me said, "If you'll buy it, I'll autograph it for you!"

"Who are you?" I asked.

"I'm Elmer Leterman," he responded.

We talked a few minutes, he invited me to have lunch with him. I stayed in touch until he retired and moved to Florida.

"How were you able to sell so much life insurance?" I once asked him.

"I don't sell life insurance," he replied.

"You don't?"

"No, I develop relationships! Then people buy life insurance."

"What do you mean?"

Eager to talk about himself, he reached into his coat pocket and pulled out a fistful of folded letter-size sheets of paper. On each sheet was printed a copy of a letter some well-known person had written him. Each one thanked him for some personal or business favor he'd extended them.

He went on, "When I hear of someone going to Europe or to Hawaii, I call ahead and have a friend meet them at the plane or dock and make sure they get into their hotels comfortably.

"Or, I send plaques ... like I'm going to send you ... "

"What kind of plaques?" I asked.

"Plaques with motivational statements on them."

As he talked he unfolded the sheets and sandwiched in information about the person who wrote the letter to him.

"Another thing I do," he went on, "is every day I have a table at The Four Seasons Restaurant. I invite up to eight people to be my guests for lunch.

"I don't do it to sell them anything," he emphasized. "I do it to bring people together.

"I invite business people, sports figures, show business people, politicians . . . all kinds of people.

"I just bring people together." He smiled. "I just develop relationships! Then lots of people buy life insurance from me!"

This was a terrific lesson for me. I've thought of it many times. I've tried to do the same thing—develop relationships!

And it's paid off! It's put me in a bigger league than I was before.

How about you? How can you develop stronger relationships with people that would provide a steady inflow of business for you?

What can you unselfishly do for people that benefits them—without sticking out your hand and saying, "Pay me back!"

What can you do to help people so they'll *want* to buy from you, refer their friends to you, and have an interest in your success?

Can you think of at least one specific action you can begin doing now that will show your customers or prospects that you're interested in them? And not ask for a "pay back"?

When will you begin doing it?

Like Elmer did, what will you do that says, "I don't sell, I develop relationships and people then buy from me"?

The Magic Wand

Most people only hear what they want to hear and see what they want to see. The trick in sales is to get your prospect to *tell* you what he'll accept. One of *Personal Selling Power's* readers, David E. Geldart of Boston, Massachusetts, wrote to tell us he's come up with a way to do this:

"It took me a long time to discover that the best way to convince people and to make sales is to feed back to them what they tell me. One of the most effective ways to do it is to ask open-ended questions.

"I am in the insurance field. If I am selling a life insurance policy, I might ask a question like this: 'Mr. Jones, if you could wave a magic wand and create a perfect policy to satisfy all your needs and concerns in this situation, what kind of policy would you design and what would you want the policy to do?' Once I get the customer's feedback, I match my product to the feedback and play back as much as possible."

Once you know what the prospect's *wishes* are, you're in a good position to *grant* them. And you're not limited to the *proverbial three wishes*—you can grant as many wishes as your products, services and imagination can fulfill.

Matching the Prospect's Language

by Dr. Donald J. Moine

Did you know that in a group of people, all speaking English, there may be three different languages being used? We're all aware of the wide range of vocabulary individuals can use to communicate their thoughts. But you may not have realized that customers can cue you in to the kind of information they want by their use of *visual, auditory,* or *action* words—the three universal languages.

Prospects who love visual information use visual words continuously in their speech: "That's not *clear* to me," "Can you *show* me how that works?" "That's a *bright* idea." Customers who prefer auditory information use sound words such as: "That *rings* a bell." "That *sounds* good to me." "Can we get a little more *harmony* into this discussion?" Customers speaking the third kind of language use action words like: "I can't get a *grasp* on what you're saying." "I really had to *lean* on my boss to get the okay." "I get a *kick* out of these fast cars."

While we speak and understand all three universal languages, we also each have a favorite language. Top salespeople automatically pick up on this in customers and then utilize the customer's favorite language in their sales presentation.

For example, if you find that your prospect prefers the visual language system, you could use this knowledge to your advantage at each step of the sale:

1. *Opening.* "Let me *show* you what an increase in productivity your office could experience with this new computer system."

2. *Needs Assessment.* "Ms. Smith, you can *look* at the success your company has enjoyed and you can *see* for yourself where the problems are and what machinery needs to be replaced."

3. *Presentation of Benefits.* "It is *clear* that this new addressing system will reduce by 20 percent the time it takes you to get a mailing out."

4. *Handling Objections.* "I can *see* your *point of view* about the safety issue in these government bonds, and it *shows* that you are a sophisticated investor."

Why is matching the customer's language so effective? Study after study has shown that we tend to like people who are like ourselves; that bosses tend to hire and promote people who are like they are; and that all of us trust people who behave and speak the way we behave and speak. Also, when you use the customer's language, the line between you and the customer becomes more blurred. There will be fewer reasons to be critical of you, since you are so much like him or her.

Careful attention to the types of images a client emphasizes will *focus* your attention on the information he wants to *hear* so that you can *grab* the advantage his cues present. Getting the feedback he wants will impress your client. It assures him that you know what he needs, which is the most important step in convincing him that these needs can be met by *your* product or service.

You can get everything in life you want, if you help enough other people get what they want.

Zig Ziglar

Shut Up—and Sell

Salespeople are great talkers. Talking is a big part of their job. But knowing when *not* to talk is equally important. A reader of *Personal Selling Power,* Chester Brainard, described to us how he put silence to work for him:

"Some years ago, I obtained a commission sales position with Dasa Corporation of Andover, Massachusetts. This involved selling automatic telephone dialers to businesses, door to door.

"I was 65 years of age at the time, and the young man who interviewed me for the position was very reluctant to hire me. He said I was too old, and as I had never sold electronic equipment before, he didn't think there was much chance of my being successful. However, after I had returned to see him three or four times, he finally gave me a kit—more to get rid of me than anything else.

"After a week of not doing very well, but learning something about telephoning and automatic dialing, I took time out to write a pitch. Having sold encyclopedias, I knew the value of a good pitch.

"Upon placing the unit I was attempting to sell on the desk of the prospect, I would say: 'This is an attachment for your telephone that will enable you to dial anyone, anywhere, by pushing one button once. Isn't that fantastic?'

"Then I would keep still—not saying a word until the prospect had spoken. Sometimes the wait was almost unbearable. The prospect's first words, ending the silence, usually gave me a good idea of his or her interest, or lack of it."

After introducing himself and the main benefits of his product, Mr. Brainard gave his prospects time to evaluate their need for the item. Once they broke the silence and voiced their concerns or interests, it was easier for him to explain any details pertinent to these needs. Mr. Brainard's "golden silence" pitch paid off, and the young man who hired him was very pleasantly surprised. Think about how you can put silence to work for *you*.

Your Buyer's Motivation

Understanding what motivates a buyer's interest in a particular product or service helps a salesperson tailor his sales talk to the specific concerns of the client. Rather than a long discussion of *all* of a product's features, the sales pitch can zero in on the main concerns of the customer. This gives a personal touch to the sales presentation, which makes the customer feel like he is being treated like an individual, not like just another commission check.

You can use your own words to ask three basic questions which go directly to the heart of the buyer's interests:

1. "Of all the products you can choose from in today's market, what in particular interested you in _____ ?"

    Most shoppers are surprised to hear questions like this. Most people are so disarmed by buyer-motivation questions that they just tell you the truth. If the buyer says he is looking for quality, you must now dig deeper.

2. "What do *you* mean by quality?"

    You need to ask the prospect to define what he means by quality. Definitions can be very different from one buyer to another. For example, one prospect may think that quality means that a car is easy to service, and the next one thinks that quality stands for superior workmanship. If you make the same presentation to both of them, they'll each get frustrated because they're not hearing about the right "quality" features and benefits.

    Once you have discovered the buyer's definition of his or her most important motivation, go one step further and ask:

3. "Why did you put that point at the top of your list?"

    At this point, you may get a more detailed answer like, "Well, the last car gave me all kinds of headaches with the transmission, the radiator ... " So when you describe your product's features, you'll simply add, "Unlike your present car, you will be able to save yourself a lot of headaches with a (company or model name).

Tailoring the specific product benefits to match the buyer's primary reasons for coming to you makes your presentation more personalized. When you focus only on those features the buyer is interested in, you don't frustrate him by wasting time on topics that won't affect his decision to buy. You zero in on what *does* matter to him. Why not put buyer-motivation techniques to work for you?

Presentations

Decide on the best way to deliver your presentation. A prefabricated sales talk may disappoint the client. Size up your customers' tastes. Don't show them designs for a mansion if they want a small summer cottage.

This section will give you a number of suggestions for presenting your product with class—whether the customer wants top of the line products or bargains. Key elements of well-constructed presentations are: effective communication (verbal, vocal and nonverbal), listening skills, selling benefits and a variety of attention getters. And don't forget safety devices—knowing how to handle a manipulative client will keep your presentation from collapsing.

Are You Really Selling Benefits?

by James F. Evered, CSP

The buying decision is made in the customer's mind... not yours! Based on this premise, what can you do to influence the buyer's decision-making process?

In training and observing salespeople over the past twenty-five years, I have had the opportunity of working with some of the best—and some of the worst. Among the top producers, I have always watched for those common threads woven among them, i.e., those techniques that seem to have the highest degree of success frequency.

Laying aside the obvious value of a good personality, proper grooming and communicative skills, I will concentrate this writing on the one basic skill I find among all the top producers, and find blatantly missing in the low-volume salespeople. The top producers have learned to speak the right language, the only language a customer understands—*customer benefits*.

Before you jump to any conclusions, let me tell you what I invariably find while observing salespeople in action. Ninety-nine percent of them *think* they talk in terms of customer benefits—about ten percent of them actually *do* it. Scores of times I have had to prove this point to a sales representative. They are often shocked when they realize how few benefits were actually presented to the customer. Implying a benefit and stating a benefit are not the same.

Let me share a simple model I use in my sales seminars to help salespeople conceptualize the how and why of benefit selling.

The Sales Scale

The "Sales Scale" helps us understand what goes on in a customer's mind when he is considering a purchase. And this understanding is essential to the selling process, for it is in the customer's mind that a buying decision will be made.

In essence, the customer is mentally comparing two things—what he will have to pay for the product (or service) versus the benefits he will gain from owning or using the product. He is simply questioning whether it's worth the exchange.

If the customer feels the price outweighs the value, he isn't going to buy. It isn't worth it to him. If he feels the price and value are equal, he *may* decide to buy. If, however, he feels that the value outweighs the asking price, he'll make the exchange and the sale will close. The salesperson's job, obviously, is to get the value side to outweigh the asking price—and right here is where the majority of salespeople fail. They sell on the wrong side of the scale.

Think for a moment where a price comes from. It is an accumulation of everything up to the point of sale, including materials, labor, research, transportation, warehousing, handling and profit margins. The cost of every single feature of the product is packed into the price—at a profit. Feature selling does no more than justify the price. Benefit selling, on the other hand, justifies a purchase in the customer's mind.

Feature selling tells us *how* the product was made, what's in it, what's on it and how it is put together. Benefit selling tells us *why* the product was made that way, or in other words, what it is going to do for the customer. Benefit selling answers the most important question in all of selling, "What's in it for me, the customer?" Benefits are the only things that add value to the right side of the scale. Features add to the cost—benefits add to the value and create desire in the customer's mind.

Breaking Old Habits

There are several reasons why salespeople push features, leaving the translation up to the customer. In the first place, they feel more comfortable talking about product features. Frequently, features are stressed in advertising and product brochures. But there are two assumptions salespeople make that cause them to ignore the customer benefits. The first assumption is, "The customer already knows that stuff, and I'd sound silly if I talked about them." To a degree, this is true. Most customers really do know most of the basic benefits a product offers.

But the deadly assumption is the second one, i.e., when the salesperson assumes the customer is *thinking* about the benefits. Those benefits are somewhere back in his memory bank and he has never been disciplined to retrieve them. Unless the customer is *thinking* about the benefits, they aren't even on the sales scale. They weigh nothing toward offsetting the asking price.

The total amount of value the customer perceives in the product or service is mentally weighed against the cost when it comes time to make the buying decision. The total value perceived by the customer will be in direct proportion to the salesperson's efforts in talking about the customer benefits. A top-producing sales representative never leaves it up to the customer to translate the features into meaningful customer benefits.

As a sales representative, you have two choices: (1) You can present the features and *hope* the customer will voluntarily put enough value on the scale to offset the price, or (2) you can take a professional approach and build a high perceived value by presenting as many benefits as time will allow. If you leave it up to the customer to make the translation, your sales volume will be determined by "buymanship," not "salesmanship." Don't leave it to the customer to determine your income.

A customer doesn't buy a product for what it *is*. He buys because of what the product will *do* for him—nothing more. A customer doesn't buy a three carat diamond ring—he buys an image of success, proof of achievement, a source of pride, the gain from investment, a source of conversation, one-upmanship, an ego trip. The customer doesn't buy film. He doesn't even buy pictures—he buys memories, the ability to capture a precious moment and have it forever. He doesn't buy motor oil—he buys engine protection, longer engine life, less repairs, a better investment, peace of mind, greater resale value. He doesn't buy theatre tickets—he buys entertainment, an escape from reality, the ability to forget the outside world for a couple of hours, relaxation.

Regardless of the customer's motive for buying, e.g., gain, fear, pride, imitation, love, affection, appreciation, and so on, that buying decision will be determined by the result he perceives he will get from the product—not what the manufacturer built into it. But he won't perceive much value unless you, the salesperson, make him aware of the value by talking about the benefits, by discussing them, by "putting the benefits on the scale." The customer simply won't do it alone. That's *your* job.

Influencing the Customer's Mind

To prove this point in my seminars, I use a series of slides that present a variety of common products with one single feature of that product listed under it. I try to use products that are totally unrelated to the group. I want them to concentrate on the mechanics of converting features into benefits, without getting hung up on the language they are used to.

One is a picture of a high-powered rifle that carries the caption, "It's perfectly balanced." Naturally, the rifle has many features, but the group discussion sticks to the one feature listed. At that point I ask the group, "What would good balance mean to me, the hunter?" Invariably, someone will say, "Greater accuracy." Let's stay with "accuracy" and see what that means to me. The list seems almost endless, including such things as more meat on the table, more pride in hunting, more trophies, less cripples, cleaner kills, less misses, less wasted ammunition, more economical, less chance of accidents. Someone will mention that good balance means it will be easier to carry and less tiring.

At this point in the discussion I abruptly stop and ask, "Do you *feel* the mental gymnastics you're going through, thinking up all the customer benefits from a well-balanced rifle?"

The reply is *always* affirmative.

"What you are doing right now is the very thing a customer has never been disciplined to do. Those things were all in his memory bank—they were not on the scale at all—they were worth nothing as far as helping him reach a favorable buying decision."

I then ask the group, "When the slide first came on the screen, how many of those customer benefits came to your mind immediately? . . . Then what makes you think *your* customer is any different?

"What brought the benefits to mind, put them on the scale so they were worth something and created desire in the customer's mind?" *Talking* about them—that's all. And *that* is the salesperson's job, not the customer's job. The customer doesn't want to buy balance, he wants more meat on the table, more pride, more trophies, less misses, greater economy, etc. If that's what he wants, doesn't it seem obvious that's what you and I should be selling?

Don't sell features to justify the price—sell benefits to justify a purchase!

I have no quarrel with the man who has lower prices, he knows better than anyone else what his product is worth.

Elmer Wheeler

How to Enhance
Your Sales Presentation
with Persuasive Eye Contact

When you present your product, you translate product features into customer benefits (verbal selling power). You can increase the impact of your benefit statement by synchronizing your eye movements with the discussion content. The key to successful presentations is to maintain eye contact when stating your customer benefits (nonverbal selling power).

Example of persuasive eye movements:

"Mr. Prospect"	eye contact
"This is a vinyl-covered chair."	your eyes move toward chair
Pause for a brief moment.	
"The reason I mention this is"	eyes moving back to prospect
"because"	eyes now firmly on the prospect's eyes
"it's easier to clean."	Smile, observe prospect's reactions . . .

Remember, when you describe a product feature, you have to lead your prospect's eyes to your sales literature, your spec sheet, your sample or your product itself. When you translate the feature into a customer benefit you have to maintain eye contact.

Our studies have shown that salespeople who avoid eye contact when explaining product benefits, send two conflicting messages: (1) a verbal message that explains the benefit, and (2) a nonverbal message that neutralizes the benefit. The prospect may get the impression that you don't believe in your own product. (People who purposely avoid eye contact may give the impression of not telling the truth!)

Back to Basics

By Paul Sullivan

Last fall, the kids and I went camping. It was just a weekend trip, long ago promised to them. We took along tent, small stove, sleeping bags and a few odds and ends. We had more, but left it home... intentionally. The trip was a big hit with the boys. Although it was just a weekend trip, there was plenty of time for them to hike, explore, look for wildlife and just mess around. When we got home, all agreed we hadn't missed all the other camping gear that usually goes along and preoccupies our time with packing, setting it up, fixing it when it doesn't work right, repacking it, and cleaning it.

We learned a lesson from that little outing: You can become a slave to your equipment, most of which is supposed to save time and make life easier for you. Isn't it supposed to be the other way around?

We noticed many others who had come to that pleasant meadow campground the same weekend. Some had huge motor homes, some had station wagons or pickup campers. Most, like us, had simply sought to escape to the country for a short time. But with a few exceptions, most of those campers spent a large part of their weekend performing chores, and many of those chores seemed to involve fooling with camping gear.

It's the same story in so many fields of endeavor. The tools, equipment, conveniences that are supposed to help become instead a hindrance. Selling is no exception. Things that should assist become barriers to success and, in certain cases even form dependencies we feel we can't do without—crutches.

Not too long ago I watched three sales presentations that illustrated this point. Representatives of three companies were seeking an order from a small town to replace a fleet of trash trucks.

The first two presentations seemed too slick, like canned productions. The men who made them had rehearsed their lines well enough, but they relied heavily on their audio-visual slide-and-tape

67

shows to do the selling for them. The salesmen themselves were
unimpressive, lifeless, grim. They seemed to have little grasp of the
art of salesmanship, little background on their clients' needs or the
nature of small town operations.

But the third guy was a different story. He took advantage of
his lack of a slide show or other props by playing the role of the poor
cousin, who explained that he hadn't come to entertain his clients
but just wanted to tell them about the best vehicle for their bucks
that a small town could hope to buy.

That man exuded confidence, knew his product and answered
questions with ease. He knew his clients and had done some homework on their needs. His only props were a handful of snapshots and
a specification sheet.

Contrary to what he told his clients that night, the third sales
representative was really the showman of the three. It was no
surprise when he got the order.

The successful salesman that evening was successful because
he was not leaning on an expensive professionally made audio-
visual presentation to do his work for him. Not that he couldn't have
used one. But when the show is over and the lights go back on, it's
still the salesperson who does the selling, not the tools he has
brought along to help.

Whether you are camping or selling, keep in mind that what
counts is results, not the baggage you bring along.

Four Principles to Impress Customers

by Nido Qubein

Recently I asked a number of experienced salespeople, "What's the biggest change you've noticed in selling over the years?" Most of them gave me a two-word answer—"the customer." They told me that buyers today are more professional and better educated, that they're bombarded by sales pitches on television and radio. Buyers have cultivated the habit of tuning out all sales presentations.

The sales professional can break through all of this resistance only by individualizing his presentation. *Play to each customer as if that person is the first and last client you'll ever sell to. Make that customer want to do business with you.*

It's a tough assignment. In fact, it's one of the most difficult parts of selling. But I guarantee that these extra efforts will pay off big! To get started, here are four principles that you can use to create presentations that will impress every customer and reward you with more sales.

Principle 1—People Buy from Salespeople They Trust

Psychologists have shown us how animals behave when their territory is invaded. Some run and hide, others make a lot of noise to scare off the invader, and still others turn and fight. Almost any animal, if he feels sufficiently threatened, will rise up to defend his territory.

People sometimes feel threatened, too. Some have emotional comfort zones, and others have physical ones, but the result is always the same. Invade that comfort zone and tensions rise. That's why everything the salesperson says and does will produce either tension or trust.

Unfortunately, some salespeople get all hyped up in a sales meeting and then go out and corner their first prospect. They back the customer into a corner, roll up their sleeves, knock down all objections and close, close, close! That's far from building trust. It's building walls.

I asked an old pro, "How do you know if you have built trust with a client?" He explained, "I'm sensitive to my customers. When they're tense, I do something to ease the tension. And when they're comfortable, I move in."

Go slow, create trust, then move into your presentation.

Principle 2—People Buy
from Salespeople They Respect

When something goes wrong with my car, I take it to a competent, well-qualified mechanic—someone whose professional skills I respect.

He's expensive. But he has convinced me that he can always find the trouble and fix my car. He's gained my respect. I also trust my banker, my attorney and my wife—but not to fix my car.

When you ask a busy executive for an appointment, that person asks himself a very important question. "Why should I spend my precious time listening to this person?" Only when they can answer, "This person has something to say that is important for me to hear" do you get that important appointment.

You listen to people you think will have something important to say. You look for signs of self-confidence and success. Well, that's exactly how your prospects look at you.

If you look, act and talk like you have something to say that they need to hear, customers will give you the time to say it. Once you've got their attention:

1. Respect the prospect's time—even if the prospect doesn't. A salesman once spent three hours with a busy executive on the first visit. Then the prospect refused to see him again. Finally, the salesman asked why, and the executive said, "I have a tendency to talk too much with some people ... and you're one of them!" Don't be abrupt or discourteous, but do be businesslike. Make your point and when you're finished, leave.

2. Respect the prospect's territory. Remember, you're a guest so act like one. Ask permission to move around the room or come closer to show a brochure. If you invade the prospect's space, you're likely to get one of those "animal" reactions.

3. Respect the prospect's intelligence. Sometimes you can gain entrance by trickery, but you won't gain respect. Be straight with your prospects so you don't have to worry about slipping up later.

Principle 3—People Want
to Make Their Own Decisions

Professional salespeople don't try to impose their decisions on clients. They try to help them reach their own decisions. Their sales calls are *client*-oriented, rather than *salesperson*-oriented; they seek to *discover* needs rather than *create* needs; they *discuss with* their clients, rather than *talk at* them. They are adaptable and flexible. Harsh statements like, "You're foolish if you don't take this offer," or "Take it or leave it" put the sale first. Ideas and suggestions, on the other hand, put the client first.

When the client makes a decision to buy, the pro reinforces that decision with positive comments. If the client decides not to buy, the top seller will try to resell the client by offering new information and suggesting alternative solutions. Your aim is to lead the client, not push the product.

Principle 4—People Buy
from Salespeople Who Understand Them,
Their Needs and Their Problems

The secret to closing many sales is to help the customer discover the real need behind the expressed need. When a prospect says, "I don't need life insurance," saying "Everybody needs life insurance" isn't the solution. It's much more productive to help that customer explore needs that life insurance could meet.

You can't move prospects from "I don't need it" to "I'll take it" by bombarding them with all of the wonderful features of your product. Instead, guide customers to discover how your product or service will meet needs—needs they might not even know they have.

When you help people discover what they want and how to get it through what you're selling, your sales potential will zoom upward. Establish trust and respect, then sell clients based on their needs. When you play to the customer, you play to win.

We Are What We Say

Paul J. Micali describes a common mistake that can cost you precious sales—poor speech habits. To make the best impression, Micali suggests increasing your awareness of the following image destroyers:

1. Poor enunciation. Mumbling, speaking too fast or too slow, or in a monotone are all careless speech patterns that will convey an unprofessional image.

2. Filling up space. A pause between thoughts is very effective, but often, out of insecurity or habit, those pauses are filled with sounds and words such as "er, ah, right, okay, you understand, ya know, and like," that can lose, bore, or offend the listener.

3. Highbrow vocabulary. Speaking over your client's head using ten dollar words is more likely to irritate than impress him. Because he doesn't want to seem stupid, he won't ask you what you mean and therefore won't understand what you say.

All of these speech mistakes can be corrected—if you know that they exist. Tape yourself or have a friend listen to you. Then concentrate on eliminating bad habits that can ruin even the best presentation. Your speech will improve and so will your sales.

How to Communicate Confidence
While Standing:

The two biggest mistakes salespeople make while standing are:

1. Communicating nonverbal expressions of insecurity by moving their bodies from side to side.
2. Communicating aggressiveness by putting both hands on their hips, standing directly opposite the client.

To avoid "swaying" from side to side, put your feet approximately one foot apart. It will give you increased physical stability and personal confidence. Try this experiment: Stand up and put your legs four inches apart, then put your legs one foot apart. Notice the difference in stability. It's astounding!

To avoid expressing aggressiveness, choose a 45 to 90 degree angle to your prospect. Further, maintain a distance of approximately one and a half feet to four feet. Distances less than one and a half feet are reserved for intimate contact. Distances of more than four feet indicate impersonal interactions. Be sure your arms and shoulders are relaxed when you stand. (Raised shoulders signal tension!) Avoid putting your hands on both hips.

You Can't Listen Yourself Out of a Sale!

by Ron Willingham

A couple of years ago I did several sales training seminars for U.S. Army recruiters. Upon a referral, I arranged an appointment for 10 o'clock one Tuesday morning with a recruiting commander.

When I walked into his office at 9:50 the Colonel's secretary seated me in his office and told me that he'd be in on time. As I sat scanning his office, it was very revealing. His desk was angled so that his back was in a corner and he could command the whole scene. Predominant was a large photograph of Alexander Haig.

In another corner was a table with a television set on it. Stage right on the TV set was a small American flag. On the other was a crystal decanter of red, white and blue jelly beans. Hanging above his desk, from the ceiling, was a huge banner entitled, "Army, Be All That You Can Be!" Artillery pictures hung on another wall.

I was seated on a small two-place settee—across the room from his desk. There were no other chairs in the room.

At exactly 10 o'clock the Colonel marched in. He shook my hand once, showing no feeling or emotion. Then he sat down in his desk chair and said, "I'll have to be honest with you and tell you that you've probably wasted your time coming all the way out here to see me!"

That was certainly a happy thought!

Without giving me any chance to respond, he went on, "You see, if there's anything we don't need around here it's sales training! I don't want my recruiters running around glad-handing and slapping people on their backs. They're soldiers, not IBM salesmen!"

Ducking his opening shot, I unbuttoned my coat, popped down the lid of my briefcase, crossed my legs and smiled, "Colonel... I appreciate your being honest with me... "

"How long have you been in the service?" I asked. I found out he'd been in 27 years. "I'll bet you've been in some exciting places! Where all have you been stationed?" He began talking. His

74

gestures were choppy and definite. He loved to talk.

"Where'd you enjoy living the most?" I asked when he ran down. He said Hawaii. He told me that his kids liked to go down to the beach.

"How many children do you have, Colonel?" I found out he had three. Two were boys. The delight of his life.

"How old are they?" They were both graduating from high school that year. They wanted to go to college. It was going to take $10,000 a year to send them. He didn't know how he was going to come up with the money.

"What are their goals?" I asked. He talked . . . and talked. About himself, of course. Never did want to know anything about me. Could've cared less.

He talked for an hour. I occasionally asked a question and . . . listened. Then out of the clear blue sky, he said, "You know . . . some good sales training is exactly what we need!"

Stunned, I tried to compose myself. "Oh . . . how do you feel it would help you, Colonel?"

"Well . . . " he replied, and for the next 15 minutes told me *why* his recruiters needed sales training.

I just listened and let him convince me.

Then I asked him, "Well, when and where would you want to hold these seminars, Colonel?"

In the next three minutes we set up three seminars. All his idea. If I'd tried to "sell" him I'd have been tossed out immediately.

Analyze this story and you'll see that I didn't do a traditional sales presentation. I just asked questions and listened. Had I tried to make a presentation, overcome objections and close I'd have been dead.

Think about it and you'll see that most of my selling took place in the approach and interview!

I sold by listening more than I talked!

The Sounds of Selling

Many salespeople are afraid of silence. To ease their anxiety, they fill the gaps with nonwords, meaningless phrases, and noise.

Below are some common fillers and sounds people use to string words, sentences, even paragraphs of dialogue together to eliminate uncomfortable silences.

1. single syllable sounds: uh, um, ah, eh, oh.
2. sometimes these are combined with connecting words: and uh, so um, but ah, like eh.
3. a word or group of words that adds nothing to the meaning of the sentence: you know, you see, well so then, ya understand, so really, ok?
4. hedge words: I guess, maybe, perhaps.
5. qualifiers: just, that's all, only.
6. noises: throat clearing, shuffling, tongue clucking, sighs, yawns, coughing, chuckling.

Many clients will judge your level of confidence and product knowledge by the fluency of your speech. They will interpret fillers and sounds as nervousness or uncertainty. Your clients won't care whether you're using them because of nervousness or habit—they'll simply get a bad impression. Here's how you can improve your sounds of selling.

Step One—Eliminate fillers.

Ask your family and friends to listen for fillers when you are talking. Have them stop you in midsentence every time you use one. This may ruin the flow of a conversation, but it will make you keenly aware of how often you rely on these verbal crutches. Soon you'll be stopping yourself before the nonwords or sounds are out of your mouth.

Step Two—Add silence.

Ronald Reagan is a master of the purposeful pause. He knows that it gets the listener's attention and gives the speaker an increased image of credibility. A slight pause between important statements has a wonderful effect on clients as well. They will believe that you are intelligent, analytical, and confident. Another plus is the opportunity you give to your client to make comments and ask questions. Instead of not being able to get "a word in edgewise," the buyer will feel that his opinions are being taken seriously.(However, customers can be afraid of silence, too. They may feel compelled to fill up the pauses themselves, thus giving you more information about their interests and concerns.)

One more advantage to using silence is this: It gives you a chance to listen. You understand more clearly what the client is saying, and can think about what you are going to say in a more relaxed manner if you aren't worried about immediately filling every little pause. Silence is a powerful selling tool. Use it to make a good impression, gain information, and listen to the buying sounds of your customer.

Nothing Is More Deadly
Than a Monotone

by Paul Micali

Recent college graduates are quick to recall which classes they cut most—the ones taught by professors with boring monotonelike deliveries. The lectures would seem twice as long as they really were and the student's mind would slide into daydreaming sessions. The same effect on a prospect or customer can spell disaster.

Speaking in a monotone is related to poor inflection . . . failure to vary the pitch of the voice.

A fan won't keep you awake on a warm night. In fact, it helps you go to sleep. The noise it makes is constant and at the same pitch. It's a monotone. An air-conditioner's pitch, on the other hand, will change when the compressor cuts in and will hamper your departure to slumberland. The monotone has been broken. Much like the commercial on TV that wakes you up with a start when you have dozed off. It's much louder than the programming.

To avoid speaking in a monotone, make an effort to speak enthusiastically when the point you are making warrants it, and to return to normal tones when it does not. In the latter case you still can avoid a monotone by using inflection. For instance:

The traffic problem is HORRRible.

Reduced to very simple terms, the formula to avoid a monotone delivery follows:

1. Whenever possible, speak enthusiastically.
2. When enthusiasm per se is out of place, make certain that the strong words are properly emphasized.

It's been said that an old form of Chinese torture was to place a person in solitary confinement, in the dark, listening to slowly dripping water. The monotony of the dripping water was the worst aspect. If, even on occasion, your sales presentation slides into a monotone . . . STOP. You will be torturing your prospect.

Listening Is the Key

Thomas L. Koziol, in his recent presentation, "Is too much talking costing you sales?", makes some suggestions to help improve your listening skills.

First, remember that listening to your client will tell you his needs, wants, and buying potential. If you listen you will avoid the pitfalls of *dominating the interview* (give *him* a chance to talk) and *assuming you know what he wants* (ask him questions and restate what he has said).

Secondly, pay attention to what he tells you. Most people *speak* at 150 words per minute but *listen* at 450 words per minute. This allows lots of time for *distractions*. Concentrate solely on your client, and don't show *indifference* or *boredom*. Put yourself in his shoes and show that you really care.

Finally, exhibit *control*. Instead of reacting negatively to a negative comment, listen for the tone and meaning of the objection. His hostility may mask a simple, easy-to-overcome problem.

Steil's Law of Listening

Nobody ever listened himself out of a sale!

Source unknown

Giving a sales presentation is not the same as giving a speech. Your customer will expect opportunities for asking questions and making comments *during* the presentation. If he is forced to wait for a question-and-answer session after you've talked for any length of time, he will either lose interest, or forget his questions. Clarification must take place as you go along. But even pausing and eliciting questions is not enough—you need to *listen* to what the client is saying.

Dr. Lyman Steil, founder and past president of the International Listening Association (St. Paul, MN), ranks as the country's leading authority on listening. He's known for his famous Steil's LAW of Listening: $L = A \times W^2$, meaning *listening equals ability times willingness.*.

Dr Steil, who conducts workshops on listening around the world, discovered a surprising relationship between people's attitudes and their ability to listen.

Over several years, Dr. Steil has asked seminar participants to identify the best and worst listeners they have ever known. Below is a sampling of their descriptions:

Description of the worst listeners:

abrasive	disinterested
absent	distracted
anxious	dogmatic
arrogant	inconsistent
biased	insecure
busy	limited
closed	moody
competitive	narrow
conceited	opinionated

deceptive	shifty
defensive	unconcerned

Description of the best listeners:

advisor	genuine
alert	helpful
approachable	informed
calm	inquisitive
caring	interactive
challenging	kind
clarifier	mature
concerned	open-minded
confident	patient
considerate	perceptive
enthusiastic	understanding

Dr. Steil, who heads the St. Paul, MN based consulting firm, Communication Development, Inc., comments on his findings:

"Our attitudes determine how well we listen. In selling, listening becomes central to sales success."

Look at both lists and ask yourself two questions:

1. From which type of listener would you rather buy?
2. Which words seem to describe you, your listening attitude and selling behavior?

Ten Ways to Improve
Your Sales Presentations

There are ten classic subjects that always create attention and attract interest. While reading them, think about which of your customers can relate to each type of approach, and how they can be used to meet your customers' needs.

1. *Drama and Action*. Make the prospect a hero.

   "I can see you six months from now when you walk to your assembly bay and talk to the machine operator. Glancing at the service record, he'll announce, 'Harry, we've finished this job three weeks ahead of schedule because we've had no downtime.' You'll smile, remembering today and the good decision you've made by investing in our product."

2. *Opposite Views*. Give the prospect an attractive choice.

   "Our product is a little more expensive compared to some of the others you've looked at. However, when you figure the reduced maintenance, the better trade-in value and the higher productivity, our product is actually the least expensive in the long run."

3. *Oddity*. Create an unusual, memorable mental picture.

   "This glue is so strong that you could put it between these two-by-fours, press them together, and not be able to break them apart."

4. *Progress*. Make the prospect an industry leader.

   "With the help of electronic circuits in the new unit, you'll be able to increase current production by 23 percent and outpace competitors."

5. *Timeliness*. Give a compelling reason to act now.

   "If you place your order today, you'll save 11 percent, because tomorrow our new price list goes into effect.

6. *Prominent People*. Elevate the prospect to prominence.

   "By the way, the President eats this brand of jellybeans."

7. *Personal Experience*. Put yourself on the same level.

   "I know what you mean. Building your own sailboat is

quite an undertaking. I built a small sloop in my back yard, and it took over two years to complete."

8. *Money.* Tap into the prospect's need for saving money.

"I know you're interested in saving on your new purchase. I can show you a way to cut the total bill by $900."

9. *Convenience.* Appeal to the prospect's need for comfort.

"This toll-free number gives you access to our computer data bank 24 hours a day. You can call with any question at no charge."

10. *Emotional Impact.* Show how you care for your clients.

"Our warranty saved a product manager's performance bonus. It depended on the replacement of an entire unit—which we did within four hours of his call. He couldn't believe that the product was still under warranty. But that's the kind of service you can expect from us."

By using the subjects that fit each customer best, you draw him into a position where he can really see the benefits of your sales proposal. Make your presentation stimulating and informative and the customer will see you as someone worthy of his order.

The Power of Analogies

Jim Sweeney is a superachiever. In one and one-half years, his beginning multilevel marketing company grew to 5,000 employees. He was one of the few salespeople in the U.S. with an estimated income of over one million dollars for the recession year of 1982. A prime factor in Jim's sales success in his use of analogies during a presentation.

In an article for *Personal Selling Power*, Dr. Donald J. Moine, a leading authority on psycholinguistics, analyzed a 50-minute presentation by Sweeney. He cited Jim's use of "the magic of analogies" as one of the most dynamic aspects of this sales dynamo's success. Dr Moine wrote:

"For thousands of years, analogies, parables, and metaphors have been used to inspire, to guide, and to teach. They are a wonderful way of influencing other people. They have several special persuasive advantages. First of all, analogies relax people. Secondly, since the persuasion is indirect and hidden, it is difficult to identify it and resist it. Third, analogies are very memorable. Your customer may not remember the facts you presented, but he will remember that down-home story you told which summed it all up for him. An example from Jim Sweeney:

'In order to explain to you, I'm gonna draw a building. The most important factor in a building is the foundation. Building a business is just like building a building. Exactly the same kinds of things apply. The hardest work you may very well do on a building is in the foundation. It may even take a good portion of time if not most of the time. It's the dirtiest part of the work you're going to do. It's the part that one day will be covered up and nobody will ever see and one day somebody will forget all about it, but nevertheless, the building stands on the foundations. It either stands or crumbles on the foundation.'

Jim goes on to explain that it takes four months to build the foundation for the business. He could have said that directly, but it would have been cold and hard and dry and much less motivating and inspiring than telling it through the above analogy. By the use of such analogies, Jim keeps the audience always alert, entertained, motivated, and excited.''

Try writing out one analogy each week that describes an important selling point. Once you have a collection of material to draw from, you'll find it becomes easier to see new ideas in the form of memorable tales. Stories are much easier to remember than a list of features and benefits. Why not start presenting your product in this age-old format? It may begin your own tale of success.

Ask Questions and Listen

by Ron Willingham

One of my most important sales lessons was taught me by a gentleman named J. Henry Thompson.

Mr. Thompson was a District Manager for Diebold, Inc. He lived in Dallas, Texas and called on dealers in a several-state area. From 1954 to 1959 I worked for an office equipment company that was one of his dealers.

He was a real pro!

One day he was up making calls with me. One of our calls was on the office manager of a large grain company.

I was young and green. I'd never been able to get to first base with the office manager. He was unresponsive, abrupt and had a flinty look out of his eyes that would have penetrated a Sherman tank.

The previous times I called on him I averaged lasting about two and one-third minutes before he threw me back out into the cold, cruel world.

Looking back, I did everything wrong. I'd go into his office with a new product in my hand and try to sell it to him. Nervously, I'd dominate the talking, try to act brave and then when I'd finish a paragraph . . . swish . . . he'd lower the guillotine blade and I'd be left headless and bleeding.

I blew it the day Mr. Thompson went with me.

The prospect pulled his usual trick. When I began talking he'd look at me showing no emotion, reach into his pocket, and pull out a nonfiltered Pall Mall cigarette. Looking me straight in the eye he'd roll the cigarette between his thumb and forefinger—attracting my attention to the motion.

Then for a couple of minutes he'd silently roll the cigarette so that pieces of tobacco would flake out on his lap. When enough had flaked out, leaving unfilled paper on one end, he'd put the other end in his mouth and fire it up.

A big flare would go up. He'd then stand up to dust off the tobacco from his lap, and dismiss me.

Mr. Thompson observed the whole show. He didn't say anything, but just thanked the man as we left.

When we got out to my car he said something to me that I've never forgotten. I've related, assimilated and applied it in hundreds of sales calls! It's been a major point in seminars I've conducted over the years.

Mr. Thompson said, "You may want to try asking questions and listening, rather than doing all the talking!"

He was very kind and sensitive about saying it so I wouldn't be offended.

His words hit me like a bolt of lightning! I was ripe to hear them. If anyone ever needed them, I did!

"Ask questions and listen." I tried it. I developed approach questions like, "How long have you been with this company?" "What are some things that helped you get where you are today?" I asked ice-breaking questions about things I saw in people's offices. About their interests.

Then I learned to ask indirect questions that got people talking about their needs. I developed trial-closing questions that gave me feedback as to people's opinions and feelings.

I learned that more selling was done when I listened that when I talked.

As I asked questions my confidence rose. My call reluctance decreased. My sales went up. Customers seemed to like me more. My communication skills increased.

I'm still learning how to ask them!

"You may want to try asking questions and listening, rather than doing all the talking," was some advice that hit me right where I needed it.

Ten Thoughts on Good Listening

1. Most people listen but few hear.
2. A major index of emotional maturity is the ability to listen.
3. Pretend you have no voice. Not only will you interrupt less, you will hear far better.
4. If it's worth saying, it's worth listening to.
5. Notice how often a poor memory goes with a poor listener.
6. Speak with enthusiasm but listen with calmness.
7. A top professional at anything is a master listener.
8. If you must speak, ask questions.
9. There is no such thing as an unpopular listener.
10. To succeed, one must understand. To understand one must hear. To hear, one must listen.

Using Gestures:
Say What You Want to Say

Some people never stop moving when they talk to you. They shift around, wave their arms and tap their fingers, catching your attention—your *visual* attention. But do you remember what they *said*? Other people appear to be carved in stone. And their delivery *sounds* as cold as they *look*. Most people are somewhere between these extremes, expressing their thoughts and personality nonverbally through posture, body movements and facial expressions. Anxiety, boredom and dislike can show through even the most dazzling sales presentation. The customer becomes *suspicious*. He or she may not be able to figure out what you're really thinking but knows that it's *not* the same as what you're *saying*. People who are suspicious of a salesperson don't buy.

To help *Personal Selling Power* readers make the most of nonverbal communication, we interviewed Suzy Sutton, a professional speaker, entertainer and trainer. She gave us some suggestions for improving the *way* you say what you *want* to say WITHOUT words.

Notice the way others use gestures. Make mental notes of gestures that are "relevant, expressive and effective. Analyze, scrutinize and appraise everyone, every chance you get."

Get some honest feedback. Have a friend or peer accompany you on a sales call to observe you and take notes on everything. "Honest feedback can mean the difference between stagnation and progressive professional and personal growth."

Beg, borrow or buy a videotape machine. You'll "really see yourself as others see you." Roleplay sales presentations, set up simulated panel discussions, practice any situations you normally encounter.

Relax. "A rigid body triggers a rigid mind." Make sure you're telling your clients "Go," not "Stop," with your body language.

Practice your facial expressions. Let your bathroom mirror tell you how to put on your best smile. "Try raising and lowering your

89

eyebrows to show disdain, skepticism, approval, acceptance. Practice looking surprised, displeased, happy, sad." Facial gestures are easily seen and read—use them.

Stop restricting yourself. If you tend to keep gesturing to a minimum, practice exaggeration. Describe things that are little or big, short or tall, "pound the table" or "jab a finger in the air." And remember that "open-handed" movements generally are positive gestures and project sincerity. Closed movements seem defensive.

Practice eye contact. Really *look* at prospects, friends and family. "Try to talk with your eyes as well as your hands."

In essence, you can learn to "project a personality that's pleasant and appropriate if you take time to analyze, understand and improve" your body's vocabulary of movement. Time spent refinishing your gestures will be one of the best investments you can make to increase your sales success.

Perform Your Way into the Sale

by Craig Bridgman

You don't have to open a sales presentation with an exhibition of knife throwing to cut through the prospect's protective layers of indifference. But it should have verve and animation, and engage the prospect's attention the same way that a good dramatic performance holds an audience. In fact, the prospect expects the salesperson's physical presence to provide an element of interest that a brochure or direct mail piece could not. That's why he's seeing you.

On every sales call, keep in mind that just as an actor makes a part come to life by putting himself into it wholeheartedly, a salesman must, through the blend of personality, enthusiasm, sincerity and craft that he brings to his work, make his product come alive in the mind of the prospect. The salesman who has a little bit of the actor in him, who has a certain flair for showmanship, who can win the prospect over through a convincing presence, gains the advantage. Think of the best sales professionals you know, and ask yourself if this is not true.

But, you say, drama has never been your thing. As far back as third grade, you flunked an audition for a walk-on part in the class play, and it's been downhill ever since. Deadpan and dour, bland and uninspiring, that's you. Well, fret not. A simple trick of the imagination will enable you to add all the excitement and emotion any good sales presentation needs.

Think for a minute about your favorite sport or pastime. You may be mad about mountain climbing, or passionate about ping-pong. Perhaps you love to hunt, read good books, take in the opera, or do hang gliding. Just the thought of this favorite activity puts you in a good frame of mind and triggers a surge of enthusiasm. Now, imagine telling someone else about, say, the highlights of a baseball game you attended, or a good book you read recently. Because your own interest is profound and active, your manner will be animated

and your commentary lively, and you will communicate your enthusiasm to the other person in the most natural and unaffected way
possible. Without even realizing it, you will invite your listener to
become interested.

When you pay a sales call, if you imagine that you are telling
your prospect about this favorite pastime, your enthusiasm will
transfer itself to the presentation. The result will be a persuasive,
credible performance that excites interest and draws in your prospect. The result of *that* might just be an order that otherwise
wouldn't have come your way.

It's Time for Q's and A's!

by Jim Savage

Have you ever heard a presentation that was informative, educational and inspirational and then had the whole program fizzle during a question and answer session? Countless business communicators have "retreated" from the room in defeat after performing in the question/answer session.

Handling these sessions isn't hard! The Effective Business Communicator uses the following steps:

1. Step forward and lift your hand while saying, "Are there any questions?" Stepping forward says that you have confidence and are willing to "step up" to the challenge. By lifting your hand, you signal the audience to lift their hands rather than just call out questions. The executive who retreats from the group, rocks back on his heels and folds his arms is certainly not signaling for open dialogue.

2. Listen carefully to the entire question: listen... listen, listen! Formulate your answer after the question is finished!

3. Answer the question to the group. Restate a key part of the question and include all the listeners in your response. Engaging in a debate with the questioner will *exclude* others... answering the group will help you control the situation.

4. Save a "power phrase" for your close. Don't "slink" off the platform with apologetic comments. Save a strong comment or challenge such as, "Use these concepts and principles in your life, and you too, will be successful!" Don't wilt like a dying flower at the end of your presentation.

Superior communicators have one or two common questions in mind to use if audience questions are slow in coming. With no response to their initial offer to accept questions, they say, "A question I am frequently asked is..." Q/A sessions are often slow to start and difficult to end—be prepared for both.

There are some cautions in conducting a Question and Answer session. The Effective Business Communicator avoids:

1. Losing control of the audience. You must use your Vital Skill Area (i.e., gestures, posture, eye contact, etc.) while answering the questions. By doing so, you will come across as competent and confident.

2. Putting down the questioner—Be courteous and considerate of the person asking the question. Remember, the questioner is a member of the audience; you are the visitor.

3. Using the question to begin another speech. Answer the question in a brief, to-the-point way. As a professional, you want to stay on the subject. Make sure your answers are specific, short, and answer the question to the satisfaction of the audience.

If you will use these basic steps, and remember the cautions, you will add power to your Question/Answer sessions.

Handling
the Manipulative Client

by Dr. William D. Brown

Abraham Lincoln once said he had anticipated most duties associated with the presidency, the exception being the innumerable requests made of him. He found these difficult to refuse, and there was little secret in Washington about his dislike of responding with a "No." Summing up his feelings he exclaimed, "It's a good thing I wasn't born a female, such is my inability to say 'No' or to refuse any but the most blatantly dishonest request!"

President Lincoln suffered from an affliction common to many sales professionals: the inability to say "No" to a prospect, client or customer. After all, the customer is always right. Right? Wrong! If the client is trying to manipulate the salesperson, it's wrong for the salesperson to act as if the customer is right.

Manipulation is a psychological defense designed to manage and control another or a situation for one's own purposes. Healthy sales personalities avoid this behavior by developing their persuasive skills. (See also "The High Cost of Manipulation" in the April 1984 issue of *Personal Selling Power.*)

Many times the manipulator is the sales prospect, with the salesperson on the receiving end. In many instances, salespeople not only allow, but sometimes *invite* manipulation. The cause? First, they are anxious to please. Second, they are afraid to offend, and third, their ego strengths may be battered. All three result in lower self-concepts. After all, pressured to perform by superiors, the last thing they want is to lose customers.

Further, salespeople are, by instinct, socially cooperative. Some social scientists argue that it is the experience and training that shapes the sales personality. Other scholars are convinced that people-oriented personality types gravitate toward the sales field because of their inherent other-oriented drives. Regardless of the cause, two main factors prevent salespeople from being more effective at handling the manipulative client: (1) Salespeople need and

95

seek constant stroking, and (2) their greatest fear is that they won't be liked.

In approaching the manipulative customer, it is little wonder that the salesperson's self-esteem is threatened and his anxiety level rises. Responding to the double threat, he tends to choose unhealthy defense mechanisms that almost always amount to explaining away failure. Healthy defense mechanisms protect the ego from unwarranted attack or ultimate rejection. An example of a healthy defense mechanism is the way a salesperson determines to solve the problem by renewing his efforts to remove or get around frustrating obstacles placed by the manipulative client.

The next time you visit a manipulative client, consider using the following techniques: (1) compensation and (2) assertiveness.

Compensation

The salesperson tries to offset a deficiency in one area by substituting a skill in another. For example, you want to make a sales presentation to a particular client, but do not feel comfortable verbally communicating with him because of his presumed advantage with manipulating words. You might compensate for this deficiency by writing up your proposal, using flip charts and other visual aids as a means of persuading your client to make an affirmative decision.

When a customer is known to be prone to say "No" to nearly all proposals, you could get him in the "habit" of agreeing with you on several minor points before attempting your first "trial close." Persuasion is your most useful tool against the manipulative client.

Assertiveness

A salesperson named Dow procrastinates in calling on Mr. Pessimist because when he leaves the customer, he always feels worse than when he arrived. True, some sales have resulted from these calls, but Dow feels emotionally exhausted just by recalling how much these past calls extracted from him. Each week, he reassigns a lower priority to the call on Mr. Pessimist, promising himself he will get to it just as soon as he has the time. Dow suffers from low assertiveness.

Salesman Jones, on the other hand, considers Mr. Pessimist as a typical purchasing agent, the kind who consume their young as hors d'oeuvres, saving their main appetites for the salesman entree!

Nonetheless, he assigns Mr. Pessimist the highest priority on his list of "must call today." He approaches the obstacle head on. First, he knows he is at his best early in the morning and can better counter the doom and gloom he will face in the presence of this customer. Second, rather than expecting to be manipulated, he imagines in his mind how he will skillfully manage Mr. Pessimist. The goal is not to change the pessimist's personality. Rather realistically the stage is set by Jones to allow him to play the role of the professional salesperson he is. He will focus on the task, making the sale and leaving with his own ego intact, with benefits accruing throughout the rest of his day from his sense of accomplishment.

Rather than withdrawing, Jones goes on the offense with a task-oriented behavior. Because of his assertiveness, he also develops a healthier personality in the process, further complementing his role as a professional in the sales field.

The best way to increase your ability to handle the manipulative client is by relying on your own intuitive judgment—listen to your inner voice.

Watch that you aren't used—consciously or unconsciously—by customers who are nice people but who have emotional needs far greater than those you are prepared to handle. Being empathetic with an understanding and perhaps sympathetic ear may occasionally be required. Yet, make certain you aren't mainly counseling (for which you aren't adequately compensated) at the expense of selling (for which you are).

Learn from your own experience. Keep a diary and record how you handle manipulative clients successfully. Test new responses and techniques. Study and choose your response strategies with care.

Finally, don't allow a manipulative client to decrease your self-esteem. Be firm and assertive and you will increase your sales success.

Selling by Seminar

Let the prospects do the walking

by Dr. Milt Grassell

If you are looking for a better way to increase your sales and profits, you should try selling-by-seminar. Here are the advantages:

- You'll be giving your sales presentation to a group of prospects rather than to one person.
- You'll have a guaranteed period of time to give your complete sales presentation without interruption.
- You'll be able to see prospects you'd not be able to see by appointment.
- You'll be able to bring satisfied customers and prospects together in the same room.

While selling-by-seminar has been used primarily to sell intangibles, it works just as well with tangibles.

Location

It's usually best to have your seminar in a "neutral" place like a hotel, restaurant, college, etc., rather than at your firm's offices.

Don't cut cost! Hold your seminars in only the best places. Select a location:

- That's easily accessible from the freeways and has adequate well-lighted parking facilities.
- That has neat, clean, attractive well-lighted and well-ventilated seminar rooms.
- That serves good food if you'll be including meals.

Length

The length of your seminars depends on how much you need to say to get your message across. However, you should be able to do this:

- During a breakfast, luncheon or dinner meeting.
- During a nonmeal function such as midmorning, in the afternoon, or after dinner in the evening.

I've scheduled successful sales seminars during all of these times. The key is how they are promoted.

Give Two Choices

Schedule the same seminar on two consecutive days. This won't double your attendance, but it will make it possible for more people to come.

Seminar Promotion

The best way to get prospects to attend your seminars is to use this three-step approach:

- Direct Mail
- Phone Follow-Up
- Last-Minute Reminder

You can often purchase adequate mailing lists or you can build your own. Putting together a good prospect mailing list isn't difficult because you already have a number of readily available sources:

- Your Own Records
- Chamber of Commerce Membership and Industrial Directories
- Trade Journals
- Telephone Directories
- Various Directories and Other Sources in Your Local Library

Written Invitations: First, mail out written invitations and enclose postpaid return response cards. Emphasize benefits! Give the place, dates, times, and a simplified map if the location is difficult to find.

Follow-Up Calls: Don't be disappointed if everyone doesn't respond. They never do.

Just pick up the phone and have your secretary do the calling for you. *Note!* The written invitation—whether your prospect has read it or not—will take the curse off the call.

The prospect may say, "I didn't receive the invitation" or "I wasn't interested," etc. Say, "It's a good thing I called ... " Continue! Never pause! Emphasize benefits.

"Last Minute" Reminders: One day before your seminar, phone and remind each prospect. They'll appreciate this.

The Seminar Presentation

Make a professional sales presentation. Use good quality audio-visual aids. Do your best in making stimulating demonstrations!

Be sure to involve your participants. After giving an overall view of what my seminars are all about, I ask each participant the one thing they want to get from the presentation. This forces me to present my material from their viewpoints. These viewpoints are written on large chalkboards in front of the room.

Invite some of your more enthusiastic customers and clients to share their own experiences with your product and services. These statements are powerful endorsements in your behalf. And, of course, throughout your presentation encourage and answer questions.

How to Hold Prospects
after Your Sales Presentation Ends

Prospects tend to rush out after the formal presentation thinking that's the end. But for you it isn't. This is the time that you need to greet as many as possible of your prospects individually, even if it's just for a few moments.

Here's the secret to holding your prospects. Serve your refreshments now and suggest that they stay at least long enough to talk to your present customers (whom you've introduced during your presentation) as well as to give you time to visit with each one personally.

Another secret is to hold your attendance to about 15 to 20 prospect-guests. This helps in two ways:

- Your guests will feel your presentation was really presented for them rather than for the multitude.
- You'll be able to talk individually to most of them at the end of your presentation.

Follow-Up

Mail out thank-you-for-attending notes immediately after the seminar and start calling each prospect for an appointment.

Selling by seminar will give you quicker and greater market penetration, sales and profits.

Objections

Objections are like termites. When left unattended they threaten the stability of your entire building, but with proper treatment, you're soon back in business. In fact, objections can focus your attention on the customer's problems and provide you with opportunities to discuss more benefits.

We've included some vital methods for getting your customers' objections under control. They include avoiding self-defeating nonverbal responses, recognizing the most common objections, reassuring nervous clients and disarming hostile ones, dealing with price objections, and handling stalls.

Don't Close Up—
Open Up to Objections

What does your body communicate when your buyer says, "Your price is too high!''? How did you react to your customer's objection in your last sales call? Try to remember specifics such as your leg posture, hand movements, and changes in body posture or angle.

In analyzing videotapes of thousands of selling situations, we found that most salespeople show negative changes in their body postures when hearing objections.

Many salespeople, faced by objections, may tilt their back, move slightly back in the chair, cross their arms, cross legs away from the client, scratch their head, put a hand under their collar, frown, jiggle their legs, rub nose, or sway from side to side.

These nonverbal signals communicate "Yellow" to the prospect. (The prospect may think: "Ah, *now* I've come to the weak spot!) Even though the salesperson's verbal reply is flawless, his or her nonverbal expression may have said simultaneously: "I really have doubts about this" ... "I am uncomfortable about this, you've found my weakest spot" ...or "I don't know if I can sell to you ..."

The key to success is to control your own body expressions. Relax when you hear an objection. Use open postures. Your mind should focus on your strategy. First, uncover the reasons for the objection, next ask questions, then reply. When you answer, use subtle hand gestures (palms up), and express understanding. Avoid communicating "Yellow."

Turning Old Objections into New Orders

Picture yourself outside a prospect's office following a lost sale. There you stand, numb and perplexed, the briefcase like lead in your hand. Overhead the fluorescent light hums and glitters. The receptionist chuckles quietly into the telephone receiver cradled between her chin and shoulder. Rushing down the corridor with an armload of reports, the office boy nearly bowls you over. But you barely notice this or any of the other activities as you turn slowly to leave the lobby.

What are you thinking? Not much. In fact, nothing. Your mind's eye focuses on the scene in the prospect's office just a few moments past. "This product seems a bit expensive," the buyer had said, "I'd like time to think it over." You relive your vague efforts to turn aside his objection. Now you realize something else: there's an empty order form. Your mind churns over in frustration, and again you return to the scene, reconstructing the dialogue.

What happened in the buyer's office is quite simple, and, alas, all too common. He or she presented an objection you were unable to meet. Brooding about the misfortune won't help. You'll have to improve your techniques for handling objections. Otherwise, you're destined to lose more sales.

It is crucial to tackle any objection *when it arises*. If you let it go by, it appears to the buyer that you've accepted the objection, which then becomes an oft-repeated factor in his argument denying you the sale. Remember, if you're prepared, you can actually view objections as closing opportunities. It's the client's way of saying, "I'll buy, if you'll first solve this problem for me ... "

Through the years, expert sales psychologists have recognized four classes of objections. These are:

- *Misunderstandings.* The prospect is inhibited by a minconception about the product, the sales representative, or the company.
- *Stalling.* The prospect claims to like the product, but wants more time to make a decision.

103

- *Price*. The prospect likes the product, but thinks it too costly.
- *Negativism*. The prospect may like the product, but won't open up.

There's not a single objection that, properly analyzed, won't fit into one of these categories. With minimal practice, you can become adept at recognizing each type. Then what? When the prospect objects or turns aggressive, do you want to respond in kind? In most cases—though there are exceptions—the answer is "no." If you "butt heads" with the prospect, either verbally or by mimicking his nonverbal messges, you'll merely reinforce his attitude and lose the sale.

"That's why I'd like to talk to you now. We need the quiet season to take a look at what we'll be needing when it is time to buy."

Your best friends in this situation are:(1) positive nonverbal messages, e.g. leaning forward, level posture and head angle, open hands, smiling; and, (2) the open question. These two tools take the prospect by surprise and get under his defenses. The objection is turned aside, and attention is focused on the issue of real concern to the prospect.

Let's examine strategy case by case for the four types of objections.

Misunderstandings. Is the customer unfamiliar with technical terms? Is he unaware of your company's superiority in this line of product? Your role is to inform and educate. The customer has to understand first before he can objectively make a decision.

Example

*Prospect:*I don't think this prescription product will improve my patients' condition.
Seller: What do you mean?
Prospect: This disease is simply incurable!
*Seller:*There is no cure for this disease, only relief from discomfort. What's significant is that your patients will feel far fewer side effects with this new drug.

Here, the sales rep asks the buyer for more information. "Why do you say that?" or "I'd like to know what made you think of that?" Then he clarifies the misunderstanding, reinforcing his explanation with visuals, testimonials, *and,* most importantly, positive nonverbal messages. The sales rep doesn't argue or make a point of drawing attention to the customer's ignorance. Both would be fatal mistakes. He wants to win a decision, not an argument.

An objection that stems from *misunderstanding* is probably the easiest to overcome. Because of a misleading preconception or a simple lack of knowledge, the prospect honestly fails to see why he should buy from you. That's perfectly valid, unless, of course, he continues to object *after* you've provided the missing information and cleared up his apparent confusion. If that happens, you know the first objection is a ruse masking something else. The prospect is stalling.

Stalling or indecision signals the presence of a conflict within the buyer. The prospect is uncertain or afraid, perhaps of making a bad purchase. The objection is *not* valid—if it's agreed that the product is good, needed, and reasonably priced.

Once the prospect has engineered a stall, he may never get back to you. The suggested technique: don't respond to what the prospect says, but concentrate attention on his reason for stalling.

Example 1

Buyer: I want to think it over.
Seller: Perhaps I could help you. What are the points you seem to question?

Example 2

Buyer: I don't buy anything until I sleep on the decision first.
Seller: I understand that you want more time to think. I'd be interested in hearing your thoughts about the reasons for and the reasons against buying now.

In both cases, the buyer is not being open with the seller. He's trying to give him the old "brush off," with an excuse of wanting more time. But that's not the real reason for his indecision. Note that the sales rep immediately turns aside the objections, and looks for the reason behind it. He wants to know what a buyer is afraid of.

Objections to price are harder to meet. Such instances may mean that the buyer is an aggressive bargainer, that the competition is cheaper, or that he doesn't see your product justifying the cost. These are all potentially valid objections requiring a well-rounded response.

Analyze the facts. Look for the reasons behind the price objection. A good opener: Check if the customer understands (and agrees with) the values you've offered. Then stress quality.

Example 1

Buyer: Your price is too high.
Seller: How do you compare the price?
Buyer: I can't see how you can get away with charging so much.
Seller: Yes, we are in the higher bracket, yet we do over $3 million a year at these same prices. That wouldn't be possible if our customers weren't convinced of our benefits. Our product may seem expensive at the time of purchase, but it's a better buy since it's the cheapest in the long run.

Example 2

Buyer: I can get a similar product 10 percent cheaper. If you cut your price, I'll buy from you.
Seller: It wasn't my impression that your products are the cheapest in *your* industry—or was I wrong? Our policy is to quote the best price first and be as fair to our new customer as to the ones who buy this product on a repeat basis."

Note the seller doesn't appear to disagree with the prospect, yet he doesn't accept the objection. There's no way a sales rep can deny the strength of numbers, if for example, a competitor's product costs 10 percent less. That's irrefutable, a valid objection. Instead, the seller focuses on an alternative merit, in this case long-term value.

Negativism. When the prospect is extremely negative, it's a clear indication of one thing: You're dealing with an individual burdened by past experiences. The sales rep, again, must find the motive behind the objection, then draw the prospect into the present.

Example 1

Buyer: I really don't have time to listen to this.
Seller: I can save you time. In only 11 minutes, you and I can find out how this product will save you time and money in your operation.

Example 2

Buyer: It's the wrong season of the year for buying this product. I don't know why you people come around when you know things are slow for us.
Seller: That's why I'd like to talk to you now. We need the quiet season to take a look at what we'll be needing when it *is* time to buy.

In both instances, the sales representative persuades the buyer to give him fair consideration in the "here and now." Nobody wants to be judged according to bias. The sales rep draws the reluctant buyer out of his shell by focusing on the issues immediately at hand.

Think you've got the idea? It's really a simple concept: Use the buyer's strength to your advantage: The important thing is not to be rattled by an objection, but to analyze it, then to act quickly to counteract it, thus turning the objection into an opportunity to close the sale.

Reassuring Your Nervous Customer

Dentists and their staffs are aware of the anxiety their services produce. They also realize that those who say they're not nervous may be the most jittery patrons. So they look for "displacement gestures." Tapping fingers, flipping quickly through magazine after magazine, fishing for something at the bottom of a purse, and chain smoking all indicate a large amount of nervous energy. To calm their patients, dentists know that they need to reassure them through pleasant music, calm, low-key conversation, and light humor. The main goal is to assure the patient, through their own actions, that everything is fine.

In selling, you may notice similar displacement gestures being communicated by the hesitant prospect. On these occasions you need to learn to proceed with caution. How would you respond? How can you help your apprehensive or nervous prospect to relax and feel comfortable about buying? It's simple:

1. Avoid "mirroring" the client's negative nonverbal gestures or movements. Resist the subtle, unconscious urge to respond to the clients' displacement gestures by scratching your head, fiddling with a match, jiggling coins in your pocket, or shifting your posture. When you imitate negative nonverbal expressions, you only maintain or even reinforce the client's existing level of tension. This can become an insurmountable barrier on your way to the sale.

2. Lead the client to imitate your own expressions of confidence and reassurence. Begin communicating relaxed gestures and postures. Maintain a comfortable distance between you and your prospect (four or five feet). Express open gestures and totally relax your body: shoulders down, head slightly tilted (to express interest and understanding), your eyelids slightly closed (wide-open eyes signal fear!).

Approach your nervous prospect with a warm and reassuring attitude. Don't say: "Come on and relax." Your words will hardly be heard. Let your body carry the message instead. Positive body language can be five times more persuasive than words. Your own calm and confident attitude will help your prospect become men-

Self-touching indicates need for reassurance.

tally available for the purpose of your visit. Earn your client's trust
and confidence with positive nonverbal expressions. Helping him or
her to relax is the key to a good relationship and a comfortable
atmosphere, and is essential to getting the order.

Rephrasing Customer Objections into Questions

by Dr. Milt Grassell

Contrary to popular opinion, it's a critical moment whenever objections pop up. The way you handle them determines whether you'll continue to keep the door open or lose the sale at that point.

If the rebuttals taught in traditional sales training through the years have ever worked, those kinds of answers don't work in the mid-1980s. Buyers today are too astute to listen to this nonsense.

Instead, use this four-step procedure whenever your prospects object:

1. *Keep Calm.* Always keep calm after an objection pops up. Show empathy and never show resentment.

2. *Get In Step With Your Prospect's Thought-Pattern.* Demonstrate that you heard and understood what your prospect said. This doesn't mean you agree. Use statements such as:

- "I'm not surprised you say that. Many customers do."
- "I understand. Many of my present customers felt that way before buying."
- "I'd never thought of that. It's a good point."

3. *Restate the Objection in Question Form.* Whether the objection was expressed as a question or as a statement, the secret is to restate the objection in question form. This is an absolute must! Examples follow:

- "The question, Mrs. Smith is, 'Will solar heat really cost you less?'"
- "The question, Mr. Jones is, 'Do the extra features on the industrial model warrant the price?'"
- "The question, Ms. Brown is, 'Can you invest now?'"

4. *Get the Prospect's Confirmation.* Find out whether this is or is not the question. Simply ask, "Mr. Jones, is that the question?"

If Mr. Jones says, "Yes," now you know what his objection is and you can handle it directly rather than shooting in the dark.

Just suppose Mr. Jones had said, "No, that's not my question." Then say, "Well . . . if that isn't the question, Mr. Jones . . . then what would you say is the question?" Most prospects will tell you.

If you've been stumbling over too many objections and losing too many sales, why not start using this successful sales tactic now.

The Over-Response

When you are feeling down and under you are most tempted to overcome feeling overwhelmed by over-responding.

The over-response is self-defeating. Here are ten reasons why: The over-responder

- overfocuses on the problem instead of the solution
- overestimates the power and worth of others
- over-reacts to normal, everyday frustrations
- overturns all realistic and sound ideas and suggestions of others
- uses overkill to get his/her ideas across
- oversleeps and becomes irritable and overbearing
- overeats and gets overweight
- overlooks that his low self-worth is an overinflated myth
- overdoses on vitamins, drugs, alcohol, or sex
- overkills time watching TV, which overstresses the overexposed nervous system

Stop over-responding. You can't get over whatever it is you want to overcome by over-reacting. Think it over instead. Thinking is an inexpensive form of action. Thinking before acting prevents over-reacting. Think it over and over and over again.

You've Got to Do Better Than That

In a recent issue of *Purchasing Magazine,* a leading expert on negotiation explained that there are seven magic words that drive salespeople crazy. They are: *You've got to do better than that.*

The author, Dr. Chester L. Karrass, says that the uninhibited use of this crunch technique ultimately results in false economy because sellers soon learn to add 10 percent to bids in order to have something to shave later when the crunch comes.

Personal Selling Power collected responses from selected readers who have handled the crunch technique with success. They used answers like:

1. I understand that you want a lower price, and we will be more than happy to lower it to the level you have in mind. Let's review the options that you'd like to cut from our proposal, so we can meet your needs.

2. We are building a product up to a quality, not down to a price. A lower price would prevent us from staying in business and serving your needs later on.

3. Yes, we can do better than that if you agree to give us a larger order.

4. It was my understanding that we were discussing the sale of our product and not the sale of our business.

5. I appreciate your sense of humor—how much better can you get than rock-bottom? You see, our policy is to quote the best price first. We have built our reputation on high quality and integrity—it's the best policy.

6. I'd be glad to give you the names of two customers so you can find out how much they paid for our product. And you'll see it's exactly the same as we are asking you to pay. We could not develop our reputation without being fair to everyone.

7. I appreciate the opportunity to do a better selling job. Obviously, you must have a reason for looking exclusively on the dollar side of our proposal. Let's review the value that you'll be receiving . . .

Overcoming the Client's Fear
of the Unfamiliar

A new product may meet resistance because it appears too complicated, too unfamiliar. Here is a tip from an office machine sales rep who developed an effective method to explain the unknown in familiar terms.

Before I explain this machine to you, I'd like to ask you a few questions. You are familiar with operating a television set, aren't you?

Yes.

What do you do to turn it on?

That's obvious, I turn the switch.

But what do you do when the picture is too dark?

I turn the dial to make it brighter.

And if you want to watch a different channel?

I turn the channel selector.

What do you do if the sound level is too high?

I turn down the volume control.

Can you explain in detail how and why the television picture appears on your screen?

I have no idea.

You see, my point is that you have not wasted your time learning about how and why it works. You have learned how to operate a few dials on your television set to get good results. The same is true with this new word processor. You don't need to be concerned about the advanced technology found in this equipment. If you follow a few simple instructions, you can easily learn how to get good results.

Disarming the Hostile Customer

by Joseph A. Pershes

A number of years ago when I was national sales manager of a middle-sized consumer company, I called on a major account we had lost. Our local sales representative had set up the appointment for me.

When I walked in, it was a hostile situation from the very start. Hanging on the firm's wall was a letter from our company's old credit manager. It was nasty, indignant and insulting to our prospect. To top it off, that old credit manager was now our company's general manager and my boss.

Thus, when I began my sales pitch, there were many strikes against me. But all of a sudden I found the vehicle that would both disarm my prospect and get him to listen to me. Two "Batakas" were in the corner of the room. Now "Batakas" are padded aggression bats used in martial encounters and group therapy sessions. They are usually owned by aggressive people who need a physical outlet without hurting others.

I knew I was getting nowhere with the owner of this company so I blurted out: "You want to fight?" He answered "Yes," so we went at it with the "Batakas" in hand. After five minutes of grueling combat in coats and suits, my adversary won. Of course he felt a lot better.

He sat down and wrote one of the largest orders my company had ever seen!

The *Personal Selling Power Tip* in this story: Don't be afraid to take a risk and do what some would say is foolish. Be willing to do the outlandish to get the order. The buyer might even turn out to become your best friend.

Refocusing Techniques
for Better Sales

by John H. Herd

The Chairman of the Board, an ex-Congressman, was the subject of highly partisan newspaper articles, which labeled him high in integrity, outspoken, opinionated, ultraconservative and unbending. After attending our three-day management seminar, he invited me to address his management team for the purpose of voting "yes" or "no" to our services.

There were fifteen yes votes and one "no." His was the "no." Since he felt more equal than the others, he won. After lunch we returned to his office to review his decision. Here is how it went:

"Bob, I want you to know I was pleased at your people's decision and disappointed at yours. I'd also like you to know that this does not affect our personal relationship in any way. I know you to be a man of integrity and personal courage, and I respect you for it."

"Thank you. I appreciate that. And I wouldn't have it any other way."

"Bob, when you decided to cast your ballot 'against,' you had your own good reasons for doing so. Now that that's behind us, would you mind sharing them with me?"

"Not at all. What would you like to know?"

"What is the single most important reason, Bob, for voting no?"

"That's easy. We have a good group of managers here. They are capable and hard-working. There is no reason why we should need an outside consultant to turn things around. I can't remember when my father (founder of one of the state's largest corporations) ever used a consultant."

"Bob, I was very impressed by the people I met this morning. It's easy for me to believe that they are professionals and that they do a good job. And I know you to be a person who doesn't do things without good reason. Let me ask you, what did you have in mind when you invited me here?"

"Well, I watched you in front of groups and I wanted you to address my people and put a little fire under them. Quite frankly I was surprised at the way they voted."

"Thanks for your candor, Bob. Frankly, I was a little surprised at their response myself. Now here you are; you've excellent people, and they're willing to work hard. My question to you is: Why do you think they wanted to bring me in?"

"Because they are not making bonus. We aren't doing very well."

"What will happen to them and the rest of this company, if things continue the way they have been going?"

"Well, I'm afraid if we don't turn the boat around and I mean soon, we might have to relocate down South."

"When will that be?"

"Oh, in about nine months from now."

"Bob, how long do you want to wait?"

He fell silent for a moment, then said, "Get your appointment book out. When can you start?"

"What will happen . . . if" is one of many refocusing techniques that can cause your listeners to alter their perspectives of reality. "What will happen . . . if" specifically makes your listeners reflect on the consequences of their decisions. It gets them to focus more clearly on the future, on outcome. In an age of instant gratification, this has wide application.

Jack Nye had a chip on his shoulder. A good salesman, he was careful only to let his company's people see his critical attitude. Repeated confrontations with the sales manager brought no lasting change, so that the company was seriously considering dismissing him. At their request, Jack and I spent some time together.

"What will happen, Jack, if they tell you they have had enough and let you go?"

"I don't care. I'll get another sales job."

"O.K. What will happen then? Things probably won't go as well there as you expect, either. So sooner or later, you'll be driving them up a wall, too. Is that a good possibility?"

"It's a possibility."

"And then what?"

"I'll get another sales job."

"Right. About how old are you, Jack?"

"Thirty-seven. Why?"

"Well, let's say it takes three years before you get yourself canned, how much longer do you expect to go through those cycles?"

There was a long silence. Finally he said:

"This may sound silly, but I never thought of it that way before. I better do something about it, or I won't ever get anywhere."

"Right."

Jack has high standards and when the company's internal support group fails him, he bares his teeth. Now that he is a little wiser, he treats the support people with the same persuasive skills he normally reserves for his customers. The reason for changing his behavior was the dour prospect of a lifetime of job-hopping, a refocus on his part.

Another refocusing technique is "Just suppose . . . " It is one that sounds particularly comfortable to your prospect's ears, because it feels so nonthreatening.

A giant corporation wanted its service personnel to do some selling when making service calls on business and residences. The people resisted, however, because they believed selling was hustling people. They also believed that their high technical competence would be besmirched and that their lack of sales expertise would color the customer's perception of them and their service. "Just suppose . . . " came to the rescue. After considerable training and coaching, they acquired the confidence to use it.

Martie Campbell was completing an installation.

"Just suppose, Mr Goodenough, you can have another unit anywhere in these offices, where would you put it?" she asked.

"You realize, young woman, that I'm not buying anything."

"I understand, but just suppose you can have another unit anywhere on these premises, where do you think you'd have it?"

"Well, in that case, at the desk near the entrance."

"Hmm, interesting idea. Why there?"

"Why? Because it is the most accessible spot, you don't have to interrupt anyone and we probably would improve our service with it."

"Good reasons. What model would you pick?"

"What model? The off-white, medium size."

"Why not the smaller one?"

"Because it's too small for our workload."

"Say, that's a good reason, let me ask you . . . so long as that is the most accessible spot and you don't have to interrupt anyone, and at the same time you improve your operation and have the workload for it, why not save yourself some money and get it installed while I'm here? If you ordered it later and I had to come back to do it, there'd be another service charge. This way you know you'll save $80."

"That so? Hmm. O.K. Good idea. Let's do it."

The "Just suppose" is a multiservice tool. First, it seems so harmless that the prospect permits himself to discuss it. Second, the service person expands the prospect's thinking and makes him focus on positive reasons for owning the unit. Third, she gets the customer to come up with and voice the sales points himself, a sure convincer. Fourth, she uses an imbedded command when she states "Just suppose, Mr. Goodenough, *you can have another unit.*" Top sales producers do this unconsciously most of the time. Fifth, she hits home on saving $80 now, a minor decision point. Sixth, she discovers the prospect's buying fingerprints and seizes many opportunities for stroking his judgment.

There are a variety of techniques for refocusing other people's view of reality, including objections on price, delivery, quality, a prior bad experience, personality issues and others. All of us have but five senses and filter what we take in through a welter of experiences and psychological biases. Often we are biased to a point where we hurt ourselves. Refocusing helps you expose your prospects to the significant factors they have failed to consider. Refocusing also enables you to be of better service to your customers.

"We Want to Think It Over"

by Thomas G. Winninger

Prospect's Objection: "We want to think it over!"
Salesperson: "How long do you want to think it over? Six months or two years!"

You can't say that, but what do you say? After selling over $10 million worth of my product, I have learned that a statement like "We want to think it over!" is a friend, not a foe. If you can learn to view this so-called objection as a "reach out," to see that the prospect is "reaching out" to you for help, you will have an inner power to rely on when you hear your next objection.

The following strategy is easy to learn, easy to use and very effective in increasing your closing ratio. (Follow each step in order.)

Step 1—Listen to the "Reach Out."

Step 2—Offer a softening statement.

Step 3—Rephrase the "reach out" into a question, then tie it down.

Step 4—Answer it.

Step 5—Close.

The following is an example of how to word each step:

Prospect: We want to think it over!"

You—Step 1: (Pause for a moment)

You—Step 2: "I understand how you feel! Many of my customers felt the same way prior to buying this product.

You—Step 3: "And you probably have several questions you still need to have answered before you make a decision, isn't that correct?"

Prospect: "Yes, that's right!"

You—Step 4: "Let's make a list of some of them." (At this point, take out a small piece of paper and list the questions they give you, then say . . .) "Which one of these is

120

actually the one that's keeping you from going ahead?'' (This is the "Eliminate to One" close. Note: If the prospect has a lot of negative responses, you haven't done your qualifying job effectively. Go back and qualify the wants and needs again, then continue by answering the one question.)

You—Step 5: (Close) "When would you like us to deliver?"

Practice this example on a friend or relative. The five-step strategy should be automatic whenever a prospect reaches out to you with, "We want to think it over!"

Closings

When you've done your best, from your opening through meeting objections, you're ready to make your final move—*the close*. Once again, it is imperative that you read your customer's style to select the best approach. A quiet suggestion to draw up a contract or the drama of a flashy ending can either make or break a sale.

The blueprints included in this section provide you with sure-fire ways to get the order. Silence, the "Yes-Set" Technique, and a variety of closing questions work. So does the dramatic $100 close. Confidence in the choice you make will mean a successful outcome to your sales call—an order.

Create Your Own Objections and Close

by Bill Bishop

One way to prevent a prospect's objections is by creating your own. If you introduce ridiculous terms of the sale—terms you can easily eliminate—you often can get the client to agree on a purchase.

Let's see how it works.

Ridiculous terms can be anything from a crazy time schedule ("If I put in your application today, I can get it approved in three or four months.") to outlandish demands ("It's company policy for me to get twenty referrals from each of our clients.")

Naturally the client will object. Now you can say, "You mean I don't get your order unless I can have your application approved immediately?" or "Are you saying that I won't get your account unless I agree to accept only three names?" (or however many he indignantly tells you he can provide.)

In essence, the client has said that if you agree to his (reasonable) terms, he'll buy. So go ahead, agree to be reasonable, and close. Rather than wait for the client to come up with an objection you *can't* eliminate, hand him one that you *can*.

The "Yes-Set" Technique

A sales executive, in a hurry and hungry, too, was looking for a fast and accessible, but quality, lunch. He spotted a great looking restaurant at a national chain motel and driving by the underground parking saw the sign which read, "Sorry, FULL." At the same time, a car was just clearing the exit gate, so our hungry executive drove in and found the just vacant spot.

Upstairs he dined at a hearty and filling soup and sandwich bar for $4.50 and in record time walked out past the receptionist's desk, with the parking ticket in his hand.

"Now," he mused, "how am I going to get this thing validated? These people are busy and if I interrupt them for a validation, they'll say 'no' for sure.

"I have to get them to do something for me first so I can establish the "yes set." He pulled out a dollar bill and held it out over the counter. The receptionist said, "Oh, thank you."

Our executive replied, "Could you give me four quarters, please?"

"Yes," from the receptionist.

"Do you validate parking tickets?" queried our sales executive while receiving his change.

"Yes," came the second reply.

"Could you validate mine?" shot back our hero.

"Yes," rang out the third response. "What's your room number?" she asked as she stamped the sales executive's parking ticket.

"Oh, I'm not staying here, I just ate a delicious lunch at your restaurant," he countered.

"Well, I'm not supposed to do this," she replied, signing her name on the validated parking ticket and handing it back.

They grinned at each other, both pleased with the results of the "Yes-Set."

The "Yes-Set" technique involves making statements or asking questions to which the only reasonable reaction is—"Yes."

This technique can be used throughout the sales call and is

ideal for closing. A word of caution: The "Yes-Set" is easy to use and easily overdone, so remember that while a few "Yes" responses are great, too many can spoil the effect.

Here are some examples:

1. *Needs Analysis:*
   Average salesperson: "I would like you to tell me more about your specific needs."
   Successful salesperson: "In order to help you with your business needs, I'd like to ask you a few questions that will help me to understand what you'll be looking for. Is it all right with you if I ask them now?" "Yes."

In the above example, the salesperson negotiates for a "Yes" prior to asking the fact-finding questions. This first "Yes" will lead to a more positive discussion about the customer's needs.

2. *Presentation of benefits:*
   Average salesperson: "This is our advanced model, it comes with built-in motor drive."
   Successful salesperson: "Do you see this motor drive?" "Yes"
   "This is a feature you'll get in addition, should you decide on this advanced model. Remember what I've explained earlier about action photography?" "Yes."
   "Here is what this motor drive can do for you. . . . "

The top sales producer conditioned the buyer with two "Yes" responses prior to describing the customer benefits.

3. *Closing:*
   Average salesperson: "Well, you seem to like this product; if I were you, I'd buy it."
   Successful salesperson: "Do you like the quality of this storage building?" "Yes."
   "Do you like the colors you've selected earlier?" "Yes."
   "Can you get the financing?" "Yes."
   "Then it seems that we can go ahead with our agreement." "Yes."

The repeated "Yes" mode has a powerful psychological impact on the customer. Each additional "Yes" increases the unconscious desire to prolong the positive internal experience. The top sales producer can benefit from this phenomenon by obtaining several "Yes" responses before asking for the order.

Why Claude Can't Close

Claude is a typewriter salesman. But he doesn't sell very many machines. It's not the economy, or his product, or the price, because his fellow salesmen are doing a brisk business. It's Claude. He doesn't know how to close.

A recent sales presentation went like this:

Claude: This model is a mid-priced machine. It has a correction key and . . .
Client: Oh, that's terrific—it makes the work go so much faster!
Claude: Yes, well it also has an indexing key, and interchangeable elements . . .
Client: I bet the elements cost extra.
Claude: Well, that's true—they're not included in the price except for the top of the line model. Now this express key is a popular feature. And the price for all of this is really quite reasonable. (pause)
Client: How long would it take to have one delivered?
Claude: Well, that depends on the color you want, and the date you place the order.
Client: I really shouldn't make such a large purchase right now but . . .
Claude: Well, I can come back when you're ready.
Client: Yes, I guess I'll think about it some more.

Claude could have closed at least six different times! But he was so intent on getting through his entire presentation that he didn't (1) pick up on buying signals (a positive reaction to a sales feature), or (2) turn a mild objection into an insignificant consideration, or use it to sell the better model. He also didn't try to (3) close immediately after his presentation, and (4) overlooked the strongest buying signal: delivery. Claude did not (5) provide reassurance in response to a weak excuse and (6) was unable to turn the stall into an immediate order. There are many opportunities for closing a sale. Don't let them get by *you*.

Logic and Emotion
in Selling

Most professional salespeople are familiar with Zig Ziglar's famous motto: "You can get everything in life you want, if you help enough other people get what they want." America's foremost motivator shared one of his key sales strategies—convincing people what they want is *your* product or service by appealing to their minds as well as their hearts—in an interview with *Personal Selling Power.*

Zig started out selling cookware before he began selling people on themselves, so he used the example of pots and pans to demonstrate how you can increase your sales effectiveness by using a combination of logic and emotion:

"Logic makes people think; emotion makes them act. For example, in selling cookware, we would take the logical approach and explain that according to USDA, the average shrinkage of a four pound roast in the oven or in the ordinary pot was one pound seven ounces. Cooking it in our method, you lost 5 ounces. Logically, you could say: 'If I had a cook who stole one pound of my roast every time she cooked one, I'd fire her!' No hesitation! Here, you've got this old, beat-up pot that's been stealing from you for 20 years. I think it's time you fired it. Fire that old pot and get a new one, and it's not going to steal from you! That logically would make sense.

"Then, we would say that from a practical point of view, we are what we eat. If the food that you put in your body is short on nutrition, then eventually you are going to pay for it. Sometimes I'd say, 'Our set of cookware will help your baby grow up with a better chance at good health.'

"We combined the logic on the dollar and the emotion on the good health for better results. You need to balance these keys. If you use all logic, you end up with the best-educated prospect in town. If you use all emotion, you make the sale, but tomorrow you'll have the buyer's remorse and a cancelled order."

Closing Questions

by Jeffrey P. Davidson

Anytime two good salespeople get together and exchange ideas on closing techniques, something positive happens. Both people usually come away with valuable information, and then enthusiastically await the opportunity to put into action the new closes that were discussed. Here is some meaningful advice in closing a sale that was learned through the exchange of ideas of good salespeople.

A good time to close is as soon as you perceive a positive response to your sales presentation. Another is anytime the customer indicates verbally or nonverbally that he or she has interest in your product or service. Since studies have shown that it takes at least six *no's* in a sales presentation before obtaining that one sweet *yes,* it is strongly advised that a variety of closing questions be learned:

- Which do you prefer, cash or check?
- In view of the benefits, can you afford to put off this investment until later?
- Would you like to okay this order?
- Don't you agree that anything worth having is worth having now?
- Your pen or mine?
- Would you like it by August 1st or August 15th?
- Would you like me to stop by for the check on Monday?
- How much of a deposit would you like to leave?
- What color do you prefer?
- Will one be enough?
- Would you like it gift wrapped?
- Should we ship it directly?
- Would you prefer early morning delivery?
- Will you be needing accessory items?
- Where would you like it to be installed?

The common denominator among all great salespeople is that they are strong closers. With each close you are indicating to the customer that you have confidence, that you see a need for the product or service, and that you and your company are ready to fulfill that need. In that sense, closing is nothing less than assuring the customer that when he reposes his confidence in you and your company, he is making no mistake. And once you prove it through carrying out your work in terms of delivery, quality and other factors, you'll find that next time you meet with this buyer, closing becomes so easy it's almost routine.

Salespeople who can't close are playing a game of luck and hope. They are lucky when they happen to walk into a situation where the prospect is ready to make the purchase. Being lucky or hopeful is certainly worth something. For long-term success, however, closing depends on more than hope, which can be dampened, and luck, which can always turn sour. Only skill stands the test of time.

If you feel that you are a good salesperson in every respect, except that you lack the ability to close the sale, do not let another week go by without making plans to learn all you can about closing. As a professional salesperson, your economic well-being depends on it.

Closing the Sale

by James F. Evered, CSP

Closing the sale is the culmination of the entire marketing process. It is at this point in the process that most salespersons fail. They may do a good job of selling up to this point and then fail to ask for the business. What a waste of effort! Because of the normal doubts in the customer's mind at the point of decision, it is the responsibility of the salesperson to push the customer toward a favorable decision. The customer needs that push, followed by reassurance that it was a wise decision.

If you don't have the courage to ask for the business, get out of selling. Otherwise, you are in for a career of rejection and disappointment. Business goes to the salesperson who asks for it.

When to Close

When should you try to close a sale? Unfortunately, many salespeople think a close is a separate step at the end of the sales interview. This belief perhaps causes them to put off closing until it is too late. The close, in fact, is an integral part of the sales interview and can come at any time. The close is not something you plan to do at the end of the sales interview, but a close at the right time can bring the interview to an end.

The right time to close the sale may be indicated by the customer any time during the interview, when the prospect has reached a decision. These indications may be in the form of questions, actions, expressions, or comments. Don't make the mistake of becoming so absorbed in what you are saying that you miss the customer's signals. Above all, don't wait until you are finished selling to ask for the business. If the customer says no at that point, you have nothing left to say except to repeat what you have already said.

Try to close at each of the following points in a sales interview:

• Any time a customer indicates an appreciable amount of interest.

- Any time a customer begins asking questions about your product. As soon as you answer the questions, try a close.
- After making a strong point regarding your product.
- After overcoming an objection.
- When a customer agrees with one of your major points.
- When a customer picks up and examines your product literature, the product itself, or the sales contract.

Rules for Closing

Before discussing a variety of closing techniques, I would like to list my rules for closing sales:

Rule number 1. Ask for the business in no uncertain terms. You are entitled to ask for it, so do it.

Rule number 2. Ask for the business in such a way that it is difficult for the customer to use a blunt no.

Rule number 3. After you ask for the business, shut up! Don't say a single word until your customer responds.

Rule number 4. If the customer doesn't buy, keep selling.

Rule number 5. Reassure the customer who does buy that it was a wise decision.

Rule number 6. Don't stop selling until the customer stops buying. Often a salesman is so elated over one order that he walks away from further business. Perhaps with a little persistence, the customer would have bought more. In the oil business, we had a pseudo-acronym, "DOSEQUA SEGAL," which was a facetious way of reminding ourselves, "DOn't SEll QUArts-SEll GALlons." Don't walk away with the sale of one puppy when you could have sold the entire litter.

Rule number 7. Always, always, always thank the customer for the business. The customer should be thanked three times: verbally, immediately after the sale; by a follow-up thank-you note within twenty-four hours; and regularly during your contacts with the customer. Business usually goes where it is appreciated.

Remember, in closing a sale it is dangerous to ask for the order in an unplanned manner (see Rule number 2). Some approaches permit the prospect to give you a definite no. The customer who has made a negative decision is obligated to defend that position. Pride may keep the customer from changing. This situation brings up another excellent rule, which may alleviate your anxieties when the customer says no. You can't get a customer to change his mind, but you can get him to make a new decision based on further information. Keep selling!

If the customer gives you a blunt no, meet it with a question. "May I ask why?" That puts the ball back into the customer's court. He will begin explaining why he took a negative stance. That might just uncover his real reason for not buying. If so, you have something to work with and you can keep selling.

How to Ask for the Order

There is no one best way to ask for the order and I could not tell you exactly what to say. But there are several methods that work well in the majority of cases. Naturally, you can modify these examples to fit your personality, your product, and the people to whom you sell. These examples are not original ideas but are those gleaned from successful salespeople over the past twenty-five years. These closing techniques have a high degree of success frequency.

Assume He's Bought

You close by indicating that the customer has mentally bought and it's merely a matter of writing up the order. In this case, you don't actually ask for the order; just assume you have it. Here are some examples of the assumptive close:

I'm sure you'll be pleased with the traditional style. I can schedule it in our next production run. Okay?

This will start your protection by the first of the month. Will that be soon enough?

We can schedule delivery for tomorrow afternoon. Okay?

What billing date would be most convenient?

Would an initial order of six cases be enough?

Will this be the only item you need to balance your inventory?

It may seem that I have contradicted my own rules for closing sales, as some of these could be answered with a no. Admittedly, some could; however, I would counter with, "May I ask why?" The customer's response to that question would keep the interview open for further selling, giving an opportunity to use a different close.

Give Him a Minor Choice

Giving the customer a small choice is one of the easiest of all closes to use and seems to be the favorite of most salespeople. A decision on the minor choice is obtained in such a way as to imply or involve a decision on the sale. The customer is given a choice between something and something, never between something and nothing.

> Will you be financing it or paying cash?
>
> Would you prefer the three-bedroom or the two-bedroom model?
>
> Which would you prefer, the ten-year or the fifteen-year plan?
>
> Would you need the twenty-socket set or will the ten be sufficient?
>
> Would you rather have the four-door model or the two?
>
> Would you prefer it with or without the comfort rest feature?

None of these is an actual decision to buy, but the answer implies the purchase. It is easier for the customer to make a minor choice decision than to make a buying decision. Either way he chooses, he's bought. Stop selling and start writing.

Concession or Inducement Close

At times you may have something special to offer to get an immediate decision to buy. This could be merely squeezing the customer's order into a production schedule that is already full, thereby giving fast delivery. It could be offering something extra that is available to anyone who takes immediate advantage of the offer, such as price reduction, special discount, additional features, promotional materials, advertising assistance, display materials, or special premiums. Each of these inducements, however, should be followed with a short assumptive close, such as "When shall I schedule delivery?" or "Which packaging will be most convenient for you?" Here are some examples of concessions or inducements.

> For the next six days, this carries an additional production clearance discount of three percent.
>
> With a gross lot purchase, we will ship FOB your destination.
>
> Orders taken this week will be delivered next Monday.
>
> During March, each six-dozen-lot purchase will include this attractive display case.
>
> During this promotion, for each six cases you purchase, we ship seven.
>
> For the next sixty days we will provide installation free of charge.

Last Chance Close

The last chance close is closely allied to the concession or inducement close. It is used when you honestly state a condition arising in the near future that would make it favorable to buy now. Again, each statement of a last chance situation must be followed by asking for the business:

> Effective June first, we will have a three percent price increase.

> The special promotion will end next Monday.

> Effective October first, 11 percent rates will no longer be available.

> The tax advantage will be lost at the first of the year.

> Beginning next week, our delivery schedule will increase to four weeks.

> This is the last week we will offer this advantage.

Let me repeat: never, never, never use a last chance close unless it is absolutely 100 percent true. To do otherwise is not only dishonest but closes the door on any future sales. There is no place in professional selling for dishonesty.

The last chance close quickly develops a sense of urgency and will frequently get an order when normal circumstances would allow a customer to delay a buying decision. Human nature causes us to hate missing out on something. If it will not be available in the future, we want to get it now. Take advantage of every last chance you can, but follow each with a good strong close.

Similar Situation Close

The similar situation or narrative close is outstanding when properly used. Unfortunately, not every salesperson is a skilled storyteller. Almost everyone tries to duplicate the successes of others and avoid their failures. Following are several "success stories" that may spark an idea you could use:

- Harold Smith, one of our St. Louis customers, found, by analyzing his sales, that for 101 days in his selling season he did not have a model 70-G in stock. Now he's ordering two at a time and he still runs out before the next production run.

- The XYZ Hardware Store found that moving this item to the prime impulse buying area and increasing the display to a gross lot increased sales 11 percent.

- This particular model accounts for 7 percent of total sales in your own marketing area. If you would like to contact some similar retailers in your area, they'll be glad to verify that. Could I place the calls for you?

- I presented this same proposal to John Duffy over in Middletown last week, but he decided to think about it until my next call. He called me last night and said he had already missed four sales. That's a $260 loss to John, and I can't do anything about it until I get there week after next.

Summary Close

In using this effective closing technique, you summarize the primary features you presented and the results they will produce for your customer. It puts the total perceived value back into the customer's mind just before you ask for the order. These results must be in the customer's mind; he must be thinking about them and be aware of them at the moment. Otherwise, they weigh nothing on the sales scale as far as your sale is concerned. Review these results, get them back into the customer's mind, and go for the close.

- Mr. Simpson, as I stated earlier, this program will increase your inventory turnover, increase your return on investment, and reduce your warehousing costs by nearly 10 percent. Would shipment next Monday be satisfactory?

- Mr. Tucker, the permanently bonded finish will eliminate your need for repainting, will be long-lasting, will resist peeling, and will retain its attractive finish. If that's what you want, let's schedule you for Monday's shipment.

- Mr. Jordan, you have seen letters that prove the profitmaking potential of this model, that it will meet 60 per cent of customer demands, and will reduce your man-hours of labor by 5 percent. In view of these facts, is there any reason to hesitate?

- Mrs. Kelly, you have seen how our shipment schedule meets your needs, our pallet delivery reduces your workload, and our packaging fits your shipment procedures. Are you ready to improve your profit picture?

Three-Question Nail-Down Close

The three-question close puts the buyer into an immediate affirmative frame of mind and makes it easier for him to continue saying yes when you ask for the order. To use this technique, you ask the customer three rapid-fire questions to which you know he will agree and then follow up with a simple close. Naturally, the three questions you ask will either be about three points of agreement you had during the sales interview, or they will be based on three points the customer will have to agree to because he has already committed himself—unless he wants to look like an idiot. Here are some examples of the three-question nail down:

> Mr. Casey, are you concerned about protecting your present sales volume?
>
> Yes.
>
> Do you want to guarantee your inventory turnover?
>
> Sure.
>
> Do you want to gain a competitive advantage?
>
> Naturally.
>
> Then let's start this program now.

The three-question nail-down can be used successfully with any product, service, or proposal. Just select three questions to which you are sure the customer will agree, immediately followed by a positive close. If you pick three pertinent points of agreement, your customer will find the offering almost irresistible. If he replies yes to the three questions, he's likely to agree with your request for the order. It is difficult for anyone to reply, yes, yes, yes, followed by no.

Since We Agree That...

In this close, you recall three or so points on which you and the customer agreed, remind him of them, and ask for the order. For example:

> Since we agree that our delivery date is satisfactory, our packaging will reduce your warehouse time, and the terms are suitable, would you please approve this first order?
>
> Since we agree that gross lots are more economical for you and our guaranteed return program will protect your investment, let's get the order written up.
>
> Since we agree that time is your major concern and our shipping schedule will meet it at a competitive price, may I phone the order in right now?

This technique refocuses the customer's attention to certain items on which agreement had been reached during the interview. It also takes his mind away from points of disagreement or concern that may cause resistance.

Keep One in the Briefcase

It is an excellent idea to hold back at least one good product feature that you might need as a clincher if all else fails. Many tough accounts have been gained with this technique.

There comes a time in any sales interview when it is apparent to both the customer and the salesperson that the latter should leave. At this point the salesperson starts putting all his materials back into his briefcase. Thinking the salesman is on his way out, the customer drops his defenses. While the defenses are down, if the salesman has held back one outstanding product feature, there's a good chance he can close a sale by selling that feature's result. He might turn to the customer and try a close such as:

> Mr. Martin, isn't it possible that our oxidation inhibitor could prevent a lot of your present customer complaints?

> Mr. Sellers, would lubrication-free sealed bearings help reduce your maintenance costs?

> Mrs. Julian, would our one-year free service contract alleviate your concerns?

> Mr. Carson, since freight costs are one of your concerns, would sharing a drop shipment with another buyer be of any help?

These questions may well open the door for further selling, giving you an opportunity to restate some of your primary features and go for an additional sale.

Other Closing Techniques

No matter what close you attempt, let there be no doubt that you are asking for the business. Don't hint around that you would like to have the business; ask for it.

There is absolutely nothing wrong with, "Mr. Skelton, may I have your business?" Frankness and sincerity will accomplish your objectives more effectively than cleverness.

Don't waltz with a customer when it comes time to close. Ask for business in no uncertain terms. Here are some of the typical waltzes often heard:

> I surely would like to ship you one of these.

> I think you'll be making a mistake if you don't buy.

This will be a real good deal for you.

You can see what this plan will do for you.

This is one of our best sellers, and it will work for you.

This will sure make you a bunch of money.

These are not closes at all, just laudatory statements. Remember, you do not have a close until you have put the ball squarely into the customer's court and he is *required* to make the next move.

Regardless of what close you use, if you get the order there is still one more close that must be used every time: "Is there anything more I can get (order) for you?" Don't stop selling until the customer stops buying.

Every good salesperson gets turned down occasionally, but the difference between the outstanding salesperson and the average one is that the former always bounces back and tries, tries, and tries again—never less than seven times. If you want to be successful at selling, make this "rule of seven" a part of your professional life. It pays big dividends.

Keep Quiet and Get the Order

by Dennis M. DeMaria

One of the biggest single weapons you as a salesperson can use in getting an order from a customer or prospect is keeping quiet and patiently waiting for the buyer to answer your questions. A general rule in the selling profession is that the person who asks the questions is the person who has control of the interview. The information obtained from asking questions is the necessary ammunition you use to find the buyer's likes, dislikes, hot buttons and areas to avoid. This valuable information also informs the salesperson whether the customer is ready to buy or whether he or she should continue selling.

Experience has shown that salespeople do ask questions but they forget the most important part of this sales principle: *After you ask a question you must be patient; don't talk and let the buyer answer.* It does not matter how long it takes for the buyer to respond, keep quiet and wait for the answer. Remember, the first person to speak after a question has been asked, loses.

Handling Stalls

How do you react when a customer procrastinates? Do you become defensive or demanding? Coercive or hostile? "These are some of the common behavioral traps salespeople need to avoid," according to Dr. David D. Burns. In an interview with *Personal Selling Power,* Dr. Burns, who is Assistant Professor of Clinical Psychiatry at the University of Pennsylvania School of Medicine, discussed ways to draw out the customer's reservations by coupling empathy with firmness.

Several common stalls, and examples of nonthreatening responses suggested by Dr. Burns, include:

1. *I've got to think about it.*
   You could ask, "What are some of the issues you have to think about?" or "What are some of the things that are holding you back? Would you share some of them with me?"
   "Communicate a positive attitude, avoiding nonverbal defensiveness," warns Dr. Burns.

2. *I've got to talk to my boss about this purchase.*
   You could reply, "Of course you do. What are some of the things you would talk to him (or her) about?" or "Would you be exploring if this is a good purchase in comparison with a competitor's product, or would you be wondering about the financing?"
   "Display an attitude of genuine caring. By responding with empathy, you put yourself in the client's position," advises Dr. Burns.

Dr. Burns also cautions against reading motives into the customer by telling yourself, "He enjoys being resistant. He just wants to give me a hard time." This prevents you from uncovering the real reasons underlying his procrastination. Remember that handling procrastinators has nothing to do with getting the other person to give in to you; the solution to resolving the client's hesitancy lies in allowing it to be expressed. Showing genuine concern for your client as a human being—and not as an object to be manipulated—is as crucial to an effective sales career as it is to a happy marriage or a lasting friendship.

Guidelines

Thus, the steps for handling the procrastinating client are:

1. Prepare yourself for a possible delaying maneuver—before the call.

2. Pinpoint the reasons and show your openness, your empathy and understanding (don't judge—observe).

3. Manage your self-talk. Don't put the client down, don't put yourself down.

4. Help the client realistically appraise his reasons for and against buying now. And if it's not in his best interest to buy your product now, urge him not to. He'll respect you and you'll feel better about yourself and you'll make out better in the long run.

"Selling to procrastinators can be very rewarding and profitable," concludes Dr. Burns. "It's like Zen. When you want the sale most, it moves beyond your reach. Instead, you temporarily abandon your preoccupation with control and success. As you open yourself to your client's experience, you are creating new space which is needed to dissolve the client's hesitancy. Once the pressure is removed, your client will be able to objectively reappraise your proposals (with your guidance) and make a decision.

"No matter what the outcome, you've created a win/win situation and you're ready to make your next call without the burden of unfinished business and most likely with the satisfaction of another sale."

The $100 Close

by Robert A. Weaver

One of my favorite closes is the $100 Bill Close. It works every time I use it at the appropriate moment. There are two conditions: First, you must use a $100 bill, second, the amount of the sale should be in the thousand dollar range.

Here is what you do. As the customer rejects your sales proposal you start saying: "I would agree with you that by saying no to me today, you will keep things as they are. But by the same token, you would probably agree with me that the only way you ever make a gain is by saying yes. (Take out your $100 bill, hold it up in front of your customer's face).

"Here is what I mean. Let's assume that this (point to the bill) represents part of the new profit your decision can create from this day forward. Think of this as your money. Now let me show you what you are asking me to do to your money when you say no.

"Watch." (Now fold the $100 bill in half and with your fingernail sharpen the crease by pulling your finger across it. Then without saying a word, tear the bill in half. Wait for your customer to interrupt ... if he doesn't, put the two halves together, fold them over and again sharpen the crease. Slowly tear this doubled piece of the $100 bill and as you get halfway through this final tear, say very slowly:) "Tell me, how much longer are you going to watch your profits going to pieces?"

I don't have to tear many bills, since my prospects tend to get the point before I begin to tear. What do I do with a torn $100 bill? Simple. I use some tape and exchange it at the bank for a new one. My banker did ask me once why I keep exchanging $100 bills. I told him and he laughed saying: "I am happy to oblige, as long as the technique puts more money into your pocket ... and our bank."

The Quota

by Douglas E. Cohen

All salespeople must learn to live with some form of sales or earning quota. Whether you aim for the quota, or try to better it, will determine your success.

Visualize, for a moment, a target for pistol shooting. It has an outer ring and a bull's eye. If that outer ring is your quota, and that's what you're aiming for, you just might miss the target completely. But if you aim for the bull's eye, more than your quota, you will have a better chance of hitting the target somewhere.

In any one month, if you achieve only 85 percent of your quota, you have missed the target entirely. Aiming at 100 percent (the quota) will always result in less than 100 percent because sometimes you'll miss the target. If you aim at the bull's eye, say 125 percent, you give yourself a margin of safety. What if you're out sick for a week, had a few bad days, lost an order or an account? Instead of playing catch up, you'll still hit the mark. And if you have a month free of problems, you'll be way ahead. The wonderful thing about sales is that there's never a limit to what you can do.

Assign your bull's eye a percentage above quota and begin target practice today. You'll score way above the competition if you do.

Handling Procrastinating Prospects

by Gerhard Gschwandtner

Think about how you have handled your last procrastinating prospect. Remember the familiar objections like "I've got to think about it" or "I'll need to talk to my boss about it." How do you deal with people who delay the decision to buy?

There are two things we can look at: First, your own attitude toward the hesitant client and second, the various techniques you can use to find out why your client procrastinates. The moment you realize that you're dealing with a procrastinator, start shifting gears and respond by caring and avoid controlling the buyer.

Let's say you hear the familiar "I've got to talk to my boss about it." You could say, "Of course you do. What are some of the things you would talk to him or her about?"

Agree with the prospect and establish trust. Sales psychologists suggest that the more you try to control a procrastinator, the more you increase the resistance to make a decision. As you give up your preoccupation with control and success you're creating an open space for the buyer to step in and reconsider your proposal.

The most difficult comment many salespeople stumble over is, "I've got to think about it." The reason it's difficult to handle is because of the things you may be secretly telling yourself about the situation, such as, "He has no right to be so unreasonable," or "What did I do wrong?"

Your job is not to blame anyone. Many salespeople respond to "I've got to think about it," with "Is there anything I have not covered that you would like to know?" That's a self-defeating question.

Next time you hear "I've got to think about it," you want to respond with "What are some of the issues that you want to think about?" or "I see that this is a difficult decision for you. Would you be able to share some of the reasons for and against buying at this time?" This approach will give your prospect a chance to open up.

If you want to sell to a procrastinator, you need to be supportive and reassuring. Your attitude will make or break the sale. If you are too eager, your customers will feel pushed and will be persuaded to resist you in order to stay in control. But if you use an open attitude, show empathy and ask questions designed to uncover the resistance, you will be able to turn procrastinators into buyers.

The Force of Talking

by Gerhard Gschwandtner

One of the most important faculties of a salesperson is the ability to talk.

It's a curious ability that we all possess and one that we rarely study. Did you know that talking raises our blood pressure, increases our adrenalin production and expands the blood flow to the brain?

It's a powerful instrument that influences others while it influences us. Many of us don't recognize this interactive process and as a result, we tend to lose sight of our objectives. One of the best illustrations of this phenomenon is the story of the farmer and the preacher.

On a hot summer Sunday, a preacher realized that only one old farmer showed up for his sermon. He walked up to him and asked two questions: "Do you think there will be anybody else today?" and "Should I go on with my sermon?"

The farmer replied, "I reckon that everybody's out in the field harvestin' and nobody else but me needs spiritual nourishment today, but I'd be much obliged if you'd carry on."

The preacher went up to the pulpit and delivered the sermon he had rehearsed the day before. His voice was filled with excitement and as he hit his stride, new ideas rushed to his head, which he was only too glad to share with the farmer. He went on for nearly an hour.

After a dramatic finish, the preacher went down to the farmer and asked, "Son, what did you think of my sermon?" The farmer replied, "Well, I don't know much about religion, but I do know a lot about farming. Let's say if I went out to my fields with a truckload of hay and found only one cow—I wouldn't dump the whole load on her!"

My point is, like the preacher, we have a hard time realizing that as we try to influence our audience, we're being influenced by our own words.

Some people even get addicted to their own adrenalin high and they continue talking to satisfy their needs for excitement instead of satisfying the customer's needs for service.

Talking is indeed a challenging task that requires discipline and self-control. One of the best ways to improve our ability to become a master of words is to develop the art of shutting up.

You Can't Lose
the Order Twice

by Craig Bridgman

Sometimes a sale lingers in memory not because it was lucrative or brilliant but because you learned something from it that helped you become more effective.

I sell an employee-motivation program to industry. Just to vary the routine a little bit I decided to try my luck one day with a different kind of prospect. I telephoned the warden of the state penitentiary and asked him for an appointment. Right away I could tell this wasn't going to be easy. The guy sounded tougher than permafrost. But he agreed to see me, and that's a good beginning.

I arrived at the prison and was escorted to the warden's office by a guard through a maze of passages with heavy steel doors that clanged shut behind us. The warden, motioning me to sit down, told me he was pressed for time and requested I come right down to business. I ran through my pitch, while my prospect leaned back in his chair and listened impassively, his arms folded across his chest.

When I finished he methodically dismantled every selling point I had made. He took a long time about it, and when he was done he asked me if I'd like to know his philosophy of employee motivation. I admitted I was curious. "We run a tight ship around here," he said. "They all know the rules. If anyone breaks them, he's out—fired."

Now, in our business this was hardly what you would call a strong buying signal, but at least it didn't completely close the door on further discussion. I asked some questions and elaborated on a few points that I thought might sway him. At length though, I concluded that I wasn't going to bring him around and that the sensible thing to do was to chalk the guy up as a lost cause. I recalled then a piece of sales wisdom that my boss had once conferred on me: *You can't lose the order twice.* If the prospect has said no, a further attempt at closing him can leave you no worse off than you were already. So why not try it?

Smiling, I said: "Mr. Permafrost, has anyone ever told you that you're a real tough guy to sell? You need this program, but I'm fresh out of ideas to throw at you to convince you. It appears you've won. I'm coming out with my hands up. But I'd still like to have you as a customer. Think about it, will you? If we can serve you in any way, please call me." Permafrost said yeah, yeah, he would, and off I went back out into the bright sunshine and freedom. Consoling myself that at least I got a smile out of the guy, I resolved to put the call out of my mind and write off penitentiaries as prospects.

The next morning the phone rang. It was Permafrost calling with a purchase order. I couldn't have been more surprised if it had been the Kremlin on the line, but I recovered enough to take down the details. That was two years ago. The prison remains an enthusiastic customer to this day. I never figured out exactly what it was that moved Permafrost to buy, but I've made it a point ever since always to make one more try for the order once I've decided it's lost. You know, you get to like the extra income it brings in.

Pin-Management

A sales manager was in trouble with his sales. He decided to call in an expert to give him an outsider's viewpoint.

After he had gone over his plans and problems, the sales manager took the sales expert to a map on the wall and showed him brightly colored pins stuck wherever he had a salesman. Looking at the expert, he asked, "Now for a starter, what is the first thing we should do?"

"Well," replied the expert, "the first thing is to take those pins out of the map and stick them into the salesmen."

Many sales people talk so much they do not give the prospect who said "No" a chance to change his mind.

Gerhard Gschwandtner

Three Sure Opportunities
to Close

Closing is not a one-shot deal—it's an ongoing process. The earlier in your sales call you attempt to close, the more time you'll have to discover and dispel a client's uncertainties, objections and resistance to buy.

Three ideal opportunities for closes are:

- after major points in your presentation
- after you have completed your presentation
- after you've overcome an objection

Opportunity 1

The benefit that puts a sparkle in your prospect's eye during your presentation may not seem to shine as brightly once you move on to other points. Catch your prospect's enthusiasm by trying to close right after presenting a major benefit.

First, sum up the benefit. What will the prospect get out of it (cost savings, prestige, reliability)? Then try to close:

Sales Rep: How soon would you need delivery? (Lean forward, open palm toward client.)
Prospect: Well, I haven't decided I'll buy yet, but we'd probably need it in three weeks.

In that case, nod and avoid negative body language such as leaning back, crossing legs or arms, or frowning. Then continue with your presentation. Try again after the next benefit is explained and summarized:

Sales Rep: Do you prefer a five-year or a three-year financing package? (Use fingers to visually indicate choices.)
Prospect: I'm not ready to decide on that yet.

Again, you go on with your presentation while remaining friendly and open. In this way you can try to close as many times as you present benefits. Because you never ask a client the point-blank question "Will you buy?," you can go from one benefit to another until he says "yes." When the client does answer one of your "closing" questions in a positive way, take the order. Once he or she is sold, you'll overstay your welcome if you continue on with your presentation.

Opportunity 2

The moment you finish your presentation or a demonstration, it's time to try another close. Your summary of benefits should be like the last burst of fireworks on the Fourth of July. If your presentation is well done and you've created the desire to buy, it will be perfectly natural to ask for ordering information.

> *Sales Rep:* So you see, Mr. Smith, the use of our Model 900 will permit you to stay ahead of the competition by (use fingers to add up benefits, lean forward) decreasing your expenses in man hours and materials, increasing the efficiency and satisfaction of your employees and eliminating downtime for repairs.
>
> The sales rep now goes right into a close.
>
> I appreciate the attention you've given me today, Mr. Smith. (Smile sincerely and use open palmed gestures.) If you'll be kind enough to give me figures on your current system's usage and a convenient day for us to make delivery, I'll work up your first month's supply needs and set up an installation appointment (have paper and pen ready to record the information).

Because this is a logical step, your prospect will probably show no hesitation, and give you the information to write up the sale.

Opportunity 3

If you can successfully clear customer objections, you are at a powerful psychological advantage to a closed sale. Here's a sample obstacle, the rep's response, and the close he uses to make the most of his position:

> *Client:* We've bought from the same company for 30 years—I don't see any reason to change now. (He or she may exhibit negative body language such as crossed arms or legs, tightening of facial muscles or tightly clasped hands.)
>
> *Sales Rep:* Well, to be honest with you (hand to chest), Mr. Davis, we weren't even in business when you started ordering from Tradition, Inc. (open palmed gesture). But I think you'll

see from these testimonial letters (Raise and lower stack of letters in your hand.) that since we've been in the field, a number of customers like yourself have found that we can provide a better, more thorough service for your money.

As the rep shows the letters, one at a time, he continues,

You see, these other companies have found it more profitable to switch to our products. (Pause. Watch for positive nonverbal cues—a smile, relaxed hands or arms.)
Would you like to hear our special discount for bulk purchases? (If you get a nod or a verbal "yes," describe your discount and then continue into a close.)
Would you like to order your normal quantities, or would you rather take advantage of the special discount we've just discussed?

Don't wait until the end of a sales call to close. Attempt to close after explaining key benefits during your presentation, after you've completed your presentation, and when you've just overcome an objection.

This simple technique can literally triple your closing ratio.

Follow-Up

A sale doesn't end with the close. In some companies up to 80 percent of their business comes from repeat customers. That means that a solid working relationship must be developed through well-planned follow-up treatment. Follow-ups are the insurance of your sales call structure.

We've included articles on problem customers and problem situations, suggestions for keeping your customers coming back for more of you and your product, and a checklist for follow-up calls. Long-term clients save you sales-call costs and time. Keep them happy and protected with effective, well-timed checkups.

Do You Clean Up
or Give Up
on Follow-Up?

by George J. Lumsden

The best salesperson I ever knew seldom did much prospecting. If that sounds like the ultimate heresy, so be it, because this salesman was nearly three times more productive than the national average of his peers. What he did in place of the traditional prospecting routines was to conduct a very careful follow-up of his customers and they did his prospecting for him!

Many salespeople fail to consider why they walked into a certain account and took business away from a competitor. Was it because their product was superior? Perhaps, but most products are fairly competitively matched in quality, function and price, and buyers can generally move from one to another with considerable ease. Was it because they gave such a spendid presentation? Maybe. Certainly it had to be good enough to turn the buyer from a neutral to a positive position, but then buyers are exposed to good presentations all the time.

How about trying this scenario: You walk into ABC & Co. with the objective of unseating your competitor. You have never even gotten to first base with these people; they are polite, but keep telling you that their needs are well cared for . . . come back another time. So you do, and this time you present a secondary-type or specialty item—just a minor product your competitor pays little attention to. And, what do you know . . . you make the sale!

The following day, you send a card to the buyer, confirming the shipping date you had promised and thanking him for the order. A week later, the order is shipped. You give the buyer a call and tell him that the order is on its way. A few days later, you call and ask if the order has been received and whether the product is working properly.

Two weeks later, you're in the customer's area once again, and you drop in to see him. "I just want to make sure that everything is OK," you say. and the customer says, "It's working just fine. You people carry a line of . . . (he mentions your bread-and-butter product) don't you?"

You tell him that you certainly do, and ask if they would like to order some. The customer says, "Send me a trial order . . . we'd like to give it a closer look."

So you do. And you go through the exact routine you did before, except this time you run into a snag!

The problem is that ABC & Co. has always used your competitor's product which has certain characteristics that differ from yours. In using the sample shipment, the operators failed to read the instructions clearly printed on the package. The results: *bad*. Since your product is compounded in such a way that *less* of it is needed than your competitor's (a point you have always made in your sales presentations), their trial run was a disaster. Now what do we do, Ollie?

"Sweet are the uses of adversity," someone once said. Problems solved are triumphs; unsolved, they are disasters. If we sell, we should be *looking* for problems to solve—even if they are problems our own product helped create.

How often in running conferences with salespeople have I explored with them the reasons some salespeople don't follow up. Usually there is at least one honest person who will say, "You might run into a problem." To which I always ask, "If you didn't follow up, would there still be a problem?"

Back to your victory-turned-sour. The complaint has been discovered early enough for your remedial action to be effective. You now have an opportunity to get out into the shop and to talk to the people who are having the problem. You show them the differences in your product and that of your competitor, and you hang on until they have completed another trial run. The results are *superb*.

ABC & Co. continues to use your competitor's product, but you get a few small reorders. You check back to see how it's going. And then the orders get larger. Finally—like the old fable of the Arab who let the camel get its nose under the tent, and the camel finally moved in and the Arab had to get out—you're the prime supplier and your competitor is on the outside looking in! Months later, you're having lunch with the buyer at ABC & Co. and he lets you in on the reason for the switch: *You followed up, and your competitor didn't.*

Obviously, as your customer list grows, your follow-up efforts increase. The easy way to keep abreast of your own success is to organize yourself to do it. Here are a few suggestions:

- On a new sale, send a follow-up note of appreciation the following day. Then mark your calendar for the important dates to come— delivery date, check-up date, reorder date.

- In addition to these calendar notes, make a few others. If the account isn't regularly active, how about a quarterly follow-up?

- Do you know your buyer's birthdate? How about a birthday card . . . an easy annual contact to make.

- Develop a list of customers and the products they buy. Break this into product lists, and when any change in product application or price comes up, the notices can be sent automatically.

- Route-schedule so that you can call on inactive accounts on your way to active accounts.

Time has always been an important factor to salespeople. It has become a major cost factor to management in recent years; the cost of a sales call has gone soaring. To save both time and money, the modern salesperson has to develop good telephone and note-writing techniques. To be sure, these are poor substitutes for the personal contact, but, in many instances, they are better than widely spaced contacts.

Here's a handy checklist for follow-up calls:

- *Plan follow-up.* That means scheduling and it also means deciding in advance what is to be said.

- *Always have a good reason for calling.* You want to find out if the product is working properly; there's a new application that the customer should know about; a new price has been announced, etc.

- *Make follow-up calls short.* Your customer has a lot more to do than talk to you.

- *If you are making a call in person, make an appointment.* Drop-ins are sometimes welcome, sometimes not. Knowing your customer's schedule and habits will give you guidance in this.

- *If a problem arises, handle it.* If you make a phone call, and there's a problem that can't be cared for on the spot, make an appointment and pack a bag.

Follow-up, of course, doesn't preclude the necessity for prospecting, but it certainly makes it a lot easier. And the nice thing about following up is that when you *do* prospect for new business you're *adding* to your customer list, *not replacing* someone on it!

Your best selling opportunities, indeed, come after the sale!

The simple truth is that it is easier to convince a salesperson to make a follow-up call in pursuit of *new* business than it is to convince him or her to follow-up with *regular* customers. This doesn't make sense, and here's why:

- It's easier to *maintain* a relationship than to *begin* one.
- What was worth going after in the first place is worth preserving.
- If you don't pay attention to your customer, he or she will find someone else who will.
- Referrals from satisfied customers turn cold calls into hot prospects.

That last item is often the most difficult to believe, but it happens. Salespeople—if they're either very good or very bad—get talked about. At meetings of business associations, at chambers of commerce, at social gatherings, at the first tee on the golf course, in local bars and restaurants, the "do-you-know-Charlie?" routine goes on and on. It's the follow-up salesperson who gets talked about most... *most favorably.*

They are the real estate salespeople who call to find out if the family is comfortable in the new home... car salesmen who call to find out if the new car is performing properly... industrial salespeople who call to find out if the shipment arrived in good shape and on time. My wife recently had a short stay at a local hospital, and three days after she got home the hospital administrator called to find out how she was feeling. The doctor never bothered. But you can imagine how well talked-up that hospital is these days!

Pasted inside every salesperson's hat should be these words:

Never forget a customer... and never let a customer forget you!

When "Bad" Customers Happen to Good Salespeople

by James E. Shaw

Making a sale is like climbing a mountain. Getting to the top is a thrill, but your position is precarious. One false step and your clients can start to de-sell themselves, tumbling you down the mountainside with them. Bad customers, like novice climbers, can turn a simple problem into a rock slide, burying you both in bad feelings.

Last week, Jim Deal had made a big sale to a very important client, Sheila Gray. But when he stops in for a follow-up visit, things start to crumble. Instead of having her expectations fulfilled, Sheila feels angry, frustrated, and disappointed over problems she's already experienced with delivery and promised features.

Her complaints are too general for Jim to address immediately. Within moments he has lost Sheila's former willingness to risk trying his products as she becomes fearful of her commitment to buy and shows an impatient eagerness to try "something else." The trust Sheila had in Jim and his products turns into distrust and suspicion—she is mentally questioning everything Jim told her during his last presentation.

Before Jim knows what hit him, Sheila has lost her confidence in him, has lost her respect for him and rejects his attempts to offer solutions to the problem, persuades herself that her disappointment is evidence that Jim and his product can't deliver what was promised. Her doubts and uncertainty finally reach the point where she claims that she is well informed about Jim's company and the sales situation and is sure nothing can be done. Whether Jim is asked to leave or shouted out of the office, he feels as though he has taken a devastating fall.

If you believe that "there is no such thing as a bad customer— only bad salespeople," you're only hurting yourself. Sheila's *reaction* was not Jim's fault, even if the *problem* was. Jim could have saved the situation, though, by recognizing the trouble spots of the sales cycle—the sales mountain.

When customers begin slipping backward—losing their trust in you or their willingness to risk trying your products—you need to use a five-step process to regain their confidence and resell them on the sale.

Step One: Accommodating

It is important to acknowledge your client's right to object, instead of answering the objection immediately. Supportive listening turns the situation from a confrontation to an opportunity for mutual problem solving. This step, although difficult because of a natural tendency to defend yourself, is necessary to reduce the tension of a downhill slide.

Examples of responses can include: "Please tell me more," "I'm not sure I understand what you mean," "Would you mind going over that again?"

Step Two: Supplementing

Accept the fact that your customers have reasons for being upset, and supplement their remarks while being empathetic. Genuine concern is essential. Show your clients that you're willing to take the time to understand the problem by gathering all the information you need.

You might say: "I'm sorry that happened to you," "I know that must have really set you back and caused you to miss your deadline," "Do you mind if I sit down so that you can tell me about it?"

Step Three: Accentuating

During this step, you ask questions to pinpoint the customer's specific concerns and uncover the causes of his or her bad disposition. By probing and then verbally summarizing the client's stated annoyances, you accent any underlying reservations.

Ask the client: "What kinds of concerns do you have specifically?" "Would it be all right if I asked you a few questions?" "It sounds like you're concerned about... Have I stated that correctly?"

Step Four: Addressing

Don't offer a solution until you have gone through the first three steps. Once the emphasis is placed on the customer's bad behavior, it is time to share your thoughts and ideas on how the problem can be addressed. Propose solutions, and then ask if any of your suggestions are acceptable to the client. At this point you must get the customer's agreement before going on to the last step.

You can say: "As a possibility you might . . . " "I'd like to tell you what I would do in your situation." "I have an idea about that, would you like to hear it?"

Step Five: Acting

Now is the time to verbally demonstrate your willingness to act on your proposals. Let the client know that you will execute the agreed-upon solutions right away by giving an approximate time period in which he or she can expect results. Emphasize that you will stay in touch and continue to encourage customer feedback concerning how he or she would like to see the problem solved.

Confirm your proposals by stating: "Why don't we go ahead then and . . . " "How does that sound to you?" "What I'll do is . . . "

Bad customers can turn a slight misstep into an avalanche. When customers feel that your product or service had failed to live up to their expectations, your struggle to remain at the top of the mountain—and maintain the sale as well as the selling relationship—depends on your ability to use this five-step process as a safety line.

Instead of letting a bad customer ruin your day, save the life of your sale by rescaling the mountain and reselling the client.

Tending Your Garden

Do you have accounts that are sprouting problems or developing bugs? Like weeds and insects in a garden, they will multiply prolifically if you leave them alone. The following three steps can help you kill those weeds and bugs while making the ground more fertile for future sales.

First, follow up with your accounts. Like a good gardener, you must root out the problems and get rid of the bugs before they get out of hand. Make sure your clients are happy. If they're not, ask about difficulties, then follow up on these. You don't have time to do this? Then find a staff member who can. Just as a gardener uses peat moss and beetle traps for preventive measures, your calls to clients who have not yet complained about a problem will protect you from full-blown disasters that hit you when you don't expect them.

Second, if an account calls you, make sure that you know about it. An answering machine, answering service, or an office worker can act as your gardening assistant; someone (or something) to discover difficulties before the client multiplies the severity of the problem all out of proportion because nothing has been done about it. Pull up those weeds and spray those bugs before they present real problems.

Third, follow up on your calls. Start with the worst-sounding ones—don't put them off until last. Saving them for later will only make them seem more difficult. Once you ask the client to explain his complaint and show a willingness to cooperate with him or her, the problem can usually be rectified easily. Don't let your weeds choke the entire crop or let a few bugs become an infestation. The longer you let the problem go on, the more it will cost you in time, energy, and money to fix it.

Keep your garden well tended and you will be rewarded with a bountiful crop of successful sales and happy customers.

Get an I.O.U.
for Everything You Do

by David H. Sandler

It is always surprising to learn during our sales seminars how many salespeople are willing to perform "free" services for their customers. It seems by performing extra services, the salesperson hopes the customer will give him or her some consideration in return. Not a bad idea if the customer knows how to read minds.

Selling is one of the few professions where much of the preliminary work is "free." For instance, can you see yourself going to the local movie house, approaching the ticket counter and telling the young lady behind the glass, "I'm going inside to see the movie. If I like it, I'll pay you on the way out." Or, calling a local cab driver and telling him if you like the ride, it's OK for him to put the meter on.

This doesn't mean for you to stop performing these services for your customers. It does mean there is a way in which you can help them "see" the effort you are putting forth on their behalf. Believe it or not, some customers believe your company pays you to perform these "no charge" services.

Here is a simple scenario to demonstrate this point.

Customer: Hal, can you bring a few extra cases of 243 by the office Saturday morning? We're out.
Hal: Fred, I'd like to help, but there may be a problem. Let me ask you this, how badly do you need them? (Your intention, of course, is to take the cases to him.)
Customer: I really need them badly.
Hal: How long are you going to be in your office this morning?
Customer: I'll be here all morning.
Hal: Call you back in a few minutes. I need to see if I can reschedule a few things I had lined up for Saturday morning.
Hal: (when he calls back): Good news, I can get them to you Saturday morning sharp.
Customer: Thanks, I appreciate your help.
Hal: No problem, Fred, we appreciate your business.

Hal's first move could have been, "I'll be glad to bring them over Saturday morning." As played out above, however, the customer received a subtle message that Hal was going "above and beyond" the call of duty by having to change previous plans. After several situations like the one above, when you are "apples for apples" with the competition, your IOU's could get you the order. You don't have to remind the customer what you have done, the IOU's are there.

Extending the Sale

By Dr. Milt Grassell

Should You Challenge the Old Rule
to Leave Immediately after the Close?

We've all been told the best thing to do after closing the sale is to stop selling and leave!

That's still good advice in some situations. But it doesn't apply to all circumstances. Many successful salespeople have significantly increased their income and profit by disregarding this old rule. To them the best time to sell is after the customer starts to buy.

Remember the time you needed just one gallon of paint. That's all. But you came home with two brushes, one roller, an extension ladder, three drop cloths, some thinner, and the paint.

Salespeople in almost all fields and with most products and services have been quietly and successfully extending sales for years without endangering whatever they just finished selling. The secret is a two-part process:

- Close the first sale before attempting to extend it.
- Tie whatever you just sold to a new need your product or service can satisfy.

This two-part process applies to both tangibles and intangibles. For example, a consultant was recently hired to make a customer-relations survey for a client. Let's see how he used this process.

First, the consultant made sure the sale would stay sold before attempting to extend the sale. He did this by putting all the details in a signed written agreement.

Second, the consultant pointed out that he didn't feel it was fair to leave the client after the survey. He convinced the client that follow-through work would be necessary. The client agreed. The sale was extended to include a retainer fee for the follow-up work.

If you're not attempting to extend your sales, perhaps doing so would be the best way to increase your own profit and income.

Marry a Client?

by Dottie M. Walters, CSP

Do you marry your clients? Of course we're speaking figuratively. The approach you take can either make your clients feel like they're being wooed by a romantic suitor or violated by a grab-it-and-run one-timer.

Successful salespeople are *in love* with people. They let their clients know that they care about them by asking about their lives, their dreams, their hopes, and then doing everything they can to give the clients what they want. Just taking the time to say "Tell me about it" can mean a lot to a harried customer. On the other hand, wandering eyes, general inattention to a customer's needs, and a canned sales talk says "I don't want a relationship, just your money."

Court your clients, as you would anyone else with whom you hope to have a fulfilling long-term relationship. Make them feel cared for and appreciated, not used and abused.

The Cost of Losing Customers

The American Management Association estimates that it costs the average company six times as much to win a new customer as it does to keep an existing one.

The main reason for the higher cost of selling a new customer is the steep price of an individual sales call versus the relatively low cost of typical customer service function.

Every time you lose a customer, you may have to subtract as much as $120 from company profits.

Good follow-up service procedures are the best weapon for keeping sales costs down.

What Customers Expect after the Sale

How many times have you said to a business acquaintance, "I owe you one."? It's pretty common knowledge that we live in an era of back scratchers. If you do someone a favor, you can reasonably expect that you're owed a favor in return.

Although this is true in real life, this rule does not apply in selling.

As a sales professional you probably feel that when you go the extra mile to sell something to a customer the relationship has not only become solid, but also that the customer now *owes you* one. It may come as a surprise, but in selling the opposite is true. No matter how hard you have worked or how many concessions you have made, when you sell a customer, he or she then feels that you owe them a favor. Yes, you! Let me quote an expert. Harvard Business School Professor Theodore Levitt, in the "Harvard Business Review," writes that the seller is at a psychological disadvantage after the sale has been made. I quote, "The buyer expects the seller to remember the purchase as having been a favor bestowed. The seller now owes the buyer one."

For many salespeople I'm sure this comes as a big surprise. Some have even told me that they do not accept this premise—that the sale is a relationship in which each party gives equally. This may be true on an economic level, but it has nothing to do with the deficit relationship created by the customer's purchase.

The perception on the part of the customer is that you, the seller, have not only gotten new business but also his or her money. There were many other salespeople after the same account but he or she chose you as the recipient. Therefore, psychologically, you now owe your customer a favor. Economically you are even. Psychologically you are at a loss, even though you had to bend over backwards to get the order.

What can you do to fill the customer's psychological needs, now that you recognize the problem?

First, pay special attention to keeping the customer happy. Send a thank you note, be sure to call to find out how the product is performing and answer any questions that may have come up since the purchase. Follow up on that account as if the sale had never been made.

One of the country's leading advertising salesmen, Spencer Longshore, says, "I always approach my customers as if I were applying for a job—even after the sale is made. They're my bosses—and I make sure that I fill the time between two paychecks with special attention and superior service."

Part II

TELEPHONE SELLING

There's a terrific opportunity for increasing your sales productivity sitting right on your desk—your telephone. With today's advanced technology, every salesperson can take advantage of the vast array of equipment designed to improve efficiency and provide services to clients. But the key is often not equipment—it's technique. How you say what you say and when you say it can turn telephone contacts into long-term sales commitments or dead leads.

This chapter will help you create a plan for better telephone selling. By learning about precall planning, listening techniques, prospecting lists, and guiding the conversation to gain the most information, you'll be ready to win more customers. If you've been running into roadblocks that keep you from reaching your goals, you can find out how to get around these obstacles. There are even tips on using an answering machine for increased sales.

Increasing Your Telephone Selling Power

Want to score big in telephone sales? Don't just master the message: Master the method.

The best prepared tele-talk in the world won't make it if your client doesn't like you. But master the fine art of sizing up that person from a few moments' conversation to find out where he or she is "coming from," and your batting average just has to rise.

Take loudness. If you're a phone yeller and your client is soft-spoken, it's a strike against you. The same with other qualities; with speaking speed, willingness to listen and find out what the customer wants, even the style of your conversation—the kinds of words and images you use. These and an array of other easily overlooked human qualities will have more bearing on your success than the message you speak, according to California psychologist Dr. Donald J. Moine.

The key is empathy—what Webster's calls intellectual or emotional identification with another. When you dial a call, you dial direct into someone else's life. Hit that person the wrong way and you might as well forget the rest. But strike a harmonious note and the door opens.

We're not talking about insincere, forced chumminess. That can be the biggest turnoff of them all. But it takes only a few moments with a skilled introduction, often ending in an open question, to catch an inkling of where the person on the other end is coming from, what his or her mood is, and what signals he or she is sending. Then build on it. Get straight to the point, but with understanding.

Speaking speed is another of those key items. Try to come close to the pace of the customer. Research has shown that we don't think we have much in common with those who speak much faster or slower than we do.

Also important are the words and expressions we use. A very precise speaker may not trust someone who speaks in too many quick generalities.

Then there's brevity. Keep your talk brief, but look for those tell-tale signs that indicate the customer would like more detail. Be prepared to provide those details.

Even dialects or accents can play a part. Someone with a strong twang or drawl from one part of the country often reacts negatively to someone with a brusque accent from another region. It's something to keep in mind. Don't put on a phony accent, but make an effort to create a bridge so your minds can meet.

How about mood? Neutrality is a good starting point. There is such a thing as being overly cheerful. Ever crawl out of bed on a Monday morning only to be hit by some "grinning" telephone sales rep? That initial opener has to be positive, even upbeat, but until you've gotten the first feedback blues, don't come on too strong.

Deal agreeably with disagreeable clients. Should waves appear upon smooth waters, don't make them bigger. If the talk turns to product specifics and the customer has a bone to pick, you don't let it turn into World War III. Try some open questions. Ask about the problem. Try to be helpful and suggest a way your own product can be used to the customer's advantage.

There are more subtle points. Speech has a rhythm, a cadence. Try to pick up on the cadence of the client's speech and get into swing with it. An adjustment on your part can bring one more point of harmony. After all, studies have shown we seem to like people who are like we are. There are points of harmony to be revealed in the opening moments of a telephone talk. Find them and build on them.

Meeting a stranger you can't see offers many differences from a face-to-face meeting. Those differences can be turned to your advantage, if you are aware of them. The telephone eliminates all visual clues about people, so the caller can get to the point more quickly. However, he or she must be extra alert for clues about the person being called.

Bell's telephone was more than an invention of convenience. For the sales professional, the phone can get through doors without having to open them, and that's half the job, isn't it? When a telephone rings, it cannot be ignored.

We've all been approached by a telephone sales pitch. What are your own reactions? Which approaches did you like; which rubbed you the wrong way, and why?

When you have used the phone to open the door, and have finished with your opening, don't run on. Share the platform with the client. After all, holding a talkathon won't keep him or her from saying "no," if that's what's coming.

Be a good listener. Take a few notes to ensure you don't forget the customer's concerns. When it's your turn to speak again, show you've paid attention by briefly summarizing a few highlights of his remarks with a comment like: "In other words, your top priority is ... "

We've talked about image enhancers. But it's also important to know some items that can work against you; things that Eugene Kordahl, President of National Telemarketing, calls "Image Destroyers."

These include mumbling, speaking at the wrong speed or volume, the wrong mood, failing to promptly identify yourself, your company, and your purpose. Then too, there are those old bugaboos like carrying on a conversation with someone else in the office, chewing gum or eating, banging down the phone on the desk, and the ultimate no-no: putting someone on hold.

In a telephone sales contact, putting someone on hold is almost inexcusable. It's better to call back. If you must do it, and can't call back, make the interruption truly brief.

There is no set of rules that will guarantee success in telephone sales, but here are some key points:

1. *Voice*. Adjust your volume and speed. Harmonize and synchronize.

2. *Content*. Practice your message so you don't take too much of someone else's time. Then outline your message in your opening and save details for the follow-up.

3. *Mood*. Start out being neutral. Then listen for clues and shift to a stronger, more positive mood when appropriate.

4. *Attitude*. It's the body language of telephone sales. There is no substitute for being confident, open, understanding and knowledgeable.

5. *Listen*. Express your understanding of the customer's point of view.

6. *Practice*. It may not make you perfect, but it sure beats being sloppy. Rehearse on tape with a colleague role-playing a client. Then critique.

The phone's right there on the desk. View it as your money machine. Go to it, Tiger!

An Attitude Monitor
for Telephone Selling

A telephone salesperson for a large New York securities firm recently called our office to promote her services. When I asked to what she attributed her unusually cheerful and friendly attitude, she explained. "It's my attitude monitor. Before I make each call, I look up to a small 6 x 9 inch mirror. When I see myself frowning, I take a moment to relax; I take a deep breath, and close my eyes while exhaling. Then I use my ten-digit-smile routine, which means that I hold my smile while I punch the numbers. By the time I reach my prospect, I'm in a good selling mood."

"Any sales rep can build his or her own attitude monitor," she explained, "all you need to do is go to a glass store, buy a mirror, then use transfer letters to write 'Attitude Monitor' across the nine inch side. You can make it fancy by dividing the remaining space into two parts. I pasted a smiley face on the left with the title 'Ideal Attitude,' and titled the right side 'Real Attitude' leaving enough room for self-monitoring."

Does it work? "Attitude is the key to success in telephone selling," she concluded. "You can't present a unique opportunity with a poor attitude. If you see the tell-tale signs in the mirror, then your top priority is to work on bouncing back *before* you punch the next number."

Seven Steps
to Qualify Prospects
on the Telephone

Your first contact call, whether it's initiated by you or the customer, will set the stage for any future interactions. So you want to make the conversation as positive and informative as possible. To do this, you should include the following seven steps to ensure creating an impression of helpfulness, trust, and genuine interest in the client's needs.

1. Thank your prospect for his interest. Set the stage for a pleasant telephone conversation. Thank the prospect for inquiring about your products. This simple courtesy creates enthusiasm and prepares for a productive conversation.

Example: "I'd like to thank you for your interest in our product—you sent us a coupon, requesting information on our ... line." (Smile while you talk!)

2. State the purpose of your call and obtain permission to ask questions. Check the prospect's availability. If he's having someone in the office, it's better to call back at a more convenient time. Stating your call purpose helps your prospect to focus his attention on his needs.

Example: "Mrs. Schlegel, my purpose at this time is to ask you a few questions that will help me to understand your current needs (pause). Would you mind if I asked them now?"

3. Ask qualifying questions: Identify your prospect's needs by asking specific questions such as:

"What *type* of product ... ?" (size, dimensions, grade, etc.)

"When would you need the product?"

"Are you *familiar* with our product?"

"What *type of specific information* would you need from us in order to make a buying decision?"

"Have you considered *alternative solutions* to your current problem?"

177

"Have you thought about *financing?*" or: *"How much* would you plan to invest in this type of product?"

4. Thank the prospect for the information. Show your appreciation and understanding.

Example: "Thank you, Mr. Wolfe, for sharing this information with me; this gives me a better understanding of what you are looking for."

5. Provide encouragement. Explain to the prospect that you've been able to solve similar problems before and emphasize that you'll be able to help meet his needs.

Example: "I think you'll be pleased to hear that we've been able to solve similar problems with companies in your particular industry. I'm confident that we'll be able to present you with a proposal that will meet your approval."

6. Propose to "show" interesting information to prospect. Your final objective is to set up an appointment. You need to get a face-to-face interview. Propose to "show" some information (that can't be communicated on the telephone).

Example: "It will take me only a short time to prepare some interesting data for you, so I'll be able to show you in detail how we would be able to satisfy your particular needs. When would you like to see this information?"

7. Propose a choice of two meeting dates. Should you propose only one date, you will give the prospect the choice between meeting that day or . . . not at all. If you propose to meet either this day . . . or that one . . . you will increase your chances for getting the appointment.

Example: "Would next week on Wednesday morning be suitable— or do you prefer to meet on Thursday afternoon?"

Use these seven steps as guidelines to qualify your next prospect. After you've identified your prospect's needs and individual problems, prepare yourself for the best selling strategy. This will dramatically increase your chances for success.

Telephone Selling at a Tradeshow

At a recent trade show an exhibitor equipped several attractive models with portable telephones.

When they identified important prospects (by reading name tags), they caused the phone to ring and then informed the surprised visitor that the call was for him.

A concealed cassette recorder (in the model's purse) played a one-minute canned sales talk over the telephone inviting the visitor to come to a certain booth.

The exhibitor attracted a record number of new prospects. (Note of caution: Check with show-management prior to using a similar technique.)

Can I Put You on Hold?
...So I Can Do My Nails!

by Robert A. Weaver, Jr.

Most successful salespeople have learned that not answering the telephone can destroy a relationship.

Unreturned calls and being left on 'hold' are the two major complaints on everyone's list of telephone gripes. Since the ill will that either practice generates is not healthy for the salesperson-client relationship, let's take a quick look at some possible ways of preventing or at least defusing the potential for damage.

Suppose you're the person doing the calling. Which of the following answers do you prefer?

Good afternoon. Quick Sales Incorporated. Please hold.
Good afternoon. Quick Sales Incorporated. Another line is ringing, would you prefer to hold or may I call you back?

If you selected the call back, you have a right to expect that call within the next ten to fifteen minutes. If you choose to be placed on hold, then you should receive a status report at short intervals, say 90 to 120 seconds. And you can be sure that people placing calls to your office have the same expectations that you do!

Let's try another situation—one of your "headaches" is on the phone. How do you start the conversation?

Hello, Mr. Jones. It's always good to hear from you. How can we be of assistance
or
Hello, Mr. Jones. What's the problem today?

The focus in the first opening was on setting a positive tone for the conversation that was to follow, and your choice provides a pretty good indication of whether your telephone skills are helping or hindering your career.

Of course, this last example also points up the need for a pleasant phone personality. The first response would have been self-defeating if the same words had been said in a dull listless manner that sounded less than sincere. Sincerity should be conveyed by both tone of voice and enthusiasm. Yes, enthusiasm. It may sound strange but a lot of individuals maintain that they can hear smiles in a tone of voice, and feel the vibrations of an enthusiastic seller in their phone's receiver. Well, perhaps they can. Why not try it sometime?

Now just in case the person reading this is so perfect in his or her own telephone manners that there is absolutely no room for improvement, what about your press agent, your personal representative with your clients? *Your who?* Your secretary or switchboard operator! They speak for your organization, they represent you and they are usually the first person your clients talk to when they try to contact you. If the person taking the call gets your potential customer upset, that ill will can and often does transfer over to you. That's a liability no salesperson should have to put up with.

If you have reason to doubt the kind of telephone treatment your clients are getting, check it out. Without identifying yourself, place a call to someone in your office and see what kind of service your clients are getting. As a member of a profession that depends on the care and feeling of telephone relationships, you have a right to expect the same high standards of performance from your representative that you demand of yourself. Don't settle for less!

Phonemanship

When you call a client on the phone, you must rely on his or her imagination to visualize your product. Paul Mills, President of Mills-Roberts Associates, Inc., suggests that you help prospects create a vivid mental picture by developing a colorful sales vocabulary.

- *Use concrete action words.* Instead of "go," use specifics such as walk, run, jog, stride, or skip.

  Example: Translate "Your profits will go up." into
  "Your profits will *climb."*

- *Personalize your message.* Make "the company" or "my company," *your* company and use lots of personal pronouns in your speech—I, you, me, our, etc,

  Example: Instead of saying "The company offers these discounts." state
  "Our company gives *you* these discounts."

- *Create word-pictures.* "Green" is just a color name; "lush, tropical green" makes an impression.

  Example: Avoid "The carpet is red." and use
  "The carpet is a *deep, rich burgundy."*

- *Use emotional words.* Spice up dull phrases with descriptions such as "exciting, beautiful, thrilling, elegant."

  Example: Improve "It's a good advertising display." by saying
  "It's an *exciting* advertising display."

- *Substitute pleasant words for unpleasant ones.* Stay away from words that have a negative emotional meaning.

  Example: Change "This medicine kills pain." to
  "This medicine brings *comfort and relief."*

- *Make your sales talk sound natural.* "Cannot" sounds canned but "can't" sounds conversational, so *do* use contractions.

  Example: Switch "What will your customers do if you do not have it in stock?" to
  "What'll your customers do if you *don't* have it in stock?"

Of course, describing your product is only part of your job

182

when you telephone prospects. Knowing how to begin the conversation, elicit a favorable reaction, create customer interest, emphasize benefits over features, overcome objections, close the sale and conclude the conversation are just as important to your sales success. Mills-Roberts Associates covers these necessary phone skills in an audio-cassette and workbook course entitled *The Art and Science of Selling by Telephone*.

Being Prepared:
Telephone Listening Techniques

According to Dr. Lyman Steil, people only listen at a 25 percent level of efficiency. That means a lot of missed information, information that is vital to a salesperson's telephone selling strategy. In an interview with *Personal Selling Power,* Dr. Steil shared some of his expertise in the field of listening, gained from 18 years of research, so our readers could utilize the other 75 percent of their capabilities. His suggestions for improving listening techniques provide valuable information for both the salesperson and his customer.

In his extensive research, Dr. Steil found that most salespeople have not developed a systematic approach to telephone selling.

"A lot of salespeople get into poor listening habits very quickly," he explains. "They think because a prospect answers the phone, he's ready to listen to their spiel."

Dr. Steil suggests asking questions like: "Do you have time? Can you listen for three minutes?" or "Do you have paper and pencil ready, because I'd like to share some important things with you?"

He advises allowing time for the listener to shift gears. More importantly: Create a brief concentration phase to collect your mental energies before you make or answer a call.

Have you ever thought about exactly where to put your telephone? If you're right-handed, it's to your advantage to place your telephone on the left-hand side of your desk. Why? There are three reasons:

1. You won't have the cord dangling over your workspace, interfering with your concentration.
2. You will have your right hand free to take notes.
3. You don't waste time shifting the telephone to the other hand.

When do you answer your telephone? On the first, second, or third ring? Dr. Steil warns: "Don't answer your telephone in a compulsive fashion. The very first thing you ought to do is to stop your conversation, clear your mind and shift gears away from what you were doing. Have a pad of paper and pencil ready. Once you are ready, no matter what ring it is, answer the telephone with your opposite-handed side."

Dr. Steil feels that this approach allows you to listen more effectively right from the very first second. He suggests that during the first 15 seconds callers tell you who they are, where they are from, what company they are with, and why they are calling. Many sales executives don't hear that information, because they are still working on a project, shifting hands, or busy searching for something to write on.

New Prospecting Lists
for Increased Telephone Sales

by Eugene Kordahl

The first step toward increased sales is needs assessment. Clearly, the need is not just for more prospecting, but rather for more accurate prospecting. We all know how ineffective the "tried and true" sources (the trade magazines, yellow pages, old sales leads, newspapers) can be. Plenty of leg work and a few results.

What we need is a new and better focus, something that gives names of firms, numbers of employees, contact names, telephone numbers and addresses: a professional list prepared by a list broker or compiler. The raw material for these lists can come from membership lists; industrial directories set up geographically by manufacturing, wholesaling and purchasing functions; directories of corporate officers; and business library directories.

Avoid buying consumer lists; instead, get business-to-business lists *with telephone numbers*.

The key to accurate prospecting is in selecting a professional list broker or compiler, somebody who will spend time with you helping to segment a list. There are three types of list firms; (1) Full service compilers who rent lists; (2) list management firms which buy specific lists and (3) brokers who locate specific lists at your request.

I suggest starting with a full service compiler who can give you a small test list. It should be compiled according to two criteria: (1) sales potential and (2) relationship to your customer base. Have the compiler specify which prospects to contact in a sales territory, and ask for referral to several other list sources for current, effective telephone prospecting lists. The typical cost is $35.00 per thousand names plus $5.00 per thousand phone numbers.

Some reliable business-to-business professional compilers include Ed Burnett Consultants, Inc., New York City (business, professions by SIC size); National Business Lists, Inc., Chicago (businesses, institutions, professional firms, farms); Cahners Publishing Co., Chicago (corporate and purchasing executives, middle managers, engineers).

While compiling your list, keep the following selection options in mind; type of business, financial strength, number of employees, geographic location, headquarters/branch selection, phone numbers, and job titles. You can get any of a number of formats, depending on your need.

It generally takes three weeks to get the list in hand. With it, you're able to telephone those firms identified as having an absolute need for the product. And that means having a prospecting system many times more aggressive and effective than your old method.

When You Just Can't Get Started

How many times have you found yourself staring at the telephone as though it were a coiled serpent?

A lot of sales representatives feel that way, especially when it comes to using the telephone for prospecting. Because of personal uncertainty or previous bad experience, many would prefer not to get involved with the phone. They anticipate failure, which makes it tough to get motivated. That's too bad, because used properly, the telephone is one of your best prospecting tools.

There are a number of reasons why telephone use goes astray. Here are a few important ones:

Poor Organization. Many sales reps sit down to a telephone with no clear idea of what they're doing—they just crank out calls.

Bad Location. I've seen sales representatives attempting to qualify prospects from telephone booths in the darndest places: airline terminals, restaurants, roadside rest stops, motels and hotels. No thought was given to the essential elements of privacy and quiet.

Lack of Preparation. Some fail to think out in advance what they're going to say. They figure experience in personal sales presentations will compensate for their lack of knowledge about telephone communications.

Past Performance. All the other factors taken into consideration, it's likely that the average sales rep hasn't done too well with telephone prospecting in the past. And that past failure sets in motion his continued expectation of mishaps. Anxiety in this case is self-fulfilling. The fear of rejection or being made to feel or to look foolish strongly hampers telephone performance.

Steps for Success

The first thing you have to do in approaching any obstacle is to tear down your internal roadblocks. You *can* succeed on the telephone if you come to look upon it as your friend. Put away your anxieties and negative self-talk and follow these simple steps:

Develop a reason for calling. Make it simple. Have a prepared sales message that highlights your motive for calling. The shorter, the better—remember that to win over the prospect, you have to make a good impression on the telephone in the first 17 seconds.

Write down features and benefits for quick reference. You can't assume that the prospect on the other end of the line is familiar with your product or service. Keep a list in front of you and refer to it often.

Select a good time and place to call. Strive to make your calls in a place that has a quiet, business-like atmosphere—don't allow any interruptions. Secondly, make the calls at a time that is convenient for both you and the prospect. If you know the customer well enough, that is, if you've done your homework, you'll pick a time that doesn't interfere with his or her busy schedule.

Start with a good list. List selection is one of the most critical factors in assuring self-motivation. If the list is no good, your motivation will go down the tubes in a hurry. And make sure the list is detailed. Reasons: You can prequalify many of the cold calls you make, and thus assure a much higher success ratio.

Make a commitment to calling. It's the nature of telephone calling that you have to make a certain number of calls before you hit paydirt. That may seem frustrating at first. But remember that telephone prospecting beats knocking on ten doors and getting rejected by all ten cold calls. If you think about it, you're really limited in the number of in person cold calls you can make each day. But with the telephone you can qualify many more firms per hour.

What Do I Say?

By now, you should be chomping at the bit to start punching telephone buttons. That's great. But before you set out to conquer telephone prospecting, have a clear idea of what you're going to say into the mouthpiece. The following recommendations can give you a format for each and every prospecting call:

- Identify yourself and your firm in an enthusiastic manner.
- Establish empathy with the prospect.
- Make an interest-creating comment and listen carefully to the response.
- Ask open-ended, fact-finding questions.
- Deliver your sales message, stressing benefits.

- Ask for a commitment, either for an appointment or an order.
- Overcome any objections.
- Confirm the commitment.
- Express your thanks and let the prospect hang up first.

On your next telephone prospecting venture try this approach and see if your motivation doesn't skyrocket. Following these simple instructions, you'll find you have a more positive attitude because the task will be more business-like and natural. What's more, that discouraging record of "past performance" should turn around in a hurry.

When You Can't Be There: Tips for Using an Answering Machine

1. Get one that records your message easily.

2. Change your recording every week. People get bored with your answering routine and hang up quickly. A new recording creates a new incentive to leave a message.

3. Tell your callers when you expect to call back without leaving a clue as to whether you have left your house or office. ("I am balancing my checking account right now and need to concentrate. Please leave your number so I can call you back within the hour." Or "I am helping a group of customers right now...")

4. Make your message as short as possible. Your callers don't want to hear a long story.

5. Don't apologize for using an answering machine. If you label your device a "silly little machine" or "my silent butler," you reveal that you are uncomfortable about using the machine. If your recording is positive and enthusiastic, you will collect more messages. If your recording is hesitant and apologetic, you will get more hang ups.

6. Make sure that your machine can be adjusted so the signal for a caller's message sounds as soon as your message is over. (Don't let your caller wait for the beep. A two-second pause can feel like an eternity to your caller, enough time to decide to hang up.)

7. Make sure your caller can leave as long a message as he or she needs. (It's frustrating to get cut off in midsentence before finishing leaving your number.)

What Do I Say?

By now, you should be chomping at the bit to start punching telephone buttons. That's great. But before you set out to conquer telephone prospecting, have a clear idea of what you're going to say into the mouthpiece. The following recommendations can give you a format for each and every prospecting call:

- Identify yourself and your firm in an enthusiastic manner.
- Establish empathy with the prospect.
- Make an interest-creating comment and listen carefully to the response.
- Ask open-ended, fact-finding questions.
- Deliver your sales message, stressing benefits.
- Ask for a commitment, either for an appointment or an order.
- Overcome any objections.
- Confirm the commitment.
- Express your thanks and let the prospect hang up first.

On your next telephone prospecting venture try this approach and see if your motivation doesn't skyrocket. Following these simple instructions, you'll find you have a more positive attitude because the task will be more business-like and natural. What's more, that discouraging record of "past performance" should turn around in a hurry.

How to Overcome the 21 Most Common Internal Roadblocks to Telephone Selling

Below you will find 21 statements about telephone selling. Please review them by asking yourself whether you agree or disagree with each statement.

		I agree	I disagree
1.	I don't think I can sell as well on the telephone as in person.	☐	☐
2.	I don't think prospects will buy from me on the phone.	☐	☐
3.	I wouldn't know how to sell to someone over the telephone.	☐	☐
4.	It's too much of a risk—the prospect would never understand the value of our product.	☐	☐
5.	I am too busy to make calls. I've got more important things to do.	☐	☐
6.	My clients want to see me in person. They'd be offended if I didn't visit them.	☐	☐
7.	It's the wrong time of the year to spend the day on the telephone.	☐	☐
8.	The rejection factor on the telephone is much higher than in a one-on-one situation. I don't want to hear "No"!	☐	☐
9.	It's such a tedious job dialing those numbers.	☐	☐
10.	I am not organized for selling on the telephone. I can't make these calls in a gas station.	☐	☐
11.	I wouldn't know whom to call.	☐	☐
12.	I'm trained to sell face to face. I don't know how anyone can present the desired professional image over the telephone.	☐	☐

13. I've tried it before and it doesn't work for me. ☐ ☐

14. My situation is unique. My product/service ☐ ☐
    can't be described over the phone.

15. I don't trust that phone. I can't hear too well. ☐ ☐

16. Telephone selling is a job beneath my abilities. ☐ ☐

17. If the phone is such a perfect selling tool, then ☐ ☐
    they don't need me.

18. I don't like it. I am a pro and don't want ☐ ☐
    people to think that I am just an inside order
    taker.

19. I resent losing the time away from the field. ☐ ☐

20. How can you "read" a client's nonverbal ☐ ☐
    signals on the phone? How do I know what the
    client is doing while I go through my pitch?

21. Frankly, number-punching is not my cup of tea. ☐ ☐
    You've got no control over your prospect when
    using the telephone.

Answers to Telephone Selling Quiz

1. I need to learn how to reduce my fear of failure. The telephone does not need to become a source of failure, but an opportunity for learning. I only fail if I don't try.

2. My fear of rejection gets in the way of becoming a more effective salesperson. I can accept that not everyone will buy from me on the telephone. If someone chooses not to buy, this does not mean that they reject me as a person, they only reject my proposal.

3. I could benefit from a telephone sales training course. I have the capacity to learn new skills and techniques. I'll start learning more about telephone selling—beginning today.

4. If I can communicate my thoughts accurately in person, I can learn to be equally effective on the telephone.

5. I am making excuses. I've got to review some of the negative ideas I had in the past about telephone selling. It's the fear of the unknown that keeps me from using the telephone. I need to stop viewing the uncertainty as danger, and look at the opportunities for increased sales.

6. My fear of disapproval makes me work harder than I should. I need to remind myself more often that I don't need to put my self-esteem in the hands of other people. One telephone call to my customer does not mean that I don't care about his needs; on the contrary, he'll be glad to *hear* from me more often.

7. My fear of the unknown causes me to procrastinate. (See 5.)

8. What I overlook in my assessment is that I can make a lot more telephone calls than in person calls. Also, the ratio of actual calls to rejections remains about the same. But what's more important, since I can make more calls (in the same time), I'll be hearing a lot more "Yes" responses.

9. I need to learn more about the benefits of using the telephone as a sales tool. Once I've obtained more professional training, I'll feel more at ease.

10. I need to review my planning habits and learn how to organize myself for more productive telephone selling. I could

greatly benefit from learning more about telephone selling techniques. (Note to myself: Visit the local library.)

11. I need more training in how to use the telephone for prospecting. (See also 10.)

12. My fear of failure prevents me from becoming more productive. I can feel confident even though my prospects won't be able to see my professional appearance. I can begin to learn more about how to use my distinguished voice to project confidence and reassurance to create more telephone sales.

13. I made mistakes in the past and need to learn professional telephone selling techniques.

14. My fear of change keeps me from learning how to use the telephone as an effective sales aid. There are many steps in a sale from the needs analysis to the close. Even if I won't be able to close a sale on the phone, I can try to become more productive by using the telephone to prepare the prospect for the close.

15. I won't admit that I don't hear too well. I can handle this obstacle by using my hearing aid or by purchasing a small amplifier from the local telephone company, or a Radio Shack store.

16. I am afraid of losing my status. I need to tell myself that my pride does not depend on what I do, but on the results I obtain. Telephone selling is another opportunity to increase my customer base.

17. I need to work on my fear of change. Telephone selling does not necessarily eliminate the need for face-to-face calls. They don't want to get rid of me; I need to get rid of my reluctance to grow and learn the use of a new sales tool.

18. My fear of losing my "image" and "reputation" keeps me from taking advantage of a unique chance to enhance my status. Using the telephone puts a new world of prospects at my fingertips. Calling existing customers does not mean I'll never experience again the great satisfaction involved in a personal call. On the contrary, by developing a "telephone image," I'll enhance my professional reputation. I know that my persuasive qualities and professional appearance will be reflected in my attractive tone of voice, my ability to ask the right questions and the use of effective listening techniques.

19. I am afraid of wasting my time, but I realize that a few prepared phone calls will lead to more productive in person calls, better deals and higher sales. I've neglected to build my telephone sales power. It's the best time saver.

20. I need more training in telephone techniques. It's the client's tone of voice that reveals his feelings and attitudes. I need to shift my

mental focus from visual awareness to auditory awareness. Once I've increased my ability to listen to voice changes and speech variations, I'll sell better.

21. My fear of losing control over the client prevents me from using the telephone.

I need to realize that I cannot control my client's mind. It's in his mind that the decision is made, not in mine. I can only *influence* the decision-making process. I can do this first by using focused questions that uncover the client's needs and motivations, and second by presenting the product benefits that match these needs and motivations.

Sharpening Your
Telephone Skills

Check if you can master these eight essential techniques.

by Craig Bridgman

If you're one of those rare types who can ring up the president of General Motors and in thirty seconds land an appointment with him, cold, then working the phone probably doesn't present much of a challenge to you. Go back to your yacht and relax. But if you're like the rest of us the chances are most days you'd rather do anything—even fill out sales call reports—than make cold calls to prospects for appointments or sales opportunities. Don't feel bad. The telephone tests the nerves and skill of even the best of sales professionals. It also happens to be the most cost-effective way you can go about the job of selling in today's economy. With the cost of making a sales call steadily rising, the telephone will continue to increase in importance as a selling tool. Following are eight ideas to help boost your telephone selling power:

1. Understand the medium. The telephone cuts you off visually from your prospect. This may seem like an obvious point, but it provides the key to understanding why so many salespeople feel uneasy with phone work. Most of us rely on visual impressions to gauge our prospects' responses and attitudes. The telephone eliminates this dimension entirely. It leaves you and your prospect handicapped by denying you visual access to each other, making communication harder and perhaps even triggering counterproductive defensive responses that start the adrenaline flowing on both ends of the line. What to do about it?

2. Create a positive mental picture of the prospect. To exploit any technology requires adapting to its peculiar characteristics and constraints. In the early days of aviation, for example, only pilots with suicidal tendencies went up in fog or bad weather. The introduction of radar changed that, and flying suddenly became a more

198

productive and profitable activity, not to mention infinitely less hazardous. Creating a positive mental picture of your prospect can aid you in utilizing the telephone more advantageously. Imagine before you dial that you are about to talk to a friend or acquaintance whom you especially like. Keep the picture in your mind as you speak. This will help you to synthesize an attitude and feeling on the call likely to relax your listener and make him more receptive.

3. Be friendly. Since there is no objective reason not to feel friendly towards a person you hope to sell, begin on that basis. Use your positive mental image of the prospect to bring personal warmth into the conversation. Mark Twain once said. "The best way to cheer yourself up is to cheer someone else." It has always impressed me how when I coax myself to work the phone in a friendly, cheerful way, even when I'm in a dark humor, I soon begin to feel genuine good humor as I go along.

4. Be relaxed and conversational. In many cases, speed of delivery and tone of voice influence a telephone prospect more than the actual words spoken. Without realizing it, some salespeople, fearing rejection or interruption, rush their words on the phone. Their anxiety communicates itself to the prospect, usually with negative consequences. When you rush, your voice tends to rise in intensity, making you sound shrill. Ironically, rushing to avoid interruption or rejection will often provoke that very reaction, while talking slowly in a relaxed conversational tone almost never does.

To capture the tone and delivery you want, talk more slowly than feels natural to you and, again, imagine yourself in casual conversation with a friend. Don't plod, but be alert to speeding up. From time to time smile as you talk. It improves your voice.

5. Commit your phone presentation to paper. Think about what you want to say, then write it down. Keep the text at hand while you work.

Many salespeople balk at the idea of any kind of canned pitch, feeling that it is unspontaneous and mechanical. A good salesperson, they believe, should be able to improvise as he goes along. True. But that's no reason to rule out a prepared presentation as being without merit. Every salesperson uses certain words, selling phrases, lines of argument and closes over and over again, because they work. Once you've devised an approach that sells, get it down on paper so you can use it repeatedly. Writing your pitch down can also help to keep you from getting flustered, or losing your way, in the middle of a call. Employ everyday words, and speak them as you write to make sure they feel comfortable rolling off the tongue. Keep in mind that a canned presentation doesn't have to be dull and mechanical; it is only if delivered that way.

6. *Make each word count.* Don't be wordy. Say what you have to say in a straightforward manner without embellishment. Prefer short sentences to long. Pause from time to time as you speak (this often has the positive effect of making your words sound more thoughtful). Put the important words at the end of each sentence for maximum impact. For example, the sentence "Management priorities are easier to understand when they're written down" can be strengthened by recasting it as follows: "Writing down management priorities makes understanding them easier." Not only is this version shorter, but the power word "easier" has become stronger by being at the end. Because the prospect hears it last, it is more likely to hit home.

7. *Don't exaggerate.* I'll bet that your product isn't merely well suited to a particular application; it's *incredibly effective* or *dramatically superior.*

Now, it may be true that your product is outstanding, but because so much exaggeration goes on in the business world, a built-in skepticism has evolved as a kind of first line of defense against ambitious claims. Let's face it, in Eastern Nebraska alone there must be at least 867 restaurants that serve the world's best pizza. You come along and open up number 868, and the world yawns and says, "Yeah, so what?" It's unjust, but that's life. If you want to boost your credibility, go easy on making lavish claims in favor of simply telling your prospect the facts likely to be of interest to him in a brief, unadorned way. Your telephone salesmanship will improve as a result.

8. *Don't lock horns with the secretary.* Many more prospects have their calls screened more thoroughly than they once did. Executive secretaries can hear a salesperson coming a mile away. Instantly they leap to defend the boss against your call. If you try to bluster or finesse your way through, the chances are they'll trip you up, and you'll get mangled. You can cut the secretarial Gordian knot simply by calling when she is likely not to be in, such as early in the morning, during lunch, or after hours. Her boss, if he is an executive, will sometimes be there, and you can reach him directly. When this approach is not practical, the best tactic for the long haul is to be straightforward and businesslike. If the call sounds unhurried, natural and routine to her, *because you yourself sound that*

way, she may drop her guard, and you'll stand a better chance of getting through. Some executives will instruct their secretaries to let no call pass, even if it's from Ronald Reagan, or the Pope. They give instructions to take messages, and later they return the calls at their leisure. Leave a message and keep it brief. If you want to leave information about the purpose of your call, have a few key words written out in advance that you can give the secretary to jot down. Otherwise, you may find yourself fumbling around, drawing out the call unnecessarily. If all else fails and you know you're not going to be able to get through, make the secretary an ally. Ask her to steer you to another suitable prospect in the organization.

Today the smart money in sales is on the telephone, because, simply stated, it's the best productivity tool there is.

Part III
SELF-MOTIVATION

All the blueprints and plans in the world can't help you if you're not MOTIVATED. Knowing how to do something, whether it's riding a bike or selling a product, isn't enough. You must have the drive to follow through.

Every individual has an enormous reserve of self-motivational power just waiting to be tapped. But most people squander their resources. Write out a plan for your ongoing self-motivation. (Remember: You can't graduate in self-motivation; it's an ongoing process.) Read at least one book on self-motivation every three weeks. Listen to at least two motivational cassettes every week. And think positive thoughts at least five times a day. If you follow your plan for self-motivation and use excellent selling skills on every call, there's no limit to the heights of selling success you can reach.

Success is never found. Failure is never fatal. Courage is the only thing.

Winston Churchill

Success is simple. Do what's right, the right way, at the right time.

Arnold Glasgow

Inertia is to failure what action is to success

Unknown

Motivation ... the Inner Flame

Eleven of America's greatest motivators share their tested techniques and most powerful motivational messages. This is must reading, because in the profession of selling, motivation means money.

On June 17, 1966, **Paul E. Galanti,** an experienced Navy pilot, took off from the U.S.S. Hancock in his A-4 Skyhawk to fly his 97th combat mission over Vietnam. Galanti, who defines motivation as "doing whatever the hell you have to do to get the job done," was about to approach his target area as antiaircraft fire hit his only jet engine.

"When the engine got hit, the plane caught fire ... it was rolling and tumbling," he recalls, describing the catastrophic experience. "The last thing I remember seeing (before the electricity went out) was 3,000 feet going down on the dial." As the plane went out of control, the tail blew off and Galanti tried frantically to establish radio contact with the other aircraft.

Smoke came into the cockpit and his mind flashed the warning, "You're supposed to slow down the airplane as much as you can before ejecting." The controls failed to respond to the pilot's commands. Every split second counted as the plane approached the ground in a dizzying falling, tumbling and rolling pattern.

Galanti kept his cool. "There is a face curtain in the head rest of the seat. You simply pull it over your face to shield your face from the wind blast. That fires a rocket from under the seat, it blows off the canopy and you're ejected out of the airplane." The powerful wind resistance stretched virtually every joint in his body and Galanti felt excruciating pain.

The parachute opened safely. As he approached the ground, looking for a safe spot to land, he got shot in his neck. "The shot blew out the whole back of my helmet," he remembers. "I didn't even realize until I hit the ground that there was blood all over the flight suit."

A group of North Vietnamese captured Galanti and put him up against a tree with their rifles pointing against him. "It was a very interesting sensation—standing there, with all these rifles pointing at me. These guys were mad."

Galanti pauses and changes the subject. "Getting shot down ruins your entire day . . . (he grins) but on the bright side, I probably would have never made a parachute jump if it hadn't been for that lucky shot."

"What went through your mind when these rifles were pointing at you?" I try to refocus on the subject he seems to gloss over.

"I kept looking at all these little holes and thinking, 'I wonder if I'll ever see the bullet.' There wasn't anything I could do. But finally one guy started yelling and pushing them away and he grabbed me and took charge of me. I don't know who he was. Then a guy with a cross on his arm—a medic—came up and poured some iodine over my neck and shoulder.

"Did you have some way of dealing with this situation that allowed you to keep your cool?" I probe.

"I don't remember ever going into a cold panic. I was watching this experience as if it were happening to someone else. Like I was a bird up in the sky. I felt sorry for this guy, but it wasn't a big deal."

Paul Galanti used this visualization technique—"as if it were happening to someone else"—several times before. "I am a lot more objective that way when I am in a tight situation," he explains. "Every time something bad is going to happen, this little thing just watches and checks all around."

Galanti spent almost seven years in a North Vietnamese prison camp until his release on February 12, 1973. His photograph appeared on the covers of *Newsweek* and *Life* magazines. He remained in the Navy for another nine years, serving as the head of Navy recruiting (a sales job, as he calls it) and as Battalion Officer responsible for leadership training. Galanti's full story was featured in the September 1985 issue of *PSP.*

Paul Galanti's technique for coping with an extremely demotivating situation is known as the "as-if" technique. It consists of purposely stepping into a new role, thus releasing untapped energies made available through imagination. Imagination is a powerful source of motivation. Professional actors use their imaginations to act their way into a new role and a new feeling. All good acting starts with the mental "as-if" technique.

Galanti stepped out of his role of the prisoner of war and became—for the time period he was in danger—that detached observer in the sky, watching the prisoner being lined up against a tree. This made his prisoner's experience "not a big deal" and thus tolerable. He kept his sanity in an inhuman situation and maintained a high level of motivation throughout his ordeal as a POW. He never lost a night's sleep over his experience back in the United States and he's one of the happiest people I've ever met.

The "as-if" technique is not only used as a survival tool or as a method for professional actors, but also as an effective strategy for dealing with potentially demotivating situations in selling. *Mary Kay* recommends, "Act enthusiastic—even when you don't feel like it. I've found that acting enthusiastically causes you to become enthusiastic. If someone asks how are you, the answer is *great*— even if you aren't." Someone once said, "Fake it 'til you make it." She certainly made it.

Tom Hopkins, one of America's leading sales trainers, gives similar advice. "There's an old saying, 'the show must go on,' and there are days when I'm tired and I go up there on stage and do what I am dedicated to doing. You have no choice—you have to give it the best you've got. What happens is that when you're giving your best, all of a sudden your adrenaline kicks in and you're doing great. If you're talking to a customer and if you're not feeling good, you literally start acting as if you were happy to talk to your prospect. All of a sudden you start listening and saying to yourself, 'Hey, I am going to close a large transaction here!'"

Interestingly, Tom Hopkins and Mary Kay define motivation as an ability. Hopkins sees it as "the ability to get people to stretch farther than they are accustomed to in order to reach their goals." Mary Kay says, "Motivation is the ability to inspire a person—to reach down within himself or herself, to bring to fruition those wonderful 'seeds of greatness' that God planted in each of us. It's said that the average person uses only about 10 percent of his God-given ability. Most of us die with our music still unplayed. Motivation encourages people to do what they've always dreamed of doing."

The Importance of Mentors and Heroes

Zig Ziglar, America's number one motivator, once compared motivation to the role of a starter in a car that cranks up the engine. Without the starter, the engine would never utilize the available horsepower.

When Zig was in high school, he hated history. Zig explains, "I hated the thought of having to learn something that happened 200 years ago. So my history teacher spent some time selling me on why I had to know my history. He said that If I had any ability that extended beyond earning a living, I had a moral responsibility, an obligation to take that ability and make a contribution to my fellow man and my country."

Zig pointed to his teacher's compelling logic, "You're part of society and if everybody doesn't make a contribution towards making it better, it will fall of its own weight and consequently—regardless of how much ability you might have, or how individually successful you might be—if your society has major flaws, then it has no value."

Zig Ziglar's mentor, Joe B. Harris, may well have started the powerful engine that led the Ziglar Corporation to a level of success far beyond the dreams of its founder. A little-known fact among the many people who have known Zig for years is that his corporate mission statement begins with "The purpose of the Zig Ziglar Corporation is to help people more fully utilize their physical, mental and spiritual abilities in order to contribute to the betterment of society . . . "

It is not uncommon that even a hero's negative comments can, like a photo-negative produces a positive print, produce positive results. Tom Hopkins recollects, "My father wanted me to become a famous attorney and I only lasted about 90 days in college. I came home and told my father that I quit and he was very disappointed. He said, 'I will always love you, even though you'll never amount to anything.' This really was a tremendous emotional and psychological motivator, because I literally told myself, 'Okay, I'm going to prove I can become a success.'" Tom's father started the engine. Tom hurt at the moment, but he healed over a lifetime.

Dr. Denis Waitley, the author of the bestselling audio-cassette program *The Psychology of Winning* (Nightingale-Conant Corp., Chicago), was significantly influenced by his father at a much earlier age. "He came into my room and sat down on my bed and gave me the belief that I was special, that I had a destiny, that I had a great purpose. He blew out the light and at the same time he would lean against the switch. I thought it was magic. He told me, 'Notice how it gets dark when your light is out. It is out everywhere. The only world you'll ever know is the one you see with your eyes.' He said that life is the perception of the eyes of the beholder, 'When you are asleep, the world is asleep. When you arise in the morning, the whole world wakes up, when you feel sick, the whole world is a sick place and when you're happy, the world is beautiful. Therefore, in your journey of life, you'll notice people being different. But the thing is that they are only seeing it from their eyes—and it's unique.'"

What did Dr. Waitley learn from his hero? "You can change the outcome of the world simply by the way you view it and that's the important thing to know." After a reflective pause he adds, "That still is the greatest thing I've ever learned. That's what perception is all about."

Mentors and heroes can help us chart our course in life, yet we alone are responsible for the trip. But how do we cope with the demotivators—the currents of fear and worry in the stream of life?

Dealing with Demotivators

"The single most unrewarded of all human emotions is worry," explains **Steven McMillan,** chairman and C.E.O. of Electrolux, a company with a sales force of over 28,000 people. "It doesn't accomplish anything. There is no positive result from worry, yet all of us do it from time to time. I see it every day in our business. We tend to explode problems way beyond what they really represent. I hear people saying, 'Steve, this is really a big problem,' and they're totally overwhelmed.

"The reason problems really become overwhelming is because we don't have a methodology to sit down and think it through. Worrying about it won't help you. But if you say, 'I have identified a problem or here is an obstacle we have to get over,' then we can say, 'Fine, we've identified that obstacle, now let's get down and look at it from an analytical point of view. Let's think about what our options are.'

"If the obstacle is too high, let's get around it. If it's too wide, then let's go over it, if we can't go over or around it, then let's go under it. In all too many cases, we react quickly and superficially without thinking it through. Therefore, we worry. It's a terrible waste of time."

McMillan, a graduate of Harvard Business School—a school famous for its case study method—has added a new dimension to the word motivation. "I define motivation as a combination of four elements: One is the opportunity. You can't motivate someone without having a real opportunity. The business objective has to be real. The second element is education—the how-to skills. Motivation without education equals frustration. The third part is hype. It's fun, it's enjoyable, but hype by itself is not going to generate positive, long-term action. The last element is an analytical methodology for dealing with problems.

"Motivation is more than just having the will to solve a problem," he continues. "It's also having the methodology with which to approach a problem. To me, these elements together lead to genuine motivation and worthwhile action." (Note that our complete interview with Steven McMillan will be featured in the next issue of *PSP*.)

Dr. Norman Vincent Peale, America's number one authority on positive thinking, told us about the preventive steps of dealing with demotivating experiences. "You know, a salesperson out on the road is alone. This feeling can syphon off his motivation. I think that the best method is to go to your room and read a good motivational book. Carry such literature around. Saturate your mind with motivational material. The evening news is likely to be depressing and negative. If you fill your mind with positive thoughts, they soak into your subconscious, so that when you get up the next day, you are going to have a great day."

Dr. Peale also urges salespeople to use positive affirmations. "To me, the most powerful form of self-direction is that of affirmation. If I say, 'Oh, I wish I felt better today!' that's not an affirmation. That's a depreciation. But if you say, 'I feel good today and I thank God for it and I'm going to have a great day!' then your subconscious mind will listen to that strong declaration. I've done this ten thousand times and I couldn't get along without it."

To Dr. Peale, the process of motivation begins with self-commitment. The powerful expectation to have a great day will lead to a great day. And if problems arise? Dr. Peale quips, "The only people that I ever have known to have no problems are in the cemetery." His advice is to attack problems squarely because, "Every problem contains the seed to its own solution."

There is a certain comfort to knowing that when we think that we have reached the end of our road, we really have only reached the end of our creativity. Talking to Dr. Peale on several occasions convinced me that problems are nothing but wake-up calls for creativity.

Overcoming Disappointment

"A few years ago, I saw a slogan in a car dealership," says ***Bob Baseman,*** Executive VP of Sales for Encyclopaedia Britannica

(USA). "It was six feet wide and three feet high. The sign asked, 'Mr. and Mrs. Prospect, just what was it that you were so worried about one year ago today?'"

Baseman, who leads over 3,000 salespeople, expands: "I think this is applicable to life.

"I woke up one morning when I was 25 years old and I discovered that the world had ended because my father had died. It was a crushing blow. I looked through the window and I saw a man going to work and I saw children going to school and I wanted to scream at the top of my lungs, 'Hey, don't you know that the world is over!' But, you know what, it wasn't over. Unfortunately, it was a very, very difficult lesson to learn all at one time. But I don't think you can accomplish anything worrying about that which you can't control."

Baseman has grown from the disappointment and he has become the number one attitude builder in his company. After our interview, he sent a little note with a golden pin that he designed himself. It consists of eight capitals letters that spell ATTITUDE. It's the most overlooked secret in the face of disappointment.

Ed Foreman, the son of a New Mexico dirt farmer, is the only person in this century to have been elected to the United States Congress from two different states: Texas in 1962 and New Mexico in 1968. Ed described his most disappointing experience as follows:

"I've had a lot of them. I guess it was losing the reelection to Congress. I had done a beautiful job, but 51 percent of the people decided they wanted someone else to represent them. I had been working my heart out for what I believed was best for them and my country. I went around for about a month feeling like someone hit me in the gut with his fist and knocked all the air out of me. At night I would dream that the election had not yet been held and that I was going to win."

One day when Ed felt particularly gloomy, his five-year-old daughter walked up to him saying, "Daddy, the next time you run for office, why don't you run in an area where there are more Republicans than Democrats?"

Foreman's prescription for self-motivation after disappointment: "You must immediately occupy yourself with something that can get you excited. I started another business. I got excited about that and flat forgot about the political defeat. It became a minor learning experience." To Foreman, motivation is "excitement about and for life and for what you do."

The excitement of a new challenge has brought new meaning to his life.

Rich DeVos, co-founder of Amway, put his fight with the Canadian Government at the top of his list of demotivating experiences. "Just to be accused of wrongdoing—but you know within you that you've done everything that was right—and then to have to admit to being wrong, even though you followed expert advice, was a very demotivating thing. But finally, you have to stand up; if you're the head of the company then you have to be responsible for the action of everybody. As time goes by, you kind of get over that."

DeVos feels that developing coping strategies for dealing with disappointment is part of leadership. "You've got to be able to think while the bullets are flying. You've got to stay cool in business and keep going. I think that's a sense of knowing who you are. If you are comfortable with who you are and know you're not perfect and accept the fact that you don't have all the answers . . . you just work with what you've got and then you move forward."

DeVos and his partner built a billion dollar business with over a million salespeople worldwide.

Here is another piece of evidence which leads to the paradoxical question: Isn't disappointment at the root of every growth experience? The disappointing event leads to self-discovery and we learn another lesson of who we really are. The Socratic advice "know thyself" could be changed to "know thy motivation," for if you really discover what moves you, you'll know your direction and move forward with confidence.

As many of these compelling life stories of successful leaders, motivators and business executives suggest, resolved disappointment is the cradle of motivation and ultimately responsible for our ambitions and success in life.

Unresolved disappointment leads to cynicism, the greatest destroyer of motivation.

Dr. Wayne Dyer, the author of several international bestsellers (*The Sky's the Limit, Pulling Your Own Strings* and *Gifts from Eykis*), pointed to this fact when we talked about the requirements for an atmosphere or climate in which people can be motivated, "People who have a sour-puss attitude towards life are likely to get serious diseases."

And what are the characteristics of a motivating attitude that creates a climate of motivation?

"It's a state of acceptance of where the other person is,"

explains Dr. Dyer, "rather than where you would like him or her to be. Carl Rogers called it 'unconditional, positive regard!' It means being nonjudgmental. It means being able to provide a fun environment where life is not taken *so* seriously.

"If you look at all your most favorite people in life, the one characteristic that runs through them *all* is that they know how to laugh. It's what I call an unhostile sense of humor."

The cynical person's sense of humor is full of hostility while the accepting person's humor is disarming. Dr. Dyer pokes fun at himself in his lectures across the country, "I always talk about my baldness and the dumb things I've done in my life. When people see that you're not hostile, they open up."

Dr. Dyer sees his role as a motivator as a tour guide to our inner potential. "A good motivator helps you discover your own potential."

Dr. Dyer has recently finished his new book *What Do You Really Want for Your Children?* (W. Morrow, Sept. 1985). He feels that the only motivation there is, is inner motivation.

"I teach my children that they have an inner candle flame that must never flicker. The outer candle flame can be blown out at any time, but if you love yourself and if you are positive in that, then no matter who comes along to try to convince you otherwise, that inner flame will never flicker."

How to Catch
Your Limit in Sales

by James F. Evered, CSP

In my sales training seminars I never tell a story unless it makes a particular point. I use the following true, and almost tragic story to open every sales seminar, because I feel it has a very close parallel to business today:

Monterey, California is a beautiful city about seventy-five miles south of San Francisco. Many years ago there lived in Monterey a large colony of Portugese fishermen who took their boats to sea every day and netted tons and tons of sardines. The fishermen supplied what was called "cannery row" in Monterey.

Also living in Monterey was a large colony of pelicans. If you don't know what a pelican is, it is the large bird with a long beak which has a bucket under it. The way a pelican fishes is to soar above the surface of the water until he sees a fish near the surface. He immediately dives and catches the fish, storing it in the pliable "bucket."

The strange thing was, the Monterey pelicans didn't fish. They didn't have to. Every day they would sit around on the docks and piers, waiting for the sardine boats to come in. The pelicans were fed from the cleanings of the sardines. As a result, there was a complete generation of pelicans in Monterey that didn't know how to fish.

Then, a tragedy hit in 1941 when Pearl Harbor was bombed. Having sighted several submarines off the west coast, and fearing a possible invasion, the Coast Guard began to heavily patrol the Pacific coast. This totally curtailed the fishing industry and the Monterey pelicans began to die.

Naturally, this was of great concern to the Monterey Chamber of Commerce and they called an emergency meeting to see what could be done about the situation. Someone on the chamber asked, "How in the world can you teach a pelican how to fish?" Another member suggested, "Why don't we get another pelican to teach them?

Immediately, the Monterey Chamber contacted the Chamber of Commerce in St. Petersburg, Florida where there was also a large flock of white pelicans. The St. Petersburg Chamber reacted at once, captured 150 pelicans and flew them out to Monterey. When these Florida pelicans were turned loose in Monterey Bay, they did what came naturally—they began to fish.

Fortunately, the Monterey pelicans who still had enough strength picked up the message and *they* began to fish. As a result, the Monterey flock was salvaged and today they are thriving.

Here is the parallel I see between this story and business today. When things are going well, the money is flowing, interest rates are down, companies are expanding and building up their inventories, and customers are lining up at our doors, we begin to sit around on our docks and piers, waiting for the business to come rolling in. But when business gets tough, interest rates are high, companies are cutting back on inventory build-up, reducing expenditures on capital expansion, money gets tight, competition gets tougher, we find a lot of salespeople who have "forgotten how to fish." Their selling skills have deteriorated and they seem to be flogging the water with an empty hook, snagging a few, but not bringing in the catches they should. These selling skills, just like fishing skills, need to be regenerated and sharpened. Nothing in the world will cause selling skills to deteriorate like good times when we're in a seller's market. But the tragedy comes when times get tough and the skills are gone.

I see this skill deterioration all the time in seminars I conduct for various companies. Salespeople who had been high-volume producers during good years had deteriorated to the point they were struggling to make a living after times changed.

To me, there is another very close parallel between selling and fishing. I am thoroughly convinced that if we went about earning our living, in selling, as disciplined, as well planned and as well organized as we go fishing—we'd catch a lot more sales. I submit that about half the companies in this country could sell twice the merchandise with only half the people if they would only go at it in a rigidly disciplined manner. Let's take a look at how we go fishing:

The first thing we do is set our objective. What is it we're going after? Is it trout, salmon, catfish, steelhead, bass? That decision (the objective) will determine everything we do from here on, i.e., where we go, what we take, our plan of attack.

Once we get out to the body of water where we are going to fish, we don't just start flogging the water with an empty hook, hoping to snag something, or hoping something comes along hungry enough to grab it.

No! The next thing we do is our prospecting. Where in this body of water are my chances the best to catch whatever it is I am after? Will it be along the rocky banks? In the main stream? Out on the sandy points? Among the old dead trees still standing in the water? Where are my prospects the best?

When we finally get to the decided area, we apply every known technique to bring in a full stringer. We apply the right bait, the right lures, the right cast, and right retrieval and the right action. And if you fish for thirty minutes and don't catch anything, you don't pack up and go home. You go early and you stay late. Those are the fishermen who consistently bring home the limit. And bear in mind, fishing won't put a single dollar in your pocket.

Why, then, don't we go about earning our living in selling with the same level of discipline? Why aren't salespeople as well organized, as well planned, as well disciplined in the thing that earns their paychecks as they are in their recreational activities? When they become as well disciplined in selling, they will find that their work *is* their recreation. They will look forward to Monday morning so they can get back to it. It's all a matter of attitude.

Concentration:
An Incredible Power

Bob Marx, an experienced skin diver, felt his heartbeat accelerating when a 12-foot mako shark attacked him. "The first time it hit me, it didn't bite," Marx said, according to the Associated Press Story, "it knocked me out of the water. It hit so hard that it knocked off my mask, fins and snorkel!"

Bob, who had 25 years of diving experience, started to fight for his life. In a sudden burst of anger and fear, he grabbed the shark's snout with his right hand and started pounding on its head with his left. The giant shark pushed Bob backwards with increasing speed and its mouth got a hold of his right arm between the armpit and the elbow.

Not ready to give up, Bob concentrated his remaining energies and pulled away his arm so hard that two of the shark's teeth were left in the wound. At the same time, he pushed both his knees up violently into the shark's belly, spun away and curled into a ball. His mind raced: "Is this the end?" As he opened his eyes, floating towards the surface, he noticed that the shark was taking off; it had lost interest.

Bob was then aided by his friends and taken to the hsopital where doctors needed 150 stitches to close his wounds.

Bob Marx's story astonished many people. It is an extraordinary example of a human being, acting under stress and accomplishing feats of strength that baffle everyone. He was able to concentrate all the force of his muscular system at the one point where it was just then needed to save his life. Because he had the power of concentration, that man's strength became more effective than the mako shark's teeth and its powerful 12-foot body! The clearness of aim gave concentration; and this concentration made the lesser volume of force the more effective.

From the world of daily experience, we might draw many more such incredible examples of the power of concentration. In a word, concentration is that which makes force speedily and directly effective.

Bob's story is indeed unusual since the average reader may quickly exclaim: "If I had been in his position, the shark would have devoured me . . . " But before you come to this conclusion, you may ask yourself: "What powers could I use—if I'd only concentrate a bit more? Isn't everyone endowed with the ability to concentrate?"

There are many among us who have seen the brilliant student, with capacity to learn all things, with sound principles, with refinement of taste, equipped for the richest conquests of life—who falls short of his potential because of a wasteful or wavering dispersion of his gifts. His powers lacked the concentration on one clear purpose. They were never brought into focus.

"Jack of all trades, master of none." This is the plain aphorism into which the world has crystallized its contempt for the person who lacks the power of concentration.

Brains, talents, capacities—he has them, but the stream of his force has ever spread itself thin. And so he dwells in the world's scorn, mourning his decreasing sense of accomplishment.

People who have entered the field of selling come from many different professions. Some have Ph.D. degrees, some have taught at colleges, some have worked for the government. Many of them were attracted to the profession of selling by the many opportunities for a rewarding and fulfilling career.

Like Bob Marx, who never realized what incredible strength his body could unite for the purpose of saving his life, many salespeople never realize what strengths their minds can use for the purpose of success.

Even if you currently think that you've only modest talents for selling, concentration will soon stimulate these faint talents to grow, setting free so much more force for initiative and enthusiasm, without which one can never be a master of any craft.

The best way to succeed is to do with fervor and concentration the thing that you are not necessarily well prepared for. (Did Bob Marx have the advantage of learning how to fight a shark through role plays?)

Keep hammering away at one spot long enough and you will seize plenty of opportunities to show your powers of concentration, and above all, you'll make your mark there, be the hammer no bigger than a toothpick.

Persistence

Nothing in the world can take the place of persistence.
Talent will not: Nothing is more common than unsuccessful men with talent.
Genius will not: Unrewarded genius is almost a proverb.
Education will not: The world is full of educated derelicts.
Persistence and determination alone are omnipotent.
The slogan "Press On" has solved and always will solve the problems of the human race.

President Calvin Coolidge

Who Did the Job?

Did you hear the story about four people: Everybody, Somebody, Anybody and Nobody?
There was an important job to be done and Everybody was sure that Somebody would do it. Anybody could have done it, but Nobody did it.
Somebody got angry about that, because it was Everybody's job!
Everybody thought Anybody could do it, but Nobody realized Everybody wouldn't do it. It ended up that Everybody blamed Somebody when Nobody did what Anybody could have done!!!

Feeding Your Mind

In reading everyday news, have you ever asked yourself: "What in the heck am I reading? This is a terrible story! What an awful situation!"

Did you know that one "regular" newspaper article can create a mood of helplessness, outrage or anger?

We know very little about the effect of information on our attitudes. We do know, however, that reading can create an endless tide of emotions.

Although science has determined the effect of nutrition on our bodies, we can't pinpoint how much positive information we need to maintain a healthy mind. Nutritionists know, for example, the minimum daily requirement of Vitamin C. We also have guidelines on the maximum intake of salt to maintain a healthy body. But not one single psychologist knows how much "bad news" constitutes a hazardous level of negative information. Do you know your own tolerance for news items covering violence in minute detail? Do we know how much positive energy is needed to recover from the emotionally depleting news-shocker?

We have the right to expose ourselves to whatever information we want—that's our Constitutional right—but how about taking the responsibility for choosing the proper exposure? How about placing a value on what we read?

In selling, our attitudes are closely linked to success. Thus we know that negative information—if we let it influence us—can be hazardous to our earning potential.

We can't say that reading more than 800 words of "bad news" exceeds the maximum dose. Nor can we establish a minimum daily requirement of, let's say, 1000 words of positive information.

We can, however, choose to either stand still and read about life gone by, or we can choose to get involved in reading that which helps us advance in the direction of our goals and dreams. One spells negative conflict; the other spells positive challenge.

Each of us is operating the most brilliant computer ever built—our mind—and every moment of our lives we make irreversible decisions concerning its input. Will it be *trash* or *treasure?*

Classic Sales Wisdom

by Dr. Frank Crane

Every young man should some time in his life have experience in salesmanship.

Selling goods is the best known cure for those elements in a man that tend to make him a failure.

The art of success consists in making people change their minds. It is this power that makes the efficient lawyer, grocer, politician, or preacher.

There are two classes of men. One seeks employment in a position where he merely obeys the rules and carries out the desires of his employer. There is little or no opportunity for advancement in this work. You get to a certain point and there you stick.

Such posts are a clerkship in a bank, a government job, such as letter carrier, a place in the police force, or any other routine employment requiring no initiative. These kinds of work are entirely honorable and necessary. The difficulty is, they are cramping, limiting.

Some day you may have to take a position of this sort, but first try your hand at selling things.

Be a book agent, peddle washing machines, sell life insurance, automobiles, agricultural implements, or peanuts.

You shrink from it because it is hard, it goes against the grain, as you are not a pushing sort of fellow. And that is the very reason you need it.

Salesmanship is strong medicine. You have to go out and wrestle with a cold and hostile world. You are confronted with indifference, often contempt. You are considered a nuisance. That is the time for you to buck up, take off your coat, and go in and win.

A young lawyer will gain more useful knowledge of men and affairs by selling real estate or fire insurance than by law school.

I have just read a letter from an office man fifty-seven years old. He had lodged at $1,600 a year for twenty years, while two of the salesmen who entered the business about the time he did own the concern.

Get out and sell goods. Hustle. Fight. Don't get fastened in one hold. Take chances. Come up smiling. So the best and biggest prizes in America are open to you.

Selling things, commercialism, business, is not a low affair; it is a great, big, bully game. It is a thoroughly American game, and the most sterling qualities of Americanism are developed by it, when it is carried on fairly and humanely.

There is incitement in it for all your best self, for your honesty, perseverance, optimism, courage, loyalty, and religion. Nowhere does a *man* mean so much.

I mean to cast no slurs upon faithful occupants of posts of routine. They have their reward.

But, son, don't look for a "safe" place. Don't depend upon an organization to hold your job for you. Don't scheme and wirepull for influence and help and privilege.

Get out and peddle maps. Make people buy your chickens or your essays. Get in the game. It beats football.

Are You Proud
to be Selling?

Don W. Beveridge, a management and marketing consultant, cites two very interesting statistics: 1) Only two out of every ten people who sell for a living started out to be a salesperson; selling was an alternative to what they originally wanted to do, and 2) up to 35 percent of experienced senior salespeople continue to avoid asking people to buy their products or services because they're afraid of being seen as a salesperson, with all of the word's *negative* connotations.

These add up to a severe image problem. Don says that poor sales management—making the salesperson, or "account executive" or "territory manager" or "marketing representative" into a mere product peddler—is a big reason why such an image crisis exists. A fancy title isn't the answer—better skills are.

A.C.R.O.N.Y.M.S.—
Key to Motivation
and Memory

by "Positive" Paul Stanyard

Ever since World War II, when acronyms were useful in saving newsprint space and broadcasting time and in highlighting important government programs there has been a tremendous growth in acronyms. An acronym is a word formed from the first letters of other words. For example, RADAR stands for Radio Detection and Ranging. In 1960, there were 12,000 acronyms listed in the Acronym Dictionary. Today there are well over 2,000,000. I first started using acronyms to improve my memory and as selling points in sales presentations. Soon, I discovered that they could also be used as a powerful motivational force.

Acronyms have been a hobby of mine since 1952 when I first took the Dale Carnegie Course in Public Speaking and Human Relations. The instructor summed up the three principles to all memory in the acronym IRA. The I stood for Impression, the R stood for Repetition and the A stood for Association. Since then I have been creating and collecting acronyms for over 30 years. The first acronym I created was HASP. It stands for the four subjects I studied to become a professional author and speaker: Human relations, Applied psychology, Salesmanship and Public speaking.

For many years I used acronyms to reinforce my poor memory. My first real test on using acronyms to help memory came in 1955 when I had to give a talk on how to sell advertising. I decided to use an acronym to remember the outline of my talk. The acronym I used was SELL. The S stood for See a lot of people. The E stood for Enthusiasm makes the difference. The first L stood for Learn that selling is 98 percent understanding human beings and 2 percent product knowledge. The second L stood for Lots of ideas, ideas and service. At the end of my talk I was presented a trophy and I was offered a new and exciting job. It was then that I realized how motivating an acronym can be. The acronym SELL gave me the confidence to make a well organized and enthusiastic speech that resulted in many rewards.

I then decided to use the motivational force of acronyms and created a guaranteed-action method called Acro-action. The method took years to develop into a unique system for making people do what they dream and plan to do but never get done. It all came from the word acronym and my determination to make myself do the many things that I planned for my life . . .

Acro-action is a unique method that will keep you motivated by inventing your own acronyms and repeating them to yourself many times a day. These words act as an inspiration to get you started working toward your goal. They are inner-motivational reminders that keep you goal-directed and act as a support system.

This is how it works: ACTION is an acronym for Always Complete The Immediate Objective Now. When you think of the word ACTION several times a day you will automatically think of the phrase. This acronym-phrase will be your inspiration and motivation now.

After developing the Acro-action method I stopped using the word acronym and created another key word called *acro-gem*. I use this new word because I want to create new ways to get and stay excited about life. The difference between an acronym and an acro-gem is that an acronym is just a word, while an acro-gem is a *motivating* word or short sentence. Acro-gems give acro-action a new and more complete definition. *(Acro-action is the highest degree of self-motivation and action towards personal goals using acro-gems as the key to self-starting action and daily support system.)*

This new philosophy of action gives you a choice. You can choose to just cope with life as most normal people do or you can set concrete, affirmative, realistic targets with specific dates and have the happiness and money you want. Everyone needs a constant motivation-reminder because all motivation comes from the inside and nobody can do it for you. It's an attitude that can't be explained—you can only experience it.

Acro-gem your way to motivation. Memorize your favorite ones and use them to keep motivated. You can also write them down and pin them in places where you will read them often.

- GOALS is an acro-gem for Golden Opportunities Allowing Large Successes. If you say GOALS several times a day and think of the phrase that it stands for, it will help you keep your mind on your goals.
- ENTHUSIASM is an acro-gem for Enthusiasm Needs The High Unseen Strength Involved Around Self-Motivation. It means that enthusiasm comes from and needs the strength of self-motivation.
- TNT stands for Today Not Tomorrow. Everytime you say TNT, that's your key to motivate you to get started on some powerful action.
- Everytime you make a mistake say "SOS." That's an acro-gem for Seeds Of Success. After all, that's what a mistake is, a seed of success.
- TAP, TAP, TAP, is Take Action Persistently, Take Action Persistently, Take Action Persistently.
- LIPMO is the definition of luck—Luck Is Preparation Meeting Opportunity.
- BAM is Be Action-Minded.
- CAN is Constant Achievement Now.
- ASK is Always Seek Knowledge.

I have given you a few examples of the acro-gems that I have created but you can invent your own. Self-styled acro-gems will motivate you even more because of their personal meaning for inspiration and motivation in your own life.

From Education
to Sales Success

I find that many people get into a sales career by reading and responding to a "Sales-Help-Wanted" classified ad in the newspaper. The ad promises big bucks fast and ends with this inevitable statement: "No experience needed. We train."

Ever seen those? I decided to investigate the "Training" that was given. Here's what I found out. The rookie would get some pamphlets to read. Maybe they showed a film. Then they gave him an order pad and some sales literature and said, "Go get 'em, boy!" And *that* was the extent of the so-called "training."

At best, he or she got some product knowledge training. But no real sales training. If all it took was product knowledge, then the auto mechanic would be the number one best auto salesman, right? And the Ph.D., who researches the facts for the encyclopedia, would be the best encyclopedia salesperson, right?

Product knowledge is fine. But if you don't know how to *sell* what you know, then you're just an "expert," but not yet a sales professional. What's the solution to this closing problem? Learn some closes. Go to the library and get some books on selling. Listen to tapes. Attend sales seminars. Think about this old saying: *To earn more, you need to learn more.* I hope you'll never stop learning about this wonderful career we call "Salesmanship." The day you stop learning is the day you stop earning!

Positive Living

by Jacques Weisel

Most people have an aim in life, but no ammunition.

You're at a picnic and you spot a young man with an archery set, shooting arrows into tree trunks. Everytime he hits a tree he goes over and paints a perfect bullseye around the arrow. Passersby who only see the results of his work think he is a great archer. You smile, knowing better of course. Or do you? ... After all isn't this basically the way you run your life? You end up somewhere, and then decide that's where you wanted to be all along. As a mature individual you've forgotten the most basic concept of living which is to *plan ahead*. You'll go over the day-by-day activities for a two-week vacation (perhaps 50 times in your lifetime) as if you were involved in a forcible overthrow of a hostile government. Yet your only *once-in-a-lifetime* journey is played through without too much rhyme or reason, usually with no plan beyond today and what it may bring. The Koran says "If you don't know where you're going, any road will get you there."

It's a well-known psychological fact that man is a goal-striving mechanism. This means that whether he has goals or not he will reach them. My question is simply this: Would you rather reach goals that are yours, or someone else's? As a child we were given short-range goals to live by. "Eat your food," "go to bed," "don't step in the gutter," "go to college," "get married," etc. ... all short-range and long-range plans that someone else wanted us to execute. It's no wonder that we got out of that habit as soon as we could ... and usually end up by throwing out the baby with the dirty water. Goals are not important to Positive Living. They are *crucial*. It is not a coincidence that the word "goal" begins with "go." Daily goals give you the best reason to get up and do. Weekly goals make the months fly, and monthly goals renew your enthusiasm for life twelve times per year. Annual goals can guarantee a lifetime of successful happenings, as you maintain full control of your personal destiny.

Just as the captain of a ship does not need to see his destination thousands of miles away to know he will reach it at a certain date and time, so can you plan your life according to your own timetable. Your goals must be realistic and reachable, so that you can reap the rewards of positive reinforcement at timed intervals, and thus have the confidence to know that you're on target for the big plan.

There are literally hundreds of self-help books, but very little on the subject of proper goalsetting. Profit-oriented companies have discovered the secret. They call it "management by objectives." They make dollars and reach corporate goals by carefully preplanning the direction in which they want the company to go.

One last good thought on goals by Henry David Thoreau: "The man who goes alone can start today. But he who travels with another must wait till that other is ready." 'Nuff said . . .

Your Competitor

Your competitor is a person who spends days and often nights, dreaming up ways to give *your clients* better service.

When he or she finds out *how,* then it's *your turn* to find still better ways to keep your clients happy.

Your competitor sometimes does more for you than a friend. A friend is too polite to point out your weaknesses, but your competitor will take the trouble to *advertise* them.

Your competitor's ability should never be underestimated. Our business graveyard is filled with people who figured their competition was stupid, shortsighted, or just plain lazy!

Your competitor is hard to live with... but harder to live without. Competition brings progress by encouraging *professionalism.*

The Price
of Being "Normal"

by "Positive" Paul Stanyard

It's no big thing to be normal. Who wants a normal paycheck? Who wants to be married to a normal person? Who wants to buy a normal car? Who wants to cope with life like normal people do? Who wants to retire with a normal $900.00 in the bank? Normal salespeople earn about $20,000.00 a year. Normally that's just not enough.

It's sad to think that 80 percent of the people in this country are normal. That makes over 160 million normal people coping with normal life in this country. And because they all live in "when" time, life is very short for these normal people. Let me explain. "When" time means: when we get married, when I finish school, when I get another job, when we have a new car, when the children are grown. *When your mother moves out,* then I'll be happy.

When and tomorrow go together hand in glove. Normal people live in the future, and they're always waiting for tomorrow to be happy. But, when tomorrow comes, what do you call it? Of course, you call it today!

Normal people think that hoping and dreaming is planning. On the other hand those whom Dr. Wayne Dyer calls "no limit" people know that planning is what they have to do today to ensure a successful tomorrow.

Normal people have a mere 29,200 days of life after they are born. "No limit" people, on the other hand, have a full 80 years of this incredible experience called life. These are the winners and achievers of life. There are only 5 million "no limit" people in this country. That is two percent of the population. Now 80 percent of the population is normal. Together the normal and the no limit people make up only 82 percent of the country. What happened to the other 18 percent? Where are they? Are you ready for this?

Eighteen percent of the people in this country, or, about 40 million people, are neurotic. They live in panic, never coping with

life. Where do they live? Of course they live in the past time of
"should have." Neurotic people say "Today is the last day of my
life." Normal people say, "Today is the first day of the rest of my
life." No limit people say, "Today is the best day of my life."

Normal people waste half their lives planning for the future.
Neurotic people waste all their lives wishing things could have been
different. No limit people waste no precious life time at all. They
say, "I'll make the most of every minute of this day."

Don't wallow in the "if onlys" of the past and the "what ifs"
of the future. Focus on the *now* time. After all, it's the only time you
really have. Present moment living will give you all the happiness
you want.

Being normal is no big thing. Almost everyone is. You can be
in the no limit 2 percent. But you have to start right now. No more
yesterday and tomorrow, no more when and should have been.
There is only today and you—*right now.*

> **The value of time—Part 1** Yesterday is a cancelled check.
> Tomorrow is a promissory note. Today is ready cash. Use it.

> **The value of time—Part 2** Thinking of yesterday as a prom-
> issory note and considering tomorrow as a cancelled check is
> the best way to waste today.

Imagination: The Key
to Improved Performance

Can you imagine how your sales presentation would improve simply by assuming that you were the one who invented and produced your company's product? Can you see yourself spending countless hours developing and improving your product and talking to your prospects about it? Can you see yourself filled with that special pride and enthusiasm?

Granted, you are not an inventor, but you can visualize for a moment how this person would talk about his favorite subject. Now compare this person with the sales rep whose product remains an "alien" and "foreign matter" in his mind. Can you see the tremendous difference?

Can you imagine how your personal enthusiasm would increase simply by imagining that you were the founder or the president of your company? Can you see yourself explaining your company's achievements, your current commitments and future goals?

Of course, you are not in their place, however you can visualize their enthusiasm, pride and ambition. As long as your company remains an impersonal and separate entity in your mind, you will speak of your company as "them," "they," and "theirs" instead of "us," "we," and "ours." Your customers will follow your lead and your company will remain impersonal and separate in their minds.

Can you imagine the best sales rep in your industry? What would be the key to his or her success? The answer is simple: The best salespeople believe in *their* product, in *their* company and in themselves. Their key to success lies in the active use of their imaginations. It's *your* key to improved performance.

You Are What You Think

Sales success is not so much determined by what we say to our customers as by what we say to ourselves. Del Polito, a thought process researcher, once wrote that we experience our thoughts in streams flowing at various speeds.

Dr. Albert Ellis, a noted psychiatrist, found that we are capable of developing two or more streams of thoughts, sometimes flowing in opposite directions.

Thoughts, most researchers agree, have a powerful effect on our emotions, decisions and actions. Many consider thinking as a manageable process; yet, few effective thought management principles have been discovered and very few of us seem to apply them consistently.

The three most useful thought management tools are Awareness, Appraisal and Choice.

Awareness comes from questions like, "What am I doing?" or "What kind of thoughts am I experiencing right now?"

Appraisal means examining your thoughts objectively, like "Is this thought fact or fiction?," "What evidence do I have for my conclusions?" and "What basis do I have for my assumptions?"

An objective appraisal can lead to healthy thoughts after a sales call where the customer did not buy, such as "I'm not the one that the prospect is rejecting. The facts are that at this time he has no need, and he's only rejecting my proposal."

Choice means using your creativity to expand the number of alternatives available to you. Choice allows you to change or reverse the direction of the flow of your thoughts.

If you've read this far, by now you're probably realizing that thought management is hard work, but so are successful living and successful selling.

Dr. Norman Vincent Peale, world-renowned positive thinker, has spent a lifetime dealing with thought management. He readily admits that managing thoughts is hard work. "But, on second thought," he says, "it's harder not to."

The Winner's Law of 80/20

Vilfredo Pareto, an Italian economist, defined a number of 80/20 relationships that have become known as Pareto's Law. The fact that 20 percent of all employees usually produce 80 percent of the work is an example of this law. Apply Pareto's ideas to the subjects of pain, failure and success as self-motivational tools.

On the pain of being successful. 80 percent of all people consider the pain of personal growth unacceptable. They represent 80 percent of all failures. 20 percent of all people accept pain as a learning experience. They suffer, but change and grow. They are the 20 percent who succeed in life.

On the problem of avoiding failure. 20 percent of all failures can be blamed on bad luck. If we spend 80 percent of our time trying to control fate, we only have 20 percent left for controlling our lives. 80 percent of all failures can be blamed on ourselves. Winners invest their energies in this area, where they have control, and avoid investing in the 20 percent they can't control.

On the problem of achieving success. 80 percent of all successes are due to personal qualities and skills. Winners cultivate and prepare themselves. 20 percent of all successes are due to external circumstances, or luck. 80 percent of all people stop improving themselves because they are hoping they'll get lucky.

You can choose to gamble your life away, hoping for a smiling fortune to come to your rescue, or you can choose to increase your odds by preparing yourself. You can remain the same, and fail, or you can bear the pain of growth, and succeed. The winners have made their decision. Have you?

Failure is the path of the least persistence.

Alexander's Tears

by William J. Tobin

Historians report that Alexander the Great wept when he learned there were no more worlds to conquer. The world as he knew it represented only 2 percent of the world as we know it today. Even the greatest among us occasionally underestimates his or her potential. In a sense, Alexander the Great underestimated the size of his market.

Don't underestimate the potential of the American market. Our country's entire economic history shows that larger markets are always in the making. Recent statistics published by The Conference Board state: "The United States, with only 5.1% of the world's population, accounts for 21.3% of the world's output of goods and services." Even in the '81–'82 recession with ten and one half million people unemployed, the U.S. economy remained unrivaled in the world for its output of goods and services. No other country on the globe even comes close. In fact, twenty-five eastern states and the District of Columbia together equal the number two nation, the Soviet Union, in production. By itself, the output of California exceeds that of all Africa. Pennsylvania alone almost equals all of Australia in economic power.

Therefore, it is almost impossible to estimate the size of the market in future months or years. Don't weep over the limitations of your territory. Instead, reexamine the limitations of your thinking.

Go for It

by Howard Brinkman

When little-known Sylvester Stallone sat down to write "Rocky," he might very well have been expressing his innermost thoughts about himself and his aspirations for a successful future. Writing the movie surely took a king-size portion of courage, but seeing himself in the role of Rocky took even more. Rocky was a bum; a loan shark's enforcer sent out to collect, by any means necessary, unpaid debts. So how did he (though the opportunity to do it was a lucky chance) decide to train for and fight for the heavyweight championship of the world? It really wasn't much different than Stallone attempting to write the movie: Rocky and Stallone fuse into the same person—they both decide to *"Go for it."*

"Go for it" is the underlying theme of Stallone's gamble on his own creativity and Rocky's courage to accept the challenge and to give it his all.

Let us look closer at "Go for it": *"Go"*—start, move, begin, act; *"for"*—what, when, how; *"it"*—your goal, your dream, the utmost, fame, fortune, success, the good life, a productive life. Your own *"it"* can be any one or all of these things or whatever else you value in life. What we're saying here is: Give it everything you've got. Determine your goal or goals; make a plan; then follow it. But make up your mind to really *"Go for it"*; you probably won't make it unless you give 100 percent. Think of it for a moment—the determination to do everything you do, the very best way you can.

This will probably make every facet of your life 25 to 50 percent more productive.

The automotive industry in our country found this out, almost too late. "At Ford, quality is job No. 1" is much more than a TV commercial. If the employees at Ford wished to continue working they had to realize this. I'm not plugging Ford cars but I think that the unions and their members now understand.

The recent drop in the economy awakened and revitalized the work ethic that once was prevalent in our country. Heavy overtime and easy money led to money in the bank, big money in the union strike fund, and a "if management won't see it our way, go on strike" attitude. Management also shares the responsibility. All of this coupled with more and easier government programs and financial aid surely helped to drain the feeling of reverence and enthusiasm for working that created the posture of "give a good day's work for a good day's pay" that we all used to live by.

Competition for business may be at an all time high, but by the same token so is there a willingness, even a desire, to listen and to learn of new ways to do things.

Now is a time to sell. Forget about the bad times in the past. Concentrate on the opportunities ahead. You'll never regret using this chance to *"Go for it."*

Teaching and Selling . . .
Go Hand in Hand

After seven years of teaching in public schools, Dave Johnson decided to go into sales. He soon discovered that the two fields are not as different as he'd imagined. They both require continued learning, a quest for creativity, interaction with many different people and a constant need for renewing self-motivation.

Continued learning means keeping up with the latest advances in your field and knowing how well your product measures up to the competition. This helps you to teach your customers all the benefits they'll receive by buying your product or service. Creativity means finding interesting ways to present this information. Interacting with different people means treating each person as an individual— customers are as different as students and their personalities and needs should be reflected in your sales presentations. Finally, both teachers and sales professionals revitalize themselves, exchange ideas and share experiences through seminars, videotapes, cassettes and informal discussions.

The Practicality of Integrity

"Phonies finish last." Do you agree with this statement? According to a recent survey by the American Management Association, most American businesses do. They placed integrity at the top of their priority list for important commodities and values in the workplace. You may be saying to yourself that integrity is a good *idea,* but it's not *practical.*

Think again. Higher sales, greater earnings and stronger relationships are as much a part of integrity as quality, completeness and soundness. Why? Because people are loyal to products, services, and people they can *trust.* Consider these questions and you'll see why integrity pays off.

Would you make a major decision to buy from a person you didn't trust?

Would you give a person your full loyalty if he or she demonstrated shaky integrity?

Would you continue to buy products or services from someone who consistently supplied second-rate service and follow-through?

Would you consummate a close or continue a business relationship with someone whose spouse and children did not trust him or her?

A noted psychologist, Dr. Henry Link, states, "Principles, and people of principle, are the life blood of democracy and not something to be sneered at, as has become fashionable in our time." Principles are the life blood of selling as well. The strength of an individual or a company is directly related to its reputation and good reputations are based on integrity.

The following practical suggestions can help your company strengthen its reputation, its sales force, and its profits:

Establish in-house educational programs, seminars, and counseling.
Obtain the help and participation of men and women whose example and track record can provide substantive, hands-on teaching and mentoring.
Research and evaluate the philosophy or basic beliefs and values of your entire company and/or sales division. If a published philosophy doesn't

exist, create one.

Read the chapter "Above All Integrity" in Joe Batten's classic book *Tough Minded Management* (AMACOM, N.Y.).

Phonies may seem to be the winners, but they eventually undermine themselves. Integrity is practical and profitable. In today's competitive market, it doesn't make sense to sell any other way.

Positive Selling

Selling yourself and your ideas to others is one of the most important needs man has. How would you like to learn the secret of selling yourself and your ideas so that more people will want to do as you suggest? Here are some basic rules to help you.

The first rule: Learn to deal with people on an emotional level. Numerous studies have shown that our buying habits follow a ninety to ten formula. In other words, our thinking brain is only 10 percent as large as our feeling brain. Research continually points to the fact that success in any endeavor is determined by attitudes in life, rather than by aptitudes—on a ratio of six to one. Speaking to people using factual information will not move them toward acceptance of your ideas. To move people, you must motivate by stirring emotions. Many of us are literally short sighted when it comes to other people. As a result, the way we see them is the way we end up treating them. As we end up treating them, they end up becoming. You have the power to change people by the way you see and treat them.

Several years ago a survey of one hundred self-made millionaires showed only one common denominator that bound them together. These highly successful men and women could only see the good in people. They were people builders, rather than critics. Critics do not make the history books because they do not help make history. They are usually on a lifelong search and destroy mission. Critics leave their victims worse off for having met them. As for "constructive criticism," there is no such thing. The words belie the term. A critic could never understand what Harvey Firestone once said, "You get the best out of others when you give the best of yourself."

Here's rule number two: Do not do to others what you would not want done to you. Look at the world through *their* eyes, not your eyes. Say and do what will excite and interest *them*. Make *them* feel important. You can change lives by using these age-old concepts, and they cost you nothing. Human relations do not work, humane relations do. The difference in the word is an "E"—perhaps standing for Extra Effort. You can acquire a Ph.D. (People handling Doctorate) overnight once you begin to use this nonmagical formula.

Finally, here's rule number three: Cultivate the art of being dependable. People will pay you more both in money and attention, when you exhibit "depend-ability" over and above ability. While ability in this world is common, depend-ability is rare. So, become the rare person you were meant to be: one who is a people builder, who practices humane relations, and let people know they can depend on you.

> *"A problem is a concentrated opportunity. The only people that I ever have known to have no problems are in the cemetery. The more problems you have, the more alive you are. Every problem contains the seeds of its own solution. I often say, when the Lord wants to give you the greatest value in this world, he doesn't wrap it in a sophisticated package and hand it to you on a silver platter. He is too subtle, too adroit for that. He takes this big value and buries it at the heart of a big, tough problem. How he must watch with delight when you've got what it takes to break that problem apart and find at its heart what the Bible calls "the pearl of great price." Everybody I've ever known who succeeded in a big way in this life has done so by breaking problems apart and finding the value that was there."*

Dr. Norman Vincent Peale,
as quoted in an interview in
Personal Selling Power,
May/June 1983.

Obstacles are those frightful things you see when you take your eyes off the goal.

Hannah More

*Nature gave men two ends—one to sit on and one to think with.
Ever since then, man's success or failure has been dependent on
the one he used most.*

George R. Kilpatrick

*If you have made mistakes, even serious ones, there is always
another chance for you. What we call failure is not the falling
down, but the staying down.*

Mary Pickford

*He who bemoans the lack of opportunity forgets that small doors
open up into large rooms.*

*A pessimist is one who makes difficulties of his opportunities; an
optimist is one who makes opportunities of his difficulties.*

From Self-Esteem
to Sales Success

How often have you, following a lost sale, imagined the world was filled with hostile prospects? At the time, did you have visions of escaping to a tropical paradise, away from all career troubles? Or did you focus on and magnify your mistakes, concluding you were a "no-good failure?"

These behaviors—defensiveness, escapism, self-blame—are classic responses to rejection. It's only natural to react in any of these ways after suffering a blow to your self-esteem. However, if you persist in faulting others or yourself, or wish you could "get away from it all" every time you meet with disappointment, you're turning your back on a serious problem that will continue to hamper sales potential. Put another way, you're neglecting your most important asset as a sales representative and a human being: your self-esteem.

What is self-esteem? Macho invincibility? Humility and patience in the face of tribulation? Not really, though people with high self-esteem may at times seem to exude these characteristics. Self-esteem is simply acceptance of self. Sounds easy, doesn't it? But in reality, accepting yourself is one of life's toughest challenges, a job that if done properly can occupy all your waking hours.

Hidden Fears

Take the example of the high-powered super salesperson who always expects to make the sale. Flip the lid on this top achiever and you'll often find a very insecure individual, someone who performs out of fear of failure. While giving the impression of invincibility—and half-believing his or her own illusions of superiority—this sales rep may utterly lack self-confidence. He or she is aggressive rather than assertive, motivated by a frantic need to prove something, driven by a deep-seated need to overcome inadequacy. Does this person have high self-esteem? Obviously not. Self-acceptance requires no proof or urgency to impress.

244

What about the self-effacing sales rep who withdraws from life's fast pace by operating on the lowest denominator of job performance? Some might say that this sales rep "accepts" himself, progressing on an even keel, if slowly. Actually, this type accepts only his limitations. Scratch the surface and you'll probably find a bitter soul who needs to "get even" with customers, tough and friendly ones alike, by giving as little as possible of himself. This type of sales rep ironically finds justification in claiming he's "too good for the rest of the world!" But, of course, what he's getting even for are his feelings of self-doubt and self-rejection.

Those who suffer from low self-esteem feel badly about, even reject, themselves. Most often they reject others, too, including sales prospects.

Identifying Low Self-Esteem

A sales representative who finds himself gazing across a cold desk into the colder eyes of a difficult client may wonder three things: (1) Is the customer going to accept me?; (2) how will I be viewed when I make my presentation?; and, (3) will I be able to persuade the prospect? There are significant differences in how sales reps with high self-esteem and those with low self-esteem maneuver in this situation. Let's examine low self-esteem.

In our hypothetical situation, the sales rep with low self-esteem follows certain behavior patterns when confronting a "cold fish" prospect. His mind whips into high gear, connecting with all the unhappy experiences of the past that occurred with similar prospects. While reeling off his presentation, the sales rep hears an internal monologue that undermines any effort to look and sound convincing about the product. "This guy is just like the last prospect who turned me down," he may think. "I'm wasting my time." Whether the salesperson realizes it or not, the impact of negative self-talk is communicated to the buyer through nonverbal signals. The buyer does get the underlying message.

Wearing Masks

Sales reps with low self-esteem commonly develop a magician's chest of tricks to cope with, but not solve, their problem. Take the so-called Super Rep. This person often creates a separate persona that he feels more acceptable to buyers than his real self. With every "success," this type grows increasingly divorced from real-

ity. "They don't like the real me, only my mask," he thinks. "If
they only knew how unimportant and worthless I am, they'd never
buy from me." Regardless of the number of sales racked up, Super
Rep feels little satisfaction. Reason: Credit for his achievements
goes to the phony outer shell. That's one form of misadaptation.

Playing It Safe

Another occurs with Humble Rep. This salesperson's motto is
"play it safe, keep distant, don't get involved," or "if I don't try, I
won't fail." How true. Unfortunately, the other half of the maxim is
that if you don't try, you won't make the sale, either. Humble Rep
can float along for years, selling just enough to get by, finding a
safe, comfortable niche in the lower ranks of sales performance, and
never breaking out of his old groove. Focus on the past and negative
self-talk lead this type of salesperson into retreat. In fact, you might
say he's "mentally retired."

The negative aspects of low self-esteem permeate all phases of
one's life. Among peers, the sales rep may "put down" his customers. At home, he'll be equally critical of his fellow sales reps.
Negativism stemming from low self-esteem may surface in actively
aggressive behavior. The frustrated salesperson often loses his temper, insults others, hangs up the phone, or refuses to talk. Though he
makes every effort to avoid discussing the problem, the message
comes through loud and clear. "I feel badly about myself," he's
saying: "I need help with my self-esteem."

The solution is easy to identify, harder to implement. Super
Rep and Humble Rep have to stop wearing masks and playing
games.

Self-esteem management can hardly be learned by reading a
book or an article. Learning about one's self-esteem is part of a
personal growing experience—that's what makes it so unique and
precious.

Nurturing Self-Esteem

Returning to our model sales call, let's see how the salesperson
with high self-esteem would appraise the situation.

Is the customer for or against him? Neither, to start with. The
customer may never have seen the sales rep before, and so has no
preconceived notion of performance or reliability. The salesperson
is "starting fresh."

How will he be viewed when he makes his presentation? This is business, not a personality contest. The prospect wants to deal with someone who is competent and knowledgeable. Being a "nice guy with a winning smile" helps, but the sales rep with high self-esteem doesn't base his performance solely on the buyer's attraction to personal charm.

Will he be able to persuade the prospect? Much depends on the prospect. But the salesperson with high self-esteem will, on closing his presentation, feel confident he's done the best job possible. If the prospect buys—great. If not, the sales rep analyzes his perform-ance with an eye to making improvements for his next meeting with the buyer, then moves on to another sales prospect. He doesn't pick himself or the buyer apart.

The active ingredient in management of self-esteem is choice. You can choose to regulate your feelings or self-esteem, or let events do this for you. Recall that as a child you relied on your parents to help foster feelings of self-worth. To some degree this continues in adulthood, with employers commenting on (hopefully praising) your work. However, *you* control the quality of the work, how you feel about your performance, etc., hence *you* supervise the esteem derived from your sales career. The less you participate in this essential management function, the less satisfaction you will feel, and the lower your self-esteem.

Self-Expectations

Imagine you'd been asked to train a race horse. Notwithstand-ing the fact that you may know nothing about it, you would probably start with some basic principles of common sense. If the horse were young, you'd expect him to make mistakes initially. You'd start him running short distances, then work up to a goal, focusing on his potential. Finally, you'd recognize that the horse would need praise and encouragement in order to be motivated. Horses respond to feelings, too.

Makes sense, doesn't it? So why treat yourself with any less interest or concern than you would a horse? The expectations you have of yourself can be used to regulate your own self-esteem. Here are some examples:

- *Expectation of one's ability.* Expect to make mistakes, to lose sales from time to time—and learn to correct your errors. Expecting to be perfect is the surest route to an asylum.

- *Expectation to grow beyond the present situation.* Focus on what you can do, not on what you can't. What's more important: giving one good presentation and getting the order, or rushing through six calls and losing every sale? Concentrate on refining your present talents, then expand.

- *Expectation to focus on one's potential.* Other people tend to view us by our past accomplishments, while we tend to judge ourselves by what we will do in the future. Healthy self-esteem comes from knowing what you want, and not from dwelling on what you don't want.

- *Expectation to focus on your need to feel good.* There's no law against it. Each time we satisfy our need to feel good, we create a deposit of happiness. Each time we label ourselves bad or attack our self-esteem, we deplete our most valuable resource and risk poor personal and professional performance.

Your Own Self-Esteem Management Program

Feelings are contagious. So is esteem. Your positive self-esteem will lift the spirits of others as surely as a smile generates more smiles. Conversely, low self-esteem draws out the worst in others.

Buyers can sense the tension between your real self and any mask you may choose to wear—they, too, may don a mask in your presence, but they won't feel comfortable until all pretense is dropped.

Feeling good about yourself will be highly visible to others, positively influencing their own feelings about themselves. Your positive attitude signals that you accept others for what they are— perhaps one of the most basic human needs. Low self-esteem is almost always taken out on others, with the sorry result of alienation from colleagues and clients. Have you ever noticed how when you feel bad, you become more demanding of others? You want them to change—to fit *your* expectations. While you may be able to disguise your verbal negativism, your low self-esteem will come through via nonverbal signals.

Why go to the trouble and heartache of avoiding the problem with masks and games? Accept yourself and you'll give up your wish for others to fit your expectations. Accept your buyers and you'll become effective in selling.

Next time you're on a sales call, try concentrating on this bit of positive self-talk. It comes from an old pro who carried it in his wallet throughout his selling career of 42 years:

"I feel good about myself. I am well prepared for this call, and there's nothing I can't handle. I know my customer has a need for the product. He appears reasonable and he's good-natured behind the masks he needs to wear occasionally. He can be thoughtless at times, but his attitude has no bearing on the good feeling I have about myself. I'll accept myself, feel able to handle my customer's attitude and manage possible conflicts to the best of my ability."

There's no better way to have customers flock to you than to *reach out to them first*. The key is your own self-esteem.

The active ingredient in management of self-esteem is choice. You can choose to regulate your feelings or self-esteem, or let events do this for you.

Cynicism

Cynicism can lead to earlier death, particularly from heart disease, according to an article in the March, 1984 issue of *Psychology Today.*

Researchers have concluded that cynicism is a distrust of human nature. In a study, Psychiatrist Redford Williams, Jr. and John Barefoot of Duke University, along with Grant Dahlstrom of the University of North Carolina, have found that 9 to 12 percent of 255 doctors, 25 years after being tested and scoring above the median measures on the Book and Medley hostility scale (HO), had a coronary event. Among cynics who scored above the median, 13.4 percent had died.

Williams and his collaborators hypothesize that "stressful conditions arouse two basic response patterns. One is the classic fight/flight response. The other is a sharp increase in vigilance." Williams notes that since cynics feel they can't trust people, they are likely to go around being on their guard and vigilant. Because these cynics are going around looking for meanness, they are likely to find it. At this point, clinical studies show, levels of cortisol, testosterone, and other hormones go up, in direct response to stress. Previous studies indicate these levels can play a major role in accelerating various kinds of heart disease.

Fitness for Life
Equals Fitness for Sales Success

Dr. Kenneth H. Cooper, author of *The Aerobics Program for Total Wellness,* and founder of a 27-acre aerobics center in Dallas, was interviewed by *Personal Selling Power* about the relationship of physical fitness to sales success. According to Cooper, stress creates a chemical imbalance, prohibiting relaxation until it is corrected. Physical exercise, which dissipates stress, is, therefore, a key element in any self-management program. Cooper's ideas are not new, indeed they go back to Plato who stated: "Lack of activity destroys the good condition of every being, while movement and methodical physical exercise saves and preserves it."

Sales executives who are overweight, and do not engage in any regular form of exercise, are not only endangering their health—they are threatening their careers. The following objections to physical fitness, and questions about weight loss and exercise are typical of anyone rationalizing why he or she doesn't need to worry about staying in shape. Dr. Cooper's answers are a condensed version of the *Personal Selling Power* interview. They'll help you improve your outlook on this important topic, making you more fit—to live *and* to sell.

1. I'll just take my chances and enjoy life to the fullest *now.*

They also want to be successful in life and overlook that the important thing for achieving success is good health.

2. A few extra pounds can't affect how I feel.

Dr. Cooper reports that at one point in his life he was quite overweight, becoming very lethargic. He recalls saying to his wife, "I feel like I am dying of mental stagnation." He then states that "it was probably as much physical as it was mental." A frightening experience on water-skis provided the motivation for Dr. Cooper to begin a self-improvement plan, but he believes that education and self-motivation can stimulate anyone to become physically fit.

3. Won't a crash diet get my weight down fast, with a minimum amount of suffering?

*A low-calorie diet can help you lose weight rapidly, but you will
gain it back just as fast, only with fewer calories than it took to
maintain your weight before. Let's say your metabolism requires
2,000 calories per day. If you go on a 300 calorie diet, you may
lose as much as 15 pounds in three weeks. As a response to this
lower caloric intake, your body lowers the metabolism. After three
weeks, your metabolism may have dropped from 2,000 to 1,200
calories. As soon as you get off your low-calorie diet, your weight
will go up rapidly even if you eat less, say, only 1,600 calories. It
takes a long time, perhaps as long as a year to readjust your
metabolism back to the original level.*

4. Is there anything I can do, in addition to exercising and
limiting calories, to increase my chances for losing
weight?

*I suggest that overweight salespeople eat 75 percent of their daily
calories before 1 P.M. Try to eat 25 percent at breakfast, 50
percent at lunch, and 25 percent at dinner. I suspect that if you
take in most of your food early in the day, your body remains
relatively active during the digestive process. This reduces your
appetite and leads you to eat less.*

5. What do you mean by being physically fit? Do you have an
objective way to measure fitness?

*Historically, physicians have classified their patients as being
physically fit if they are free from disease. A weight lifter may say
it means having bulging muscles; a young lady might say it means
having a lovely figure. To me, physical fitness means a good
cardiovascular-pulmonary system, which means that you are fit
for life. I suggest to focus on the organs that you live with first.
Once you've built your cardiovascular reserves and achieved
fitness on the inside, then you begin to work on the outside, the
muscle building or the figure contouring.*

6. Exercise is too painful, and takes too much time.

*Dr. Cooper states that aerobics "literally means exercising with
air, and refers primarily to endurance types of exercise." But he is
quick to point out that it can be recreational. "Some people prefer
to jog, others walk, swim, dance, play tennis or ride a bike. It
doesn't make a difference what type of aerobic exercise you
engage in, the key is to increase your heart rate for a period of at
least 20 minutes four times a week, or 30 minutes three times a
week."*

7. How can I tell how fit I am?

I use a very simple test in my presentations. I ask each person in the audience to count his or her pulse for 15 seconds and then multiply that figure by 4 to get the number of heartbeats per minute. A resting heart rate of 50 to 60 is excellent; 60 to 70 is good; 70 to 80 is average; most American men and women are within this category. 80 to 90 is fair and over 90 is poor.

8. How can physical fitness reduce stress and anxiety?

During a stressful day, your adrenal system produces hormones which set you up for flight and fight responses. You are keyed up from a high level of these hormones. Your body can't relax until this chemical imbalance is corrected. Exercise helps you dissipate the stress and you end up feeling refreshed and relaxed. If you don't allow for a physiological release, you tend to respond to your body's demand for chemical balance by having a drink or taking a tranquilizer.

9. How can all this affect my salesmanship?

The additional benefits from physical fitness which Dr. Cooper cites are, "higher enthusiasm, better energy levels, higher confidence, improved attitudes." Cooper also notes that those who are physically fit take fewer sick days—which means more days to sell!

10. How do I remind myself that physical fitness is important?

Dr. Cooper suggests: "It is a whole lot cheaper and more effective to maintain good health than to regain it once it's gone."

Motivating Salespeople

How do you motivate your salespeople?

An effective sales manager knows that money is not the prime motivator to a salesperson, *meaning* is. In order to create a highly motivated sales team, we need to continuously reward the three "P's" of the salesperson. The first "P" stands for the performance. A good sales manager recognizes the value of good results and pays for productivity. This basic level of motivation satisfies the salesperson's economic and power needs. Reward good performance! The second "P" stands for the position. The effective sales manager recognizes the values of the salesperson's position by creating job autonomy and support systems that add greater importance and opportunity to all sales jobs. Don't give just lip service by saying "Nothing happens unless somebody sells something," but ask yourself: "What can I do today to get everybody in our company to support the sales team?" In this area salespeople don't want words, but action. This level of motivation satisfies the salesperson's achievement needs. Don't defend the salesperson's position, reward it instead!

The third "P" stands for the person. Recognize the value of each individual. Satisfy their social needs, their need for pride in belonging to your company, their need for recognition in front of their peers. Also satisfy their need for seeing their picture in your company newsletter, their need for receiving a personal letter from the company president or their need for your words of praise and admiration for a job well done.

Motivation is not a one-way street. As you cover all three levels of motivation, you'll realize that your investment is paying off handsomely. You'll see a dynamic sales team, you'll realize consistent above-quota results and realize that indescribable deep-down good feeling that you've contributed to something very meaningful.

Motivation comes in many subtle ways and speaks many different languages. As long as you cover the three "P's" of motivation, as long as you reward the performance *and* the position *and* the person, you'll be motivated too.

Eleven Steps
to Stress Management

Stress is an inescapable part of modern life. But you can change the way you react to it. The following suggestions for stress reduction will help you relax and enjoy life. As a dividend, you'll be more productive, so you'll create less stress for yourself in the future.

1. *Laugh.* Laughter is one of the best tension releasers there is. Find things to laugh about and people to laugh with. Laughter is a great antidote for taking life too seriously.

2. *Take Breaks.* Learning to interrupt a stress producing activity will help give you the break from tension that you need. You'll return to your activity refreshed and ready to be more productive.

3. *Make "Happy" Plans.* Anticipation is an exciting feeling. Plan to see a special movie, eat out with someone you like, or do something else that pleases you.

4. *Focus Your Thoughts.* The habit of thinking about too many things at the same time is extremely fatiguing and stress producing. Instead of being overwhelmed and unproductive, concentrate on one task at a time. Try making a list of other things you must do, and then put it aside, so that you don't have to think about them, but you won't worry about forgetting them either.

5. *Check Yourself.* Stop to see if you are relaxed. Are your hands clenched? Is your jaw tight? Such tension will begin to spread throughout your body, so catch it early. Let your arms hang loosely, unwrinkle your brow, relax your mouth, and breathe deeply.

6. *Tackle the Hardest Jobs First.* This will give you a sense of tremendous accomplishment, and provide momentum for finishing your other tasks. The pleasant things you must do will make your final hours at work enjoyable, if saved until last.

7. *Go Task by Task.* If you finish one task at a time, you will avoid feeling fragmented and overburdened. It is also easier to see where you're going with a job when you give your full concentration. Leave some time between activities to minimize overlapping.

8. *Move.* Speed up your body action by moving to music, stretching, or jogging. Movement helps eliminate pent-up stress by aiding the removal of chemicals that stress produces and which make you feel bad.

9. *Manage Your Time.* Use a plan of action. Schedule only as many tasks each day as you can reasonably finish without pressure. Leave time in your schedule for the unexpected.

10. *Help Someone and Smile.* Lending a helping hand or smiling can do what other methods of relaxation can't do—they give you a wonderful feeling of happiness and well-being.

11. *Enjoy Yourself Now.* Stop whatever you're doing and delight in being alive. Sense the physical processes inside you, the good in people around you, and the beauty of the world you live in.

The Traveling Salesman: The Bag of Cookies

by L.B. Gschwandtner

When you're a salesman who travels a lot, you spend much of your time in the company of strangers. You get accustomed to the slight nod, the averted eyes, the solitary thinking and the psychological space with which you surround yourself as a cushion against the threat of unwanted intrusion. You become an island in a sea as you move to each temporary place.

So it was with the subject of our story, a salesman in an airport, far away from the comfort of home and the familiar sound of a loved one's voice. At sixty-two Henry "Ham" Walker had been on the road for over forty years. He even remembered the early days when most people traveled by train. These days, it is both easier and harder on a fella. Sure, the traveling is quicker, but then the waiting between the traveling is longer, and the people are colder, and the airports can't hold a candle to the old railway stations with their hustle and bustle. They had an air of community about them, not like these jetports where you never see the same face, no matter how many times you fly from say, St. Louis to Houston.

As Henry recalled his early days, he passed a vending machine, and caught a strong smell of fresh baked cookies. He stopped and peered into the machine. This smell of real food cooking was like the old days of fried chicken and lemon meringue pie in the train depot. Eight cookies for a dollar fifty, it said on the metallic plate next to the machine's window. Henry watched as the cookies baked. Place your coins in the slot, and get eight cookies in a bag at the dispenser door.

Henry put the coins in the slot and watched as the freshly baked cookies slid off of a small track and into a waiting open bag. A metal bar slid across the top of the bag sealing them in, and then they slid into the little loading dock. A light went on inside the door and a sign said "ready" in orange letters. Henry opened the door and took his bag of cookies. The fresh smell of chocolate chips

257

filled the air around the machine. Henry marveled at the inventiveness of people.

Looking up at the big clock in the airport's main waiting area, Henry saw that he had forty minutes before his plane to Atlanta would be boarding. He looked around for a place to sit. Across the wide expanse of milling people, the waiting area was more than half full. He cut through the crowd and chose a seat under a huge plastic billboard that proclaimed the glories of a low tar cigaratte. He sat on a green plastic chair, the kind that's designed like a bucket with a back and attached to a long row of other buckets. Between Henry and the woman in the next seat was an empty bucket, the reason that he had chosen this seat.

He struggled out of his raincoat and dumped his armload of extra baggage on the free seat with his raincoat on top of the pile. Then he sat down and opened his newspaper to read about the latest drop in interest rates. After starting to read the first page, he reached over to his right and took a cookie out of the open bag.

As he munched on the fresh, still warm cookie, he saw, out of the corner of his eye, an outstretched hand to his right reach into the same bag and also take a cookie. He flinched ever so slightly and tried to reason to himself why the stranger in the next seat would do such a thing. Probably she was very hungry and couldn't resist the aroma. He took another cookie and continued to read. Again, out of the corner of his eye, a hand stretched out and took a cookie from the bag.

This was outrageous. Henry began to feel annoyed. But the woman to his right moved not a muscle and Henry felt uncomfortable making a scene about a cookie. Henry went on reading. After about five minutes he reached over and took another cookie. No sooner was the chocolate chip taste on his tongue than the woman reached over and took another one also.

Now Henry was dumbfounded. There were only two cookies left and he decided to make one last bold move. He reached into the bag and took one more cookie. Then he reached in and took the last one. He ate both together. "That should take care of that," he thought to himself.

Our of the corner of his eye, Henry now saw the woman take the empty bag, lift it high above her face, tilt her head back, and shake the last few crumbs into her mouth with much crinkling of the paper bag. This, then, was to be the last statement of passive aggression before she crumpled the bag up and left it on the seat between them.

Boarding for flight 726 to Des Moines was called and the woman got up from her seat and walked away. Henry sat very still, trying to reconstruct the events of the past half hour. He was perplexed. His own flight was called next and he, too, got up to leave. He picked up his raincoat to put it over his arm, and there, on the seat, on top of his briefcase, and his folders, and his carry on shoulder bag was an unopened bag of cookies—*his* bag of cookies.

There was nothing to do but sit back down and laugh, until the tears rolled down his cheeks. He laughed for both of them because the woman whose cookies he had eaten would never get the benefit of this incredible joke.

"If only she had spoken up," Henry told himself, and then corrected himself, "If only *I* had."

Sales Classics

In the study of History there is an old saying: "The past is prologue." In selling it is equally true that the professional builds on the knowledge of what has already been done and proven effective. It is not possible to build a future in sales without learning from the pioneers of the past. By incorporating their tried and true methods into your own style of selling, you can be on the road to sales success within a few months.

The articles that appear in this chapter were all written from the 1920s. We tend to look at the good old days with a sigh of nostalgic benevolence. After all, we reason, things were so much simpler then. But the twenties were rife with the same pressures and problems we face today—they just had different labels: Prohibition, the aftermath of World War I, The Great Depression, to name a few. Was it easier to sell then? Not likely.

As you read these sage pieces of classic selling theory, remember that the future is built on the experiences of the past, and knowledge has no time limits.

Be Somebody,
Not Just Anybody

By Dr. Frank Crane

Back in the 1920s when the country was growing up, salesmen were told that education was the key to a successful future. Today many things have changed but an education, no matter when and how you acquire it, is still one of the fundamentals to success.

No matter what a man's work, he can do it better if he is well informed. And the point here is that education, while it has a larger bearing than a mere preparation for one's trade or profession, is the very best equipment for any sort of efficiency.

Whatever your peculiar calling, your expertness is more telling if it rests upon a basis of general culture.

As a stenographer you will do better work and your chances of advancement are much greater if you are familiar with history, know your Shakespeare, and are not in doubt as to whether Botticelli is "the name of a cheese or a violin."

As a lawyer, doctor or preacher, your reputation will very likely rest as much upon your "all aroundness," your wide acquaintance with the inside of great books and the general impression that you are not a narrow-minded specialist, as it will upon your technical finish.

Culture means intellectual background.

It means accumulated force behind your stroke.

It means that you are not only capable yourself, but that you know how to absorb and use the capability of wiser persons.

It gives you perspective.

It increases your personality.

It strengthens your influence.

It keeps you from settling down to become a mere cog in the wheel, a little specialized piece of machinery to do a certain task, and makes you a Human Being, alive, vibrant, radiating.

It makes you Somebody, not just Anybody.

Many a mother has realized too late that she has no hold upon her children because of her lack of knowledge. They have grown up and gotten away from her.

Many a man has risen in the business world only to be humiliated because he has neglected to acquire that education that alone would qualify him to mingle on terms of equality with well-informed people.

In fact, no man or woman who has neglected an education does not bitterly regret it sooner or later.

And no living person was ever sorry that he had secured an education.

There never was an age in the history of the world when it was so true as it is now that "Knowledge is power."

And Knowledge is open to Everybody.

Its gates are unlocked, its door is unlatched, its road is as free as the king's highway.

The only things that prevent any person from acquiring useful knowledge are laziness, self-indulgence, weakness and procrastination.

Even if you did not get a chance to go to school, or if you failed to improve your opportunity when young, you can still set out upon the royal road to Education if you have the will.

And even in the case of those who are college graduates, the best part of their education is gotten from their studies in the ten years after leaving school.

There is no single thing so essential to Success, in whatever calling, as Education.

Knowing When
to Close

by W. L. Barnhart

Sales meetings are a tradition as old as apple pie and mother. And almost like today, in the 1920s salespeople didn't agree on the right time to close a sale.

The question recently came up at a sales meeting in 1929: "Is there a good psychological moment to close?" When the answers were evaluated, the overwhelming conclusion was:

Yes, there is a psychological moment in every sale which is fatal for the salesman to pass.

A few of the 27 salespeople in attendance disagreed. In fact, a determined minority of eight insisted that "this talk about the 'psychological moment' is all foolishness."

A still smaller minority expressed the opinion, which I believe to be the correct one, that while there is undoubtedly one moment that is the best time to close any sale, at the same time there are many moments almost as good, so that the salesman will have many other good chances to close, even if he does pass the one best moment.

Of course, everybody recognizes that a salesman who is intent upon talking will go oratorically on his way, past all the good closing points, and will talk himself clear out of an order, just as did Mark Twain's missionary, who preached so long that Mark, after feeling thoroughly "sold" at first on a five dollar contribution, became so thoroughly unsold by reason of the long-windedness of the preacher that he abstracted a dime from the collection plate instead of contributing anything.

Knowing when to close is one of the most difficult problems, especially for the beginning salesman. Not one of the salespeople's answers was wholly satisfactory on this question, but from all I have made a sort of mosaic.

"Close as soon as your man acts as though he were ready to buy,"
said nine, but the only clue as to how the salesman was to know
when this point had been reached was that the "salesman's
experience" would tell him. "He should use his inherent and
acquired knowledge of human emotions," declared one. "You
must feel it," pointed out another. While a third thought it "a sort
of telepathy."

Scarcely less indefinite were the next group of answers.
"Close when you are sure you have the consent of his mind."

"When prospect visualizes possession."

"As soon as you are sure he understands your proposition,"
asserted another, "you can start to close." "When he is very much
interested." "Watch for desire," advised one. Another believed that
"you can try to close on any evidence of interest,"—which is
contradicted by the statement of another: "Attempt to close only
when desire is at white heat."

The Comeback

by Dr. Frank Crane

The following advice on success first published in 1922, may have more meaning in today's world of jumbled values and confused ethics than it did even in the roaring twenties.

I find that the way I am treated in the day's work depends upon the state of mind I bring into it.

If I enter a circle of men whom I take to be superior to me, I am likely to be snubbed. If I impute to them the feeling that I am inferior I will not fail to be inferior.

If I am self-confident, I awaken confidence.

If I cringe, I make others want to step on me.

If I am cheerful, cheerfulness is handed me by others.

If I am grouchy and snappy, they will bite me.

People go at me about the way I go at them.

There is a law in physics to the effect that action is equal to reaction. The ball rebounds from the wall with precisely the force with which it was thrown against the wall.

And if I approach a man with politenesss, I usually receive politeness.

I get from this world a smile for a smile, a kick for a kick, love for love, and hate for hate.

Of course there are exceptions to this rule. But if there were no rules there would be no exceptions.

And the difference between the man who knows how to play a game and wins regularly—any game, including poker, business, and the game of life—and the man who steadily loses, is that the wise man sticks to the rules and the law of averages, and the fool "has a hunch" and stakes his all on the exceptions.

A good definition of a fool is one who thinks that this time doesn't count.

This is a world of law. Chance is only to be found in the dictionary. In the bright lexicon of fact there's no such word.

If I am petulant, unrestful, irritable, unsatisfied, wretched, and bored—I know the crop, and might have expected the harvest when I sowed that seed of self-indulgence, lack of will, moral cowardice, and general selfishness.

If I am lonely, it was I who drove hearts away.

If I am bitter, it was I who skimped the sugar-bowl.

If I am persecuted, it was I who brought it on by my cantankerousness.

The loving are beloved.

The generous are helped.

The considerate are considered.

The bully by and by is bullied, the smasher smashed.

And the end of the hog is the slaughter house.

There are no victims of fate. The hero always rises above tragedy. The noble soul is never more serene than when all creation thinks it has downed him.

Saul of Tarsus:
A Great Salesman
of 2,000 Years Ago

By Edgar Paul Hermann

*Whether the product is philosophy or tents, selling is an art as old
and as useful as man*

It is fitting that in this first number of a series on Celebrities of
Selling we choose a man whose influence on human thought and
conduct, and whose general sales ability, have been so great.

He was a Rooseveltian sort of a man, with energy, personality,
persistence, drive; a great psychologist, a great student of the
motives and mental traits of men. He sold his proposition over most
of the known world of his time, braving prison, shipwreck, hard-
ships of every kind, to do it.

He was Saul of Tarsus, a tentmaker and a seller of tents—and
the first and greatest salesman of the ideals and philosophy of
Christ. We know him better as the Apostle Paul.

He was born a Jew, with the natural bent for affairs, and the
other sturdy qualities which have always distinguished the Hebrew.
He also was a Roman citizen, and was well educated, well trained,
cultured.

He was a great sales promotion manager and sales letter writer.
Read his sales letters to the Romans, Corinthians, and Ephesians.
He was a sales thinker, and, to a large extent, imposed his thinking
upon those he sold. Even to this day, Paul is the official interpreter
to us of the meanings of Christ.

There are some mighty worthwhile sales suggestions in Paul's
writings. Consider, first, those great essentials of big production,
industry and energy. Paul was a living example of these qualities, as
well as an eloquent advocate of them. Said he: (Be) "Not slothful in
business; fervent in spirit; serving the Lord" (Romans, 12:11). This
great activity of his took him on trips over all his world, to Athens,

Rome, to many lands and nations—always to make a wider market for the service he was promoting.

He taught sales industry, but he also taught sales honesty. Listen: "That no man go beyond and defraud his brother in any matter" (1 Thess., 4:6).

He loved to be among people, as does every good salesman. Whenever he could you may be sure he would be at the market place, or elsewhere that people assembled, and that he would be at his job, selling them.

He was a remarkable sales strategist. The people of Athens were a proud people, with their own philosophies and religions. To offer them a new proposition, to invite them to leave the customs they liked, might be to court instant antagonism, to risk immediate defeat. Paul was too wise for that. He used a great principle of sales strategy. He agreed with them first, and then, starting from a common ground, advanced to the point he wished to make. He said, in effect:

"You men of Athens, I have noted with respect your religious attitude. The other day, indeed, I came across an altar dedicated to the Unknown God. That altar does you great credit. Now, I want to tell you about that Deity that you have wisely recognized, though you know Him not. He is a God that can and will help you."

He loved to dramatize things, so that they vividly made the idea acceptable to his sales prospects. He told with elaborate detail the dramatic story of how he was himself sold on the philosophy of the Nazarene. The dramatic miracles he performed aided him in dramatizing the power of the proposition he sold. He healed the sick, made the lame walk, and with each instance more and more people came to think his way. That is true Salesmanship—to use every asset and to mobilize every ability and resource for the purpose of making prospects think and act as you would have them, so that they will accept the goods and services that you offer them, to their benefit.

Like the salesman of today, Paul had much competition, but he dealt diplomatically and shrewdly, yet squarely, with his competitors.

How many traveling salesmen of today would stick to their jobs in spite of being stoned, robbed, beaten, and doubted by their sales managers back home? Yet Saul of Tarsus just went ahead, selling his tents and his religion.

He was always a square shooter in his selling. Suppose a salesman of today met a purchasing agent who insisted on his little bribe, how would he handle the situation? Paul made the sale and didn't give the bribe, either (Acts 24). There are many more stories that might be told of his aggressive, sportsmanlike leadership and sales tactics.

What sales manager would not like to have a man like him on the staff: absolutely reliable, fearless, brilliant, honest; sold one hundred percent on his proposition and on his own ability to sell it; a student of psychology, a great speaker and debater, especially strong in a man-to-man tilt, able to dramatize his story, and with a gift for putting it in language that his particular audience or individual prospect could understand; aggressive, earnest, mature—here was a man who had *everything,* as a salesman.

Is it any wonder he was so successful?

The Men
Who Make Good

by Dr. Frank Crane

We are full of hidden forces.

In a crisis we discover powers in ourselves, powers that have lain dormant, secret reserves of ability, only waiting for the occasion to leap forth.

You can tell just what strain a bar of iron will bear, just what weight a locomotive will pull, and just how much liquid a glass vessel will hold; but you cannot tell how much responsibility a man can carry without stumbling, nor how much grief a woman's heart can suffer without breaking.

The human being is the X in the problem of nature. He is the unknown quantity in the universe.

The frightened boy can jump a fence he would not attempt in his sober senses. A frail woman in the desire to save her child becomes a strong *Sandow*.* A soldier, battle-mad, acquires the strength of ten.

The one thing nobody knows is what he can do in a pinch.

The forceful natures are those that depend upon this hidden nerve force. These are the pioneers, to whom the danger from unknown beasts and savages is a welcome filip. They taste

That stern joy that warriors feel
In foemen worthy of their steel.

These are they that love "the doubtful ridges of the battle," that go down to the sea in ships, sing in the face of the storm, and laugh at the arrows of the sleet.

These are the overcomers.

These are the salt of the race.

These are the born kings of men—the men who can.

---

*Eugene Sandow (1867-1925), German physical culturist, noted for feats of strength.

They do not know what they can do. They only know that when the thing is to be done, possible or impossible, safe or deadly, there is some strength that surges up in them that meets and measures with the task.

Panic only calms them, clears their brain, and steadies their hand while other men go mad.

Defeat only rouses in them a dogged strength.

Slander, sneers, and curses cannot drive them from their work; success or praise does not make them dizzy.

They are not prudent, they are not wise; they are not skilled and trained; they simply make good wherever they are put.

There is no recipe for producing such souls. The choicest heredity cannot breed them, schools cannot prepare them, religion cannot form them.

They are the men who rise to the occasion. They are the unafraid. They are those who lose themselves in the thing to be done, and do it, and care not for heaven or hell or for their own life.

The supply of such has never equalled the demand. Every business enterprise wants them, every profession cries for them.

They are the heroes. They are better; they are men.

When you meet them they seem commonplace, often shy and awkward.

But don't be deceived. They are the only really Great Men. For they are the Men Who Make Good.

Overwork

by Dr. Frank Crane

Overwork never hurt anybody.

That is about as true as most generalities.

Somebody said that "all generalities are misleading, including this one." But the declaration that nobody was ever hurt by overwork will be found to be rather watertight, if you carefully examine it.

In most cases of breakdown from overwork we find the cause to be something else, such as excess, abuse or indiscretion of one sort or another.

Most of the elaborate and expensive resting that is done by people with money is really camouflaged self-indulgence. They want to go off to Newport or to Palm Beach and play highjinks, so they all tell each other it is because they are so "run down." They do not believe what they say, and neither does anyone else except the gumps who believe what they read in the society columns of the newspapers.

As a matter of fact, work is about the healthiest thing in the world for a he-man. And a good dose of it would cure the complaints of most she-women.

About the only thing that is better than work is more work.

Of course, work has to be done intelligently. You cannot neglect and abuse the human machine and expect it to produce, just as you cannot afford to leave your harvester out in the rain or neglect the care of your automobile.

Your body should be stoked up with the proper kind of fuel and not gummed up with too much meat nor overheated with alcohol nor poisoned with drugs.

And your body needs intelligent exercise and plenty of good fresh air and sound sleep.

You have to look after your mental machine also. You can no more get good results out of your mind without proper discipline than you can get good results from a stationary engine in the hands of one who knows nothing about machinery.

And you have to take care of your soul enough to keep it from worry and pessimism and cowardice and superstition and all the rest of the dirt and grime that gets into souls that never take a bath.

But if you do, if the body is sound and strong, if the mind is trained and clear and the soul is clean and sweet, no overwork in the world can kill you.

And that for the simple reason that human capacity is like an open bucket: When it gets full it runs over. A human being is not like a balloon which you can go on filling up until it bursts.

Consequently, go ahead and work all you please. If you keep healthy and cheerful and do not worry, you'll have a lot better chance to live a hundred years than the fellow who is devoting his life to new and ingenious forms of resting.

The Man
Who Gets Things Done

by Dr. Frank Crane

*The art of getting things done has not changed significantly since
this article was written in 1924*

"The Lord certainly shows His low opinion of money by the
kind of folks He gives it to," said the pale young man at the
banquet. "Look at Hiram Perkins over there—ignorant, no manners, no grammar, no anything but money." The pale young man
was a Harvard graduate, and inclined to Socialism and Poetry and
The Future.

"Well," said his uncle Tom, who sat next to him, "I'm not so
sure the Lord missed it on Perkins. To my mind he comes nearer
earning his millions than most of us."

"Why, what can he do?"

"Nothing. That's the idea. He doesn't do. He gets things
done."

"Humph!" grunted the youth.

"Yes," went on his uncle, "there's a small but lively tribe of
fellows who get things done. They toil not, neither do they spin.
They couldn't qualify for a labor union. They are not educated, not
many of 'em. They can't read Greek and Latin nor do stunts in
mathematics. They are short on Art and Literature. They are not
Socialists. They are not philosophers. When you meet them you
think they are about as common as prunes.

"And yet they are the biggest men in these United States.
Because they get things done."

"What things?" asked the young man.

"Oh, any old thing you want," replied his uncle.

"There's Hi Perkins, for instance. He came from a little town
in Illinois. He was a foundling. A poor grocer's wife adopted him.
He worked in the store. By the time he was seventeen he had
changed his foster father's store from a piddling affair to the biggest

275

mercantile enterprise in town. When he was twenty-one he had a chain of stores in the surrounding towns. At thirty he owned the street railway and the waterworks and electric plant. At thirty-eight he owned public utilities in a dozen towns. And it wasn't graft, nor the power of unlimited capital, nor anything like that. It was because, somehow, he got things done when everybody else failed.

"There are plenty of people that can do things if you tell them how. Hi Perkins is one of the kind that do things when nobody can tell them how.

"Loyalty, honesty, perseverance, training, education, and all those things are good. But there is something rarer. Something that the creator gives only to the hundredth man. It is the ability to accomplish the impossible. It is the genius for finding a way. And the Lord gave that to Perkins.

"All you need to tell him is that a certain thing needs to be done. He goes and does it. It isn't mentality nor suavity nor talent. I don't know what it is. He doesn't know. But when he puts his shoulder to the wheel it moves. When he faces obstacles they vanish.

"I see," said the young man, "a sort of typical American, crude but efficient."

"Yep," replied his uncle. "You've said it. Still, he doesn't do things, you know. He gets things done. There's a difference."

Keep Your Chin Up

by Dr. Frank Crane

I am going to tell you the truth about this naughty world; and the truth is that whichever way you're going, up or down, people want to help you along.

If you are going up, we all want to *boost;* if you are going down, we all want to *push*. That is what we call sympathy.

You hear complaints that the rich are getting richer and the poor poorer. That has always been the case, simply because it is human nature. Society has always been organized to increase the wealth of the wealthy and the power of the powerful; also to make the weak weaker.

The rule is that "to him that hath shall be given, and from him that hath not shall be taken away even that which he hath."

There's no use whining about it. It is simply one of the flinty laws of nature. The only thing to do with nature's laws is to adjust one's self to them and not to complain.

This might be called the law of the inertia of prosperity.

You are guilty yourself. Whom do you want to see? The man everybody wants to see. And you read the book everybody's reading, and go to the store where it is "the thing" to go.

"Follow the crowds," says the advertiser, with his shrewd knowledge of our makeup.

If you have a hundred dollars ahead, to whom do you want to hand it? To the poor man who needs it? Not at all, but to the rich banker who does not need it.

If I ask you for the loan of a quarter you will pass it over without a word if you think it is a trifling matter to me; but if you suspect I really am in want, and need the quarter to buy a little food with, that's quite another affair; you can't encourage that sort of thing; I should go to the Associated Charities.

Now the way to use this law is to feign prosperity even if you have it not. *Keep your chin up.*

Wear good clothes. Don't withdraw from the society of the

prosperous. Look pleasant. Don't let yourself get down at the heel. Don't get that poor beggar look on your face.

It isn't hypocrisy. It isn't pretense. It is sheer courage. It is letting the world know that while you live you propose to fight, and that like old General Zachary Taylor, you "don't know when you're licked."

Keep smiling and an unfriendly universe will not know what to do with you; so it will crown you.

Says Alfred de Vigny: "All those that struggle against the unjust heavens have had the admiration and secret love of men."

Fate is a bluff. Face her, defy her, and she will fawn on you.

Fate is cruel, *but only to the quitter.*

Selling Goods

by Dr. Frank Crane

Get out and sell goods. Hustle. Fight. Don't get fastened in one hole. Take chances. Come up smiling. So the best and biggest prizes in America are open to you.

Every young man should some time in his life have experience in salesmanship.

Selling goods is the best known cure for those elements in a man that tend to make him a failure.

The art of success consists in making people change their minds. It is this power that makes the efficient lawyer, grocer, politican, or preacher.

There are two classes of men. One seeks employment in a position where he merely obeys the rules and carries out the desires of his employer. There is little or no opportunity for advancement in this work. You get to a certain point and there you stick.

Such posts are a clerkship in a bank, a government job, such as letter carrier, a place in the police force, or any other routine employment requiring no initiative. These kinds of work are entirely honorable and necessary. The difficulty is, they are cramping, limiting.

Some day you may have to take a position of this sort, but first try your hand at selling things.

Be a book agent, peddle washing machines, sell life insurance, automobiles, agricultural implements, or peanuts.

You shrink from it because it is hard, it goes against the grain, as you are not a pushing sort of fellow. And that is the very reason you need it.

Salesmanship is strong medicine. You have to go out and wrestle with a cold and hostile world. You are confronted with indifference, often contempt. You are considered a nuisance. That is the time for you to buck up, take off your coat, and go in and win.

A young lawyer will gain more useful knowledge of men and affairs by selling real estate or fire insurance than by law school.

I have just read a letter from an office man fifty-seven years old. He has lodged at $1,600 a year for twenty years, while two of the salesmen who entered the business about the time he did own the concern.

Get out and sell goods. Hustle. Fight. Don't get fastened in one hole. Take chances. Come up smiling. So the best and biggest prizes in America are open to you.

Selling things, commercialism, business, is not a low affair; it is a great, big, bully game. It is a thoroughly American game, and the most sterling qualities of Americanism are developed by it, when it is carried on fairly and humanely.

There is incitement in it for all your best self, for your honesty, perseverance, optimism, courage, loyalty, and religion. Nowhere does a *man* mean so much.

I mean to cast no slurs upon faithful occupants of posts of routine. They have their reward.

But, son, don't look for a "safe" place. Don't depend upon an organization to hold your job for you. Don't scheme and wirepull for influence and help and privilege.

Get out and peddle maps. Make people buy your chickens or your essays. Get in the game. It beats football.

REFERENCE

Alphabetical Listing
of Major Contributing Authors

Tony Alessandra & Jim
  Cathcart
Cathcart, Alessandra &
  Associates
P.O. Box 2767
La Jolla, CA 92038
619/459-4515 (inside CA)
800/222-4383 (outside CA)

Craig Bridgman
P.O.B. 427
East Haddam, CT 06423

Dr. William D. Brown
Suite 217
1025 Connecticut Ave., NW
Washington, DC 20036
202/833-8792

Jeffrey P. Davidson
3709 S. George Mason
  Drive
#315-E
Falls Church, VA 22041
703/931-1984

James F. Evered, CSP
President
HRD Services, Inc.
Box 1450
Denton, TX 76202
817/382-7202

Dr. Milt Grassell
371 California Ave.
Oakdale, CA 95361
209/847-2951

John H. Herd
The Achievement Center
Box 261
Rochester, MI 48064
313/651-3600

Eugene Kordahl
President
National Telemarketing,
   Inc.
56 Shongum Road
Randolph, NJ 07869
201/361-3500

George J. Lumsden
Executive Communications
2694 Heathfield Rd.
Birmingham, MI 48010
313/647-2038

Paul J. Micali
President
The Lacy Institute
15 Paine Road
South Yarmouth, MA
   02664
617/394-6888

Dr. Donald J. Moine
The Association for Human
   Achievement
1728 Morgan Lane
Redondo Beach, CA 90278
213/379-3560

Nido Qubein
Creative Services, Inc.
Box 6008
High Point, NC 27262
919/889-3010

David H. Sandler
P.O. Box 483
Stevenson, MD 21153
301/653-1993

James E. Shaw
4620 Northridge Drive
Los Angeles, CA 90043
213/296-9410

Homer Smith
President
Marketing Education
   Associates
4004 Rosemary Street
Chevy Chase, MD 20815
301/656-5550

"Positive" Paul Stanyard
6013 Susan Court
San Jose, CA 95123
408/225-7424

J. Donald Staunton
Vice President
Superior Sales/Management
   Publications
P.O. Box 81C
Morristown, NJ 07961
201/540-1366

Dr. Lyman K. Steil
President
Communication
   Development, Inc.
25 Robb Farm Rd.
St. Paul, MN 55110
612/483-3597

Suzy Sutton
Park Town Place Ste
1506 S
2200 Ben Franklin Pkwy
Philadelphia, PA 19130
215/567-0713

Dottie M. Walters
18825 Hicrest Rd.
Glendora, CA 91740
213/335-8069

Jacques Weisel
P.O. Box 224
Coram, NY 11727
516/698-7760

Ron Willingham
Ron Willingham Courses,
   Inc.
P.O. Box 8190
Amarillo, TX 79109
806/372-5771

The Zig Ziglar Corporation
3330 Earhart, Ste 204
Carrollton, TX 75006
1/800/527-0306

The Wild Mare

The
Wild Mare

GLENN BALCH

HarperCollins*Publishers*

Library of Congress Cataloging-in-Publication Data

Balch, Glenn.

[Flaxy mare]

The wild mare / Glenn Balch.

p.   cm.

Summary: In Idaho, an orphaned filly, rescued by and then separated from a
young cowboy, has adventures with various owners and bands of wild horses
before being reunited with her old benefactor.

ISBN 0-06-056365-6 (pbk.)   —   ISBN 0-06-056366-4 (lib. bdg.)

[1. Horses—Fiction. 2. Orphaned animals—Fiction. 3. Idaho—History—
Fiction.] I. Title.

PZ7.B18Wk 2004   2003069144

[Fic]—dc22   CIP

                                                        AC

First Edition

Typography by Amy Ryan

❖

To Lilian

◄•One•►

Flax was foaled in the spring, when the grass of the Owyhee uplands was green and nutritious. The chokecherry, bitter brush, and white sage were sending forth new shoots on which the horses would later browse like deer. Clusters of juniper and cedar added dark gray-green touches to the rocky slopes. In pockets near the crests of the hills hardy mountain mahogany made pools of bluish color.

In the afternoon of a bright, warm day a light sorrel mare, seeking seclusion, left her grazing band of wild horses. She went slowly up the slope to the cool shade of a juniper thicket. Her cleanly chiseled head and high, well-sloped shoulders showed the influence of Thoroughbred ancestry. Probably her sire had been a prized stallion that had escaped his pen on one of the low-country ranches. The mare found a quiet place among the trees and stood patiently, her intelligent head lowered. This was her time to be alone.

Flax was born during the night. Her front hoofs emerged first from the mother's body. Next, snug against her slender forelegs, came her long head. The mare labored steadily, convulsing her strong stomach muscles. Flax's neck and shoulders, still soft boned for this ordeal, appeared, and she hung suspended a second or two while the mother rested. At this critical moment Flax had a great need for life-giving air. With her forefeet she broke the membrane that encased her head and breathed deeply through her small nostrils.

The mare took two steps forward and positioned herself for another effort. Flax's chest appeared, then her back. The mare's flanks contracted powerfully. Flax's hips and hind legs slipped out, pulled by her own weight, and the whole of her surprisingly long and slender body tumbled free. She fell in a crumpled heap, rolled on her side and struck out instinctively with her pipestem legs, at the same time jerking her head free so she could breathe easily. Then she lay still, her small chest heaving.

The mare turned and eyed this new creature with some concern, as if she didn't know just what to do about it. But instinct soon asserted itself. The mother moved forward, inspected the newborn foal, and then nuzzled it. She began to lick the soft, damp hair with her strong and comforting tongue. Starting at the muzzle, she thoroughly cleaned the foal's face and ears.

As Flax looked up, she made out a big bony head, attached by a long, tapering neck to a strong, rounded body. This interested her and she made her first effort to stand. Doubling her forelegs, she put her tiny hoofs against the ground and pushed up her head and shoulders. Then she fell back, exhausted. Her mother continued to lick her, and soon she tried again. This time she managed to straighten her front legs. Finally, with a mighty heave, Flax got her hind legs under her, too, and stood erect. She looked about anxiously and with keen curiosity. The big, reassuring creature was close by. She tried to move closer to it, then plunged forward on her tender nose to sprawl again on the gritty earth.

Young as she was, Flax's instinct told her that safety lay in being on her feet. This time it was easier to stand. Her big knobby joints already had more strength. She spread her gangly legs wide for balance, and the mare moved closer and steadied her.

Leaning thankfully against the warm body that was so comforting, Flax rested. As her confidence increased, her curiosity did too. Furthermore, there was another vital need in her. She pushed her small body searchingly along her mother's side. She fell, but got up again. This time, with some gentle direction from the mare, her mouth found its proper place and instinct told her what to do. A delectable warm liquid flowed down her small gullet, wonderfully satisfying to her stomach. Now she had successfully passed one of the most critical periods of a horse's life. As ranchers say, she "had stood and sucked," taking the special food that nature provides for newborn foals. If she had delayed even a few hours she would have died.

The filly drank only a little milk. Sucking was an effort and the space in her stomach small. Soon she took her nose from under her mother's flank and looked around with big, wide eyes. There was an instinctive wariness in her, the distrust and suspicion with which all horses are born and which has enabled them to survive as a species. Everything, to Flax, was an enemy and would remain so until experience proved otherwise, everything but her mother, already known and trusted.

The mare took a few steps, and Flax was immediately filled with fear, a fear of being left alone, which is also instinctive with horses and never completely outgrown. Now this fear in Flax found a voice, a small, anxious whinny. The mare halted, turned her head, and waited patiently. Flax teetered forward to her mother's side. When the mare started on, Flax solved the problem by going too.

Soon she nuzzled for more milk and the mare moved one hind foot back to make it easier for her to find the nipple. After nursing Flax was tired and wanted to lie down. She started to bend her knees but suddenly her courage deserted her and all the strength seemed to leave her legs. She fell. This time, however, she protected her sore nose by turning to one side before hitting the ground. Relieved, she lowered her head, and soon went to sleep. The mare stood protectively above her.

Flax's memory was still short, but it was strong. When she awoke, the good warm milk was the first thing that came to mind, and at once she heaved herself up. Balanced quite well on her long legs, she searched hungrily for the milk supply and found it.

Just as she was beginning to get accustomed to her new world, an astounding thing happened. The dark sky above turned silvery, and light stole silently across the rocky slopes. One edge of the earth became pink, and the sun, a copper disk, rose over the horizon. The forms around Flax became more distinct, the rocks and trees and the big russet shape which her senses of touch and smell told her was her mother.

The mare took a few steps and Flax jigged along beside her, bumping against her ribs. Below them, the wild horses grazed peacefully in the valley. There were a stallion, six mares, and four colts. Three of the colts were nearing their first birthdays and almost completely weaned. The fourth, wide-eyed and spindle-legged, was only a few days old, but already able to run swiftly at his mother's side. Three more of the mares had full flanks, indicating that they, too, would soon produce new foals.

The stallion, Flax's father, was a yellow palomino with white mane and tail. He grazed apart, keeping near the bunch but not mingling with it. His concern was to prevent another stallion from stealing any of his mares, and occasionally he raised his big-jowled head and looked around, prepared for a jealous display of strength and anger at the appearance of a possible rival.

The leader of the band was a wise old roan. She,

too, looked about at regular intervals. She would start moving at the smell, sight, or sound of anything suspicious or even unusual. The others knew this and, by instinct and habit, followed her without doubt or hesitation.

By late afternoon Flax had found her legs and could get about well for a creature so young. Her mother grazed along above the others, still not sufficiently sure of herself to take this firstborn, of which she was so proud, down among the older mares and the prankish yearlings.

The mare and her foal were still on the slope the following morning when, among the broken boulders, a large tawny shape moved silently on great, cushioned paws. It caught sight of the mare and instantly flattened itself against the earth. Now and then the tip of its long, thick tail twitched in anticipation and its claws emerged spasmodically from their padded sheaths. With unblinking yellow eyes, the cougar watched the mare.

A Canada jay sailed through the golden light, planed down to gain speed, and used the momentum for a short steep climb to a cedar bough. The mare, not yet recovered from her ordeal, grazed hungrily. Below her the band was scattered, the yellow stallion clearly visible in the early morning rays of the sun, far down the valley.

Cougars generally feed on rabbits, squirrels, and other small creatures, with occasional deer, colts, or calves. As a rule they do not try to kill horses, for experience has taught them that they cannot match the horse's strength and endurance. But this cat was large and powerful, weighing nearly 150 pounds, and he was hungry. He noted the mare's clumsiness and still-big belly, and he knew he had an advantage because the large, broken rocks would mask his approach. Nothing would have suited the cougar better than a newborn foal, but fortunately for Flax no wind was moving to bring her scent from the low brush where she was sleeping.

The big cat crouched, his blunt head motionless. As the mare moved in his direction, he waited patiently. Then, carefully selecting the right instant, he leaped, his taut muscles driving his body through the air in a long arc.

As the cougar came out of the shadow the mare threw up her head. She remembered her helpless foal and hesitated just a second before whirling away. Then, her hoofs gouging deeply into the coarse soil, she fled down the slope toward the other horses.

The cougar landed and bounced right back into the air as if his legs were steel springs. His body stretched its full length, from the tips of his terrible paws to the end of his tail.

From her place in the brush Flax saw this savage, flashing form and instinct told her its great danger. Motionless she lay pressed against the earth. For a moment fear seemed to stop the beating of her heart.

The sorrel mare was only in her third stride when the curved claws cut through her thick mane into her flesh. She was almost knocked from her feet, but regained her balance and ran in panic, driven to still greater frenzy by her pain.

The band of horses, after a startled instant, broke into wild headlong flight. They raced across the valley and up the shale-strewn slope beyond. There they whirled about for an instant, their heads up, and snorted in deep alarm. The mare plunged into the meadow, fighting with all her strength to dislodge the cat. But soon her pace slowed and she stumbled among the rocks. Near the far edge of the meadow she fell. The cougar leaped free, landed on his big paws, and spun back. The mare was struggling weakly to get to her feet when he fastened his teeth onto her throat.

◄ • *Two* • ►

Jim Thorne topped a ridge on Duke, his brown horse, and descended into a wide sun-drenched basin that was dotted with green meadows. His keen eyes searched the basin for the bulky red forms of Seven-K cows. Jim was eighteen years old, lean and strong, with high, narrow shoulders, almost a man in size. Born and raised in the Owyhee stock country, he was riding his second year for Ben Drake's big Seven-K outfit.

The many tributaries of the Owyhee River had carved a wide-flung maze of twisted canyons in the arid Idaho upland. Forbidding and spectacular in their vastness, the Owyhee Breaks are a last stronghold of the freedom-loving wild horses once so numerous on the western ranges.

Jim liked his assignment in Middle Creek, an isolated rock-rimmed valley where Seven-K had a summer range allotment. Thirty-five miles of rough trail separated him from Seven-K headquarters. He had a string of three good saddle horses, and a hundred head of white-faced cattle to look after.

The young rider carried a short-barreled rifle in the saddle scabbard under his right stirrup. He did not see the cougar until the big yellow shape bounded out of a chaparral clump. Quickly he clapped his spurs to Duke. Jim had no love for cougars and welcomed any opportunity to shoot one. But he seldom had the chance, because the big cats were usually too cunning to be caught in open daylight.

The cougar moved in quick bounds across the meadow. Duke knew well enough what his rider wanted and followed at a wide-open run, his iron-shod hoofs digging at the gravelly soil. Jim leaned low in his saddle to decrease the wind resistance and urged his horse to faster speed. Spasmodic lashing of the cougar's tail showed that it was feeling desperate. The cougar glanced back, then changed direction and headed for a rim of boulders on a steep slope. Jim kept Duke at a hard run, but the cougar managed an extra spurt of speed and vanished among the big, broken rocks.

"Whoa!" Jim yelled and tightened the reins. With Duke still in the midst of a sliding stop, he pulled the rifle from its scabbard and hit the ground. He raced to the nearest boulder and scrambled to its top. The cougar was nowhere in sight.

Jim drew a deep breath and waited. Nothing was visible except an eagle circling lazily overhead. Then Jim caught the flick of a long tail. He shifted the rifle muzzle to the spot where he had seen the tail. A second later the cougar appeared in a crevice between two of the big boulders.

Hurriedly, Jim found the tawny form in his rifle sight and squeezed the trigger. The cat leaped high in the air and Jim knew from the way its head snapped around that it had been hit. When the cougar did not reappear, he jumped down and walked cautiously toward the crevice, well aware that a wounded cougar could be extremely dangerous.

On the far side of a big boulder, he found a bright splash of blood. But that wasn't enough. He had to make sure the cat was dead, if he could, because a partly crippled cougar, being too slow and clumsy to catch its normal food, could become a habitual calf-killer.

Bright red drops made a trail that twisted upward among the boulders. Big round paw marks showed, too, in the thin layer of dust. Jim hurried on, worried that the cougar might still escape.

Suddenly the cat leaped from a hiding place. It tried to reach the top of a boulder but fell short, its right front leg hanging useless. Jim lifted the rifle quickly and the bullet broke the cougar's spine. Scratching feebly, it slid backward into a crevice.

When Jim reached it, the animal lay on its back, the pale yellow of its belly exposed and its paws in the air. A fullgrown male, it had recently gorged itself. Now it was quite dead.

Jim eased the short rifle's hammer forward to uncocked position. He was relieved to know that no more deer, calves, or colts would fall prey to those hooked claws and long, yellow teeth. The cat's blunt muzzle was smeared with drying blood. Jim frowned and studied it more closely, confirming his sudden suspicion that the blood had not come from the cougar. Probably it had been feeding on a fresh kill, which helped to explain why he had surprised it at close range.

He slid into the crevice and scalped the big cat, taking a section of skin that included the blunt ears from the flat, broad skull. The ears would soon hang on his cabin wall beside the two wolfskins and the smaller cougar scalp already there. Ben Drake, if he paid a visit to Middle Creek, would know his young rider had been alert to range predators.

Back with his horse, Jim levered a shell from the rifle and carefully closed the action on the empty chamber. As an additional safety precaution, he pointed the muzzle skyward, pulled the trigger, and heard the strong metallic click of the tripped hammer. Then he shoved the short gun into its scabbard and mounted Duke. Pleased by his success, he let the horse take his time walking back toward the chaparral, curious to see what had been the big cat's last kill.

He was surprised to find the body of a large horse. He saw that the animal was a mare with tightly swollen udders. Its stomach had been cut open. He guessed that the knowing cougar had been after an unborn foal, for he knew the cats had a special liking for fawns fresh from their mothers. Maybe the mare had been just ready to drop her colt, and this explained how the cougar had been able to catch her.

Jim slowly shook his head in thought. Even a big cougar couldn't eat a foal, head, legs, hoofs, and all. Some part would have been left behind. But there was not a single sign of the foal to be seen.

One hand on the rein, he glanced at the lowering sun, then turned his gaze across the high land toward the little valley which held his rude cabin and corrals. Even if he left now, it would be nearly dark by the time he reached the point where the trail angled down to his camp.

He hesitated a few seconds longer. Then, with a sigh of irritation at his own stubbornness, he tightened his hand on Duke's rein and began to search the rough ground for a sign leading to the chaparral thicket. There it was—deep, scarring hoof tracks, obviously made in panic. With Duke on lead, Jim began to back-trail them.

◄•*Three*•►

*F*lax lay still, not daring to move. Young as she was she knew there was danger during her mother's absence. She remembered the swift charge of the cougar, and the mare's frantic flight. She must wait, she knew, for her mother's return.

Time passed. The great red ball of the sun climbed steadily into the sky. Its size became smaller but its heat increased. As the sun passed its midday point Flax felt unpleasantly hot. Except for an occasional flick of her small ears to discourage a buzzing fly she did not shift her position.

Throughout the long afternoon Flax waited patiently, but her mother did not come. There was no sound save the soft drone of passing insects. Then later, from across the basin, came the loud crack of a rifle shot. Flax's ears turned toward it. A short time afterward she heard a second explosion, but the sounds meant nothing to her.

The heat drained the moisture from her body. Her flanks were pulled taut against her ribs and she became aware of a gnawing hunger in her stomach. Still she did not get to her feet. The bright light blinded her and she closed her eyes for relief. The same instinct that warned her of danger told her that her mother would return.

But her mother did not come. Flax's mouth fell open and she panted like a dog from the heat, longing for the delicious fluid that had flowed down her gullet.

The shadows were long and the heat had finally lessened when she first heard the measured fall of hoofs. It was a familiar and welcome sound.

A big creature moved into the area of her vision. Then it hesitated instead of coming immediately to her. Flax, impelled by the painful emptiness inside her, tucked her small hoofs under her body and stood up on her long knobby legs.

The big creature halted, and Flax became aware of still another form close by. For the first time in her life she heard the sound of a man's voice. "What tough luck!" it said in a soft and sympathetic tone.

Strange as the sound was, Flax's hunger was so keen that she wobbled toward it. Before her were Duke and Jim Thorne. As she approached Duke, she realized he was not her mother, but she nuzzled him for milk anyway. Duke sidestepped abruptly, leaving her unconsoled and confused.

"Good night!" Jim exclaimed. "She can't be more than a day or two old."

Another long minute passed as Jim turned over in his mind what he should do. At last he lifted his rifle from the saddle scabbard. "It's too far to the shack," he debated with himself, "and she's half starved already." To Flax he said gently, "I won't leave you here to die, little girl."

Flax made another effort to approach Duke, but he sidled away. Jim worked the gun lever, and a cartridge moved from the magazine to the firing chamber with a bright yellow flick. His lips tightened with reluctance and pity as he looked down the slope toward the chaparral where the body of the dead mare lay. His eyes came slowly back to the little filly standing before him.

He knew there was only one humane and sensible

thing to do. The little filly didn't have a chance of surviving. Completely dependent on her mother's milk, she would starve in a few days if a cougar or wolf didn't get her first.

He shifted the rifle forward and brought the butt up to his shoulder. The filly's eyes were dark pools of bewilderment. "You haven't got a chance," Jim told her.

Nevertheless, the hammer of the carbine did not fall. Jim's finger slipped away from the trigger and he lowered the gun, letting out his breath in a long, troubled sigh.

"All right," he said with irritation. "I know better, but—" He turned slowly to his horse, climbed into the saddle, and reined away, toward the crest of the ridge.

Duke moved in a nimble walk, glad to be heading home at last. Light clicks sounded on the rocks behind. The little filly was following. Jim groaned aloud and said, "You would! Don't you know Duke's not your mammy." But he stubbornly refused to look back, afraid that another glimpse of the helpless foal would compel him to get out the rifle again.

In her great need and from age-old instinct, Flax kept on, clinging to the company of the only thing she could trust—another horse. She knew that it was not her mother, but it had her mother's shape and even a smell that was somewhat the same. Somehow she sensed that this big creature, indifferent as it might be, was her only hope. From time to time she was forced to break into a trot to keep up with Duke's long stride. Mile after mile they traveled along faint trails that were sometimes narrow and twisting. Flax's legs became numb with weariness and she was weak with hunger, but she managed to keep going.

Deep shadows were gathering under the junipers when Flax discovered that she could trot no more. Duke moved farther and farther away, but she was too weary to catch up. The fear of being alone surged up in her and she uttered a thin whinny, a faint cry of desperation and panic.

With an unhappy groan, Jim lifted his hand to rein Duke up. When he looked back, Flax was swaying with weariness. She let her tired legs fold and flopped heavily down on the ground.

"What do you expect me to do?" Jim asked crossly. "It's not *my* fault. *I* can't help it."

The filly rested her chin on the ground, her eyes still on him.

Jim dropped his right hand to the saddle horn, and swung down. "All right, all right," he grumbled, and started toward her.

Separated from the horse, the man was strange and frightening. Flax lunged to her feet, but her legs were numb and stiff and she fell.

With a few long strides Jim was at her side. He leaned down and put his hand on her long, narrow head. "Take it easy," he soothed. "I won't hurt you." Gradually the filly's struggles ceased and she lay still.

Jim slid his arms under her thin body. "At least no cougar will get you," he promised, and carried her toward his horse.

The gelding cocked his ears uneasily. "Whoa!" Jim commanded. "I don't like it any more than you do, Duke, but we can't leave her here."

He placed the filly across the saddle. "Take it easy, little girl," he said to calm her. She was so weak he could restrain both of her front legs with one hand. I'm probably going to a lot of trouble for nothing, he thought. She's not going to last much longer.

The filly soon quieted. Jim spoke to Duke and swung up behind the saddle. With his free hand, he steadied the foal. He clucked and tightened his lower legs and Duke stepped out with the obedience of a good range horse. He had carried more than one weak calf in from the range this way.

Now, Jim knew, it was up to the fates that guide the destinies of men and horses. He felt better knowing he was doing all he could, more than most riders would have even attempted. If she lived until he got her to the shack, he would be surprised.

The sun sank into the western ridge, a crimson smudge that sent streamers of pink and red across the sky. Dusk came, with a cooling of the soft wind, and not long afterward stars began to sprinkle the sky.

Jim kept Duke traveling steadily. The filly's slim little head sank lower until at last it lay against her forelegs, and the beat of her heart became fainter and fainter under Jim's hand.

The moon was up when he reached the rim. The trail lay in the shadows under the wall of broken rim-rock, but Duke knew it well and turned downward without hesitation. They came in time to the bottom and crossed the meadow in the moonlight. As they reached the cabin Jim halted his horse and got down. He gently pulled the limp foal after him, catching her in his arms. The cabin door opened at the nudge of his shoulder and he made his way through the darkness to the bunk, where he put the filly down. After locating the box of matches on the shelf behind the stove, he lighted the lantern, which was hung by a piece of bailing wire from the ceiling. On the wrinkled blankets of his bunk the filly lay motionless.

Outdoors Jim quickly stripped the saddle and blanket from Duke. Then, dismissing the gelding with an affectionate slap on the hip, he returned to the cabin. Flax had not moved. "Now what?" Jim muttered to himself.

The filly needed milk, but on a beef ranch milk was scarce. If he only had a wet mare that was nursing a young colt. The closest one gentle enough to catch was at ranch headquarters, thirty-five miles across the ridges.

In the cardboard box where he kept his groceries were four cans of evaporated milk. Quickly he punctured one can and poured the thick white fluid into a cup half full of water. He stirred the mixture briefly with a spoon and carried it over to the bunk.

Jim caught the filly's muzzle with one hand and forced her jaws open with his fingers. Then he spooned the milk into her throat where it collected until, with a weak cough, she blew most of it in his face. Jim spooned in more. Finally the filly swallowed. At least she was alive. He sighed with relief.

Jim kept busy with the spoon, pausing now and then to let her swallow. Gradually the cup was emptied. Much of the milk had trickled out the corners of the filly's mouth, but some, he was sure, had gone down her throat.

He released her muzzle and her head flopped back to the blanket. Her eyes were open but dull. He made a fire in the stove, opened a can of pork and beans and put it on to heat. He moved the water bucket to a place over the fire, and then went out into the darkness.

Strong whinnies came from the corrals. Jim tossed hay to Nip and Crimpy, the two horses in the pen. Duke trotted over to the gate and nickered softly. Jim let him in the pen and watched as he lined up at the hayrack with the others.

In the cabin, Jim hungrily ate the pork and beans, and finished his meal with a can of peaches. With warm water from the bucket he mixed another cup of milk and took it to the bunk. The filly swallowed more readily, and he continued to spoon the mixture into her mouth until it was all gone.

Then he lifted her high enough to slip one of the coarse blankets out from beneath her. He folded the blanket and spread it on the packed-dirt floor. "All right, you can have the bunk tonight; I'll sleep here," he said, and undressed and blew out the light.

Two hours later he awoke. The little filly was still breathing. The water in the bucket was cold, so he made a fire to heat it before he mixed it once again with milk.

Three more times during the night he got up, rekindled the fire, and fed the foal. She had hardly moved but seemed to have less and less difficulty in swallowing.

The first light of day was stealing through the cabin's one, dusty window when he awoke again. The foal's eyes were open and seemed a little brighter. "Well," he said, "you look better." He quickly pulled on his clothes. "Just lie still. I'll get us some breakfast."

The filly's dark eyes followed him as he made a fire. When he took hold of her muzzle she tried feebly to free herself. He spilled the first spoonful of milk but the second went down her throat and she swallowed. Patiently he fed her spoonful after spoonful, pouring the last few drops directly from the cup into her mouth.

When he had finished she sighed, put her head down, and closed her eyes. The cup of thin milk was not much, but it was all he could offer.

The horses at the corral raised their heads and nickered with impatience as he came from the house. "All right, all right," he said as he opened the gate and let them into the little fenced pasture. "Get some grass. We won't be doing any ridin' today."

◄•*Four*•►

During the morning Jim fed the filly regularly at two-hour intervals. Young foals, he knew, did not take much at a time but nursed often. Near noon she drew up her legs in an effort to get to her feet.

Jim lifted her from the bunk and put her down on the floor. "You might fall," he explained when she looked at him questioningly.

There were some rails in the corral fences that needed repairing and between feedings in the afternoon Jim worked on them. He had seen most of the cows on the range the previous day and was sure they were all right. His saddle horses were enjoying the rest.

Late in the afternoon he carried his tools to the saddle shed, put them away, and went toward the cabin. Inside he halted abruptly. Flax was standing up.

"Well!" he said, surprised but pleased.

Her ears were alert.

"Don't worry, I won't hurt you," he told her. "Are you sure you're up to this?"

She took a step away from him, moving toward the bunk.

"Okay, have it your way," he said cheerfully as he walked around her toward the stove. A little later, hearing a thump behind him, he turned to find her lying down, half on and half off the blanket.

Once in the night he heard her get up. A short time later there was an audible thump as she lay down again. She was still down when daylight came, but raised her head when he swung his legs over the side of the bunk. As he kindled the fire she scrambled to her feet and watched him curiously. A short fuzz of creamy mane stood upright along her neck.

Jim smiled at her. Then, worried, he checked his grocery box. Only one can of milk remained. It and the partly used can on the table were all that was left. At best it would last only through that day and night. And the stronger the filly became the more food her body would demand. It would be weeks before she could eat hay or grass, and months before she could live on them alone.

I'll have to go to the ranch for more milk, he said to himself. But it was a long ride to Seven-K headquarters. Usually two full days were allotted to the trip there and back. By steady riding he could do it in a day and a night. He doubted the filly could last that long without food.

He tried to feed her as she stood, but she struggled and fell. With a knee pressed lightly on her shoulder, he held her down, and her lack of resistance told him that she was by no means out of danger.

He had an impulse to throw his saddle on Duke, take Nip to carry the supply pack, and start at once for Seven-K. But there was still some milk left, and common sense told him that the longer he continued to feed her the stronger she would be. He decided to reduce the time between feedings until the rest of the milk was used and then strike out for the ranch. By riding all night, he should be back in early afternoon of the next day. Would that be soon enough? And what would Ben Drake think when he learned that his Middle Creek rider was spending so much time trying to save a mustang colt? Jim shook his head, not happy with the thought.

Meanwhile, so that no one could say the cattle were neglected, he rode up for a look on the south flat. To save Duke and Nip for the long ride to the ranch, he put his saddle on Crimpy, a flea-bitten gray, sturdy and Owyhee-raised. Jim sent him up the long slope at a brisk trot.

About twenty head of cows, most of them with young calves, were on the flat. As he rode Jim studied them with a knowing eye. There were no signs of any illness, injuries, or disturbances. Near the top of the trail he noticed a fat brindle cow with a husky young calf. For a beef cow the brindle had an unusually large and well-filled udder. Maybe more milk than her calf needed. Even though cow's milk was probably not as good as mare's milk for a colt, it would certainly be better than none.

Jim touched Crimpy's neck and the gray turned obediently. The cow's head came up at once and she tried to cut away to the left. Jim headed her with a short dash and crowded her into the trail. At a swinging trot she went down the trail, and the calf, its tail stiffly upright, galloped along after her.

At the bottom the cow struck out across the meadow and headed for the creek. Jim put his horse into a circling gallop and turned her toward the corrals.

The calf ran at her heels with short jumps. The cow saw an open gate and shied away. Jim boxed her against the fence and held her there to reconsider and calm down. Then he drove her into the corral. The brindle calf followed. Jim swung down, closed the gate, and slid the heavy latching bar forward.

"Well, Crimpy, it's on the hoof—but there's milk," he said.

Flax raised her head as he entered the cabin and dropped some kindling near the stove. It was a nuisance to make a fire every time he fed her, but he was afraid cold milk might give her the colic.

At the corral he took his rope from the saddle fork. "I figured I was through milkin' any more cows, Crimpy, even broke ones," he grumbled. The brindle, big and strong, with short, tapered horns jutting from her head, was edgy and jealous of her calf. She returned Jim's stare from big, watchful eyes. "No cooperation there," he said, mounting his gray horse.

Inside the corral he told Crimpy, "Keep your eyes open. She'll fight." Crimpy knew cattle, too, and stepped about warily with an arched neck.

Jim watched his chance and tossed his loop over the cow's horns. Immediately she started to run. He made two dallies about the horn, bringing her to a sudden stop. She wheeled in his direction. Jim stepped Crimpy up quickly and threw the rope slack over the top of a strong fencepost. As the cow came along the fence he swung wide and, backing his horse, took up the slack. The brindle's head was soon held high by the rope. Jim dismounted and made his end of the rope fast to another post.

The cow rolled her eyes as he approached with a bucket. Behind her the calf bawled its concern. "Sook, girl, sook. Take it easy." Jim put his hand on her hip. She lashed out sidewise with her hind foot, and he jumped back, put the bucket down, and went to the saddle shed for another rope.

This time he got behind the cow, where she couldn't see him, and flipped a loop along the ground to catch her hind feet. She kicked angrily. Jim lay back against the rope until she stopped. Then he looped it around another post and worked out the slack until the cow was caught tight between the two ropes.

Presently the cow stopped fighting, and Jim stood well back, milking with one hand and holding the bucket with the other. It was an awkward, strained position, but he kept on until he had about a half gallon of the foamy white liquid.

The filly's head was up and she was looking toward

the door as he entered with the bucket.

"You can't be hungry again so quick," Jim told her indignantly.

She scrambled to her feet and stood staring at him.

"Don't look at me like that. I'm not your mammy," he scolded, but there was no resentment in his voice.

She took a step toward him and flicked the short brush of her light-colored tail hopefully. Jim knew the name for her then. "Flax," he said. "You're going to be a sure-enough flaxy. With that mane and tail folks'll see you coming a mile away."

He was pleased at this vision of her future beauty and put out his hand. She sniffed it and permitted him to caress her forehead, rounded by nature to make the birth process easier. In time it would widen and flatten, and the bone would become thick and hard. Her ears were small and nicely curved. She would have a shapely and intelligent head. "One thing's sure," Jim went on. "You're going to have to learn to drink."

He moved to the filly's side, put his arm about her neck, and brought the bucket up under her chin till the warm milk touched her muzzle. She started back in alarm, with surprising strength. Jim held her briefly, then let her go. She glared at him as milk dripped from her lips and long chin whiskers.

Learning to drink would take time, he knew, so he held the filly's muzzle up and fed her from the cup as he had before. She took the cow's milk readily.

If he was going to get enough milk, Jim knew he would have to keep the calf away from the cow, except for intervals after the milkings. The husky youngster could supplement his diet with grass and hay. Jim drove him outside the corral, knowing he wouldn't wander far from his mother. The calf spent most of the night bawling and the next morning he was waiting at the gate.

Jim had to tie the cow again, head and heels, to milk her. Her bag was full and tight. When his bucket was nearly full he opened the gate and let in the hungry calf to take the rest.

In the cabin Flax was on her feet. "And another thing," Jim said firmly, after a glance at the soiled floor, "you're goin' to have to learn to go outside." It was reassuring, though, to know that the filly's digestive system was working properly. When he had fed her, he gently propelled her through the doorway and closed the door behind her.

Curious but half frightened in the bright sunlight, the filly looked about her at the green trees along the creek, the crusts of dark rimrock on the slopes, and the blue skies beyond. Soon she turned back toward her place of security and whinnied softly.

"Oh, no, you don't," Jim declared. "You're a horse, not a person. Now you just stay out there." A little later he came out and walked to the pasture. A glance behind him showed the filly had not moved. The shoe on Duke's near hind foot was loose and this seemed a good time to fix it.

Looking small and forlorn, Flax was still at the cabin door when Jim returned from the pasture with the brown gelding. Jim paid no attention to her but went about his business of pulling the shoe from Duke's hind foot with the long-handled nippers. Then he decided to take the shoe from the other hind foot and trim it too, so that the hoofs would be even. All this time the fuzzy little colt watched him hopefully.

"Now I'll get you some milk," Jim told her as he pulled the string that lifted the wooden latch. "It wasn't so bad outside, was it?"

Flax followed him through the door and stood behind him as he made a fire. While the milk was warming, Jim scratched her ear. "You're a good-for-nothin' little scamp," he said, "but you're cute."

◄•*Five*•►

As the days passed, Flax's legs grew straighter and stronger, and her body rounded out. The fuzzy baby hair on her neck and shoulders loosened and began to shed. She was delighted to have Jim scratch her with his old curry comb, and she followed him about the place like a big, overgrown dog. When he was working she would often come up behind him and search along his back with her soft muzzle. Having assured herself, she would stand and wait patiently for him to give her a caress, sometimes taking the edge of his jacket or a fold of his shirt between her lips to gain his attention. Jim knew he was spoiling her but he didn't care. After what she had been through he figured that a little something extra wouldn't hurt her.

She reported regularly for her meals at the cabin door. If they were unduly delayed she became visibly indignant. Nor did a closed door stop her, for she soon learned to lift the latch from the inside or out. Teaching her to drink had not taken long. Once she learned, she gulped the milk eagerly until the bucket was empty and then scoured the bottom with her tongue for the last drops.

When Jim was absent for long hours, looking after the cattle, he left a bucket of milk outdoors for her, secured between three stout stakes driven into the ground, so she couldn't overturn it. In this he often mixed small amounts of grain—usually oatmeal from his own supply—and there was never any left when he came in. Soon she was eating all his table scraps— bacon, eggs, sourdough hotcakes, or anything that was left over.

Jim never penned her up but let her run about free, knowing full well that she wouldn't wander far. "If you were a horse colt, you'd make a good saddle critter, I bet," he told her pensively one afternoon. The ranchers, as a rule, did not ride mares because their dispositions were not as even or dependable as those of geldings. "Somewhere back of you there's some good breeding—Thoroughbred," he went on. "You can run, or I miss my guess. Given a chance, you'd sure raise some mighty nice colts."

When Jim's mother had died three years before, his father had sold his cattle and most of his land and moved to Portland, Oregon. But even then Jim knew that the rugged Owyhees was the country for him. He wanted to raise horses, good ones, and Owyhee forage made horses strong and wiry; Owyhee rocks and slopes put strong legs and hard, tough feet on them. Getting a start would require "grass" or range, some brood mares, and a little money, but Jim was sure he could manage that. There was his father's old homestead, now deserted but with a pretty good cabin on it, a shed, and a couple of corrals, and meanwhile, Jim was saving money regularly from his Seven-K wages.

The summer months were happy ones for Jim Thorne and the little filly. Despite Jim's good intentions, she still slept in the house every night, on the floor beside his bed. The nights at that altitude were always crisp and chilly, and as the fall season approached they became longer and sometimes bitingly cold.

One afternoon Jim did not return to the shack as

was his custom. Old Duke, ordinarily careful and sure-footed, had not seen an old badger hole hidden in tall grass and went down hard, trapping Jim's leg underneath him as he fell. Jim knew immediately that it was bad. There was torturing pain in his leg, and he felt dizzy and sick inside. He knew he had to have help. Fortunately he had ridden that day in the direction of the ranch headquarters; it was only a little more than twenty miles to Seven-K across the ridges.

Like the dependable cow pony he was, old Duke was still there. He was shaken by the fall, but he looked unhurt. Slowly Jim dragged himself to the horse and reached up to the stirrup. "Whoa, Duke," he said through clenched teeth.

It was a painful task to pull himself up and into the saddle, and once he almost lost consciousness.

"All right, Duke," he groaned and started the horse toward Seven-K, the nearest place he could get help.

Before the horse had taken a dozen strides Jim stopped him with a "Whoa." What about Flax? The cattle and Nip and Crimpy would be all right until someone could get back from the ranch. But what about Flax? She was eating grass now and could pick up wisps of hay around the haystack fence. She'd miss the regular feedings, but she could make it. And he'd send someone back from the ranch right away. It wouldn't be too long . . .

When Duke pulled wearily into the ranch headquarters the next morning shortly before daylight Jim was bowed over the horn in sick delirium. He babbled out "Flax" several times, but before he could make sense Ben Drake had him bedded down in the back of a pickup truck and on the way to the hospital. So a second long day passed before a rider was sent to Middle Creek to take Jim Thorne's place, and the man knew nothing about the little orphan filly.

Flax waited near the cabin door through the twilight hours. Darkness came. She whinnied impatiently, then walked inside and whinnied again. She no longer required milk for food, but she liked it, especially when a cup of rolled oats had been stirred into it. Her stomach told her that it was long past time for the man to return. She nosed the rumpled blankets and then went back outside to paw at the old bucket in its stakes.

She finally went back into the cabin, out of the cold, and lay down on her old blanket. But when morning came the young rider had still not returned. Flax went to the corrals. The brindle cow's bag was swollen with milk, and her calf was waiting hungrily at the gate. Nip and Crimpy nibbled grass in the little pasture. Duke was gone. But he would come back, and the man with him, Flax was sure. They always had.

After a time the calf wandered out to the slope and began to eat grass. Flax went to the wire fence that protected the small haystack and ate stray bits of hay that had fallen outside. The wire, she had learned, had sharp points but there were places where, being care- ful, she could push her head through and reach hay inside.

Her hunger somewhat satisfied, she left the haystack and went up the slope and grazed with the calf. Near noon two cows, who also had young calves, appeared up under the rimrock. The brindle's calf climbed toward them and Flax, lonesome, went along too. The calf tried to suck one of the strange cows, but she butted him away.

Late in the afternoon they went back to the corrals. The brindle bawled forlornly and the calf tried to push his blocky head between the rails. The cow hooked at the gate latch with her short horns and pushed at it again and again until finally, near sundown, the gate swung open. At once the calf flung himself at his mother. She stood for several minutes while he sucked, then moved on and began to feed.

Flax went up to the cabin and walked through the open door hopefully. No one was there.

No one came during the night, and at daylight she wandered up the slope, finding the brindle cow and her calf at the top of the rimrock. She was hungry and grazed with them. Close to noon, when the sun was hot, the three dozed in the shade with some other cows and their calves. Later they moved out in search of grass. The cows paid no attention to Flax, but it was better than being alone. The cool evenings, when the flies were less pestering, were good times to graze.

It was well after dark before the cows lay down, grunting as they eased their heavy, red shapes to the ground. They began contentedly chewing their cuds, and their calves, close by, curled up to sleep.

Flax felt more and more lonesome. She went back to the rimrock trail and made her way down it through the darkness. The old bucket, in its stakes, was disappointingly dry and empty. Flax moved on to the dark bulk of the old shack. The door was closed but that delayed her only an instant. Inside, she sensed immediately that a man was there. She could smell him, could hear his regular, heavy breathing. Happy and relieved, she hurried to the bunk and nosed vigorously at the covers to let the man know he had forgotten to feed her and she was hungry.

A loud, frightened yell broke the dark stillness and the blankets flew upward, one of them landing about Flax's head. She lunged backward in wild surprise. The table had been moved from its former place and she crashed into it, knocking it over and adding to the noise and confusion. The yelling continued, now more angry than frightened, and the voice was hoarse and rough, not gentle and soothing.

She whirled about, searching blindly for the door, and collided with the man. His yelling became angrier, and a blow fell on Flax's back. It was followed by more hard blows. Flax kicked back instinctively, one hoof striking the table and the other a soft body. Then the blanket slipped from her head and she saw the gray oblong light that was the door. She leaped into the night and bolted away. Well up the slope she halted to listen and try to see through the darkness. The cabin door slammed loudly, and then there was silence.

Now hurt and fear were added to Flax's loneliness. She did not know what to do. After a time she made her way slowly up the rimrock trail and back to the cattle, where she spent the night. The next morning she stood among them, her head low, dejected and forlorn.

Night came again but Flax did not return to the shack. Memory of the fright and pain there was too fresh in her mind. She stayed with the cows and grazed with them the next day.

On the third day, Flax saw a form on the crest of the ridge that brought a quick little whinny of happiness from her throat. It was a horse, one of her own kind. She was sure it would be Crimpy, or Nip, or Duke. Then more horses came over the rise.

Flax left the slow-moving cattle at an eager trot. She was full-bodied and strong for her five months. A horse on the ridge whinnied down at her, and immediately another horse came into view over the rise. Without hesitation he headed downward, his step high and his neck proudly arched. Flax halted, uncertain about this bold approach. But after a few brief sniffs, the stranger lost interest and ambled back toward the others.

Flax followed him, seeking in the band for Duke, or Nip, or Crimpy, but these horses were all strangers.

Several among them were about the same size as Flax and near her in age. She regarded them with interest, and they in turn were equally curious. One, a bright little bay, approached, wary at first but soon with the courage for a playful nip, after which he turned and scampered away. It made Flax feel welcome.

The band accepted Flax and she stayed with it. She became aware that her situation was different from that of other colts, for she had no attending mother. She remembered only a man, who was no longer there.

As the weeks passed she foraged widely to satisfy her healthy appetite, developing more independence and resourcefulness than the other colts. Often, in her constant search for grass and twigs, she would be on the outskirts of the scattered band, sometimes even temporarily alone. But she never knew the flurries of panic that the other youngsters had when they suddenly discovered that they were separated from their mothers. And Flax never became lost.

◄• Six •►

*I*ndian summer in the Owyhees lasted unusually long that fall. But finally, as the days passed, the leaves turned brown, yellow, and red and dropped from the trees. Thin rims of ice appeared at the edges of the ponds in the early morning. Then one afternoon thick, gray clouds scudded across the sky from the west and, near dark, white flakes began to fall. Flax, with the other horses, huddled for warmth in the shelter of a juniper thicket. When morning came there was a soft, white covering over the dried grass, and little ridges of snow topped the limbs and twigs. The air was still thick with feathery, falling flakes.

An old chestnut mare lowered her head and nuzzled through the covering of snow. Other mares awoke, stretched, and followed. Their backs were soon white, and melted snow trickled down their sides.

Flax looked with some concern at the snow, so soft and yielding beneath her feet. She put her head down and tasted it. It was cold and quickly vanished, leaving her mouth wet. She tried again, but the snow was gone almost before she could swallow it. Impatient, she pawed the ground until she reached the grass underneath. Water dribbled from her lips as she chewed, but the grass was pleasingly moist and tender.

The horses grazed for some time, leaving straggly furrows in the snow. Then the chestnut mare lifted her head, glanced around, and started across the valley. She neither nickered nor paused to look back, but, one after the other, the mares ceased grazing and followed her. Their foals trailed after them in little family groups.

Having no mother to follow, Flax loitered and entered the line after the last of the colts, a brown yearling. The bay stallion came behind her, loafing along and caring little where or why they were going. Few things short of a challenge to his position as the band's dominating male could stir him out of his lazy indifference. Feed and water were problems too minor and too well taken care of by the mares to merit his concern. But if another stallion came near he would show them how strong and bold and important he was.

The band traveled steadily, winding along faint trails remembered by the old chestnut. Wet snow clogged Flax's feet and made walking difficult, but it was not until midafternoon that the lead mare halted and began to nip the sprigs of grass that poked up through the melting snow-cover.

By the next morning the snow was gone, leaving the coarse earth wet and soft. The sun came out and steam rose from the meadows. The horses filled their stomachs, then gathered in a close little group to drowse in the warm sunshine.

Soon the snow came again. This time the covering was deeper, and over it an icy crust froze, hard and glittering. A bitter cold wind swept across the country and drove the horses to the protective rock walls or deep into the canyons. More snow came, riding the wind in lacy swirls down from the dark rims. Then the clouds scuttled away, leaving the skies clear. Ice, thin and brittle, reached out from the edges of the streams, and the slopes, warmed by the sun in the day, were slippery and dangerous at night. Winter had come to the Owyhees.

The coats of the horses, now thick and woolly, trapped small pockets of air which acted as insulation against the bitter cold. Long fetlocks helped to protect the horses' tender heels and ankle joints from the sharp crust, and fuzzy hair filled their ears to keep out the frost.

More ice formed along the creek banks until the quieter pools froze over, forming treacherous bridges.

The horses pawed in the snow for food. The stiff frozen crust wore down their hoofs like sandpaper. After a few days, small red traces of blood appeared in the horses' tracks.

As the weeks went by the fat melted from ribs and flanks and hips. The horses ate leaves and twigs, even tree bark. At night they huddled closely, seeking to share each others' warmth, in the lea of protecting walls or in juniper thickets, enduring the hunger and cold with the remarkable fortitude and patience of their kind. One mare, weakened by old age, quietly stood in one place for several days, then fell forward on the rough frozen surface of the snow.

Flax's forefeet became so tender and painful that she could no longer paw. Her small stomach shrank and her flanks began to settle inward. She searched among the trees for the smallest bits of bark, and stood on her hind legs to reach limb tips that were already eaten back to woody pith. There were days when she could find only a few mouthfuls to eat and the emptiness of her stomach became more and more demanding.

One day, as they were scattered along a creek bank, a memory came to her, pleasant and enticing. She lifted her head, then turned and made her way slowly up the slope. Busy with their own search for food, the other horses paid no attention to her.

At the top of the wide mesa the snow was deeper and wind-packed, but Flax continued steadily across the white wastes, pausing only now and then to nibble at the tops of some low bushes. She spent the night in a dense juniper thicket and the next day followed easily remembered trails in and out of the ravines. Late in the afternoon she came to the Middle Creek country and, from a point on the high rim, saw the shack and corrals in the valley below. With a pleased little nicker, she hurried to the old trail and made her way down it.

No welcoming whinny came from the corrals, and no smoke rose from the dark pipe protruding from the thick cap of snow on the cabin's roof. At the door, Flax hesitated, then pulled the latch string. The door swung open. Looking through, Flax could see the bunk, the table, and the old stove, but there was neither the smell nor the sound of a man. She saw a battered bucket and went in, only to find it dusty and empty, and unpleasantly cold to her nose. Disappointed, she turned back outside.

Some of the corral gates had been left open, and now were held fast in that position by the crusted snow. Inside, Flax found a manger that had some hay in it. The hay too was covered by the hard white crust but she discovered that she could get at it by pushing her small muzzle through the openings between the side slats. The hay was old, dry, and bleached, but to her it tasted wonderful.

Because of the slats she had to eat slowly and it was after dark before her stomach began to feel comfortably full. Then, weary and sorefooted, she returned to her favorite sleeping place, the shack. Again she listened and sniffed, but there were no breathing sounds or any fresh smells of a man. Flax lay down on the dirt floor and was soon asleep.

In the morning, with the early light coming in through the door, the place was even more familiar and reassuring. Flax rattled the old bucket impatiently.

Where was the man with the gentle hands and the kind voice? Why didn't he come with the milk and grain?

She went back to the corrals, wedged her nose between the manger slats and ate more hay from under the snow. She stayed there most of the day, eating, and resting her sore feet.

In the afternoon a gray wolf trotted silently across the slope behind the shack and disappeared into the dark leafless brush along the creek. There was no other sign of life in the snow-whitened valley.

Flax ate the last of the hay from the manger and picked up the small bits that had fallen through the slats. She found an ice-free riffle in the creek, had a good drink, and made her way back to the cabin through the early winter dusk.

The next morning she went back to the empty manger and nosed the slats hopefully. Then she remembered the haystack, from which the man had carried big forkfuls to the corrals.

Where the stack had been there was now a white mound of snow, much higher than Flax's head. She approached the protecting fence and found that it still had its sharp barbs, but in one place the wires had been trampled down. Flax went through the opening, and on that side of the mound there was a dark hole, like a small cave but big enough for Flax to enter easily. And inside there was hay, walls of it, green and fragrant, just as Flax remembered it.

She had been eating steadily for some time when there were sounds outside. Quickly she backed out, ready to run if necessary. Two large elk were coming through the opening in the fence. Flax had seen elk many times on the high, brushy ridges and she had no fear of them. They, in turn, were not afraid of her. They came on steadily, and the larger one swung his big, dark head at her in a threatening manner, but at that time of the year the elk's new horns were only short round stubs, still soft. Flax still scrambled quickly out of his way.

The elk went on into the cave, only their yellow rumps visible from the outside. Flax knew they were eating, and waited patiently. After a time they backed out and, with hardly a look at her, went through the fence opening and disappeared among the trees along the creek. Flax then returned to the cave to eat until she was full.

The hay would have lasted Flax until spring had she not had to share it with the elk. But they were hungry, too, and came every afternoon, burrowing deeper and deeper into the mound. The hay above their heads loosened and fell, and they ate that too.

One morning as she entered the cave she found that no hay was left. Only the hard, frozen walls surrounded her. But she did not starve, for there were layers of firm flesh on her ribs now and her feet had grown long and tough again.

A few days later the snow softened and a soft breeze brought warm pungent smells down from the ridges, reminding Flax of the high meadows. She turned up the old trail through the rimrock and struck out across the wet spongy slopes. Two days later she found the old chestnut's bunch. They were grazing their way across a rock-strewn incline when she saw them. With a pleased nicker of recognition she rejoined them.

◄• Seven •►

*T*he coming of spring was evident on the south slopes first, for there the sun's rays struck most directly and lingered longest. The horses climbed out of the canyons to feed on the pale new grass, and the snow line moved back toward the higher crests. Water plunged down the rifts, swelling the streams and sweeping the ice away. The spruces put out bluish-green shoots of new growth and the willows turned from faint yellow to soft green. Ground squirrels came from their burrows and sat saucily upright on their tails. Birds appeared in the trees, their voices breaking the winter's long silence.

The old chestnut mare led her band to the flats. The horses' tender feet healed and their flanks started to fill out. They traveled slowly, grazing long hours each day. Their thick, woolly hair began to loosen and was rubbed off in the thickets and wallow beds. Once again the clear air rang with the challenges of the stallions.

With the extra feed from the range shack, Flax had come through her first winter well. She entered the spring lean but strong and she grew rapidly. Among the largest of the yearlings, she soon became a leader in their games. Now it was of even less importance that the others had mothers and she didn't. Many of the yearlings would soon be supplanted by fuzzy new brothers or sisters anyway. As an orphan, Flax had made her adjustment long before. Now she was carefree and independent, bolder than the others and more mature.

Spring passed and summer took its place on the brushy uplands. The horses' new coats were short and bright. Flax's color darkened to a light chocolate, strikingly highlighted by her creamy white mane and tail. She was indeed a "flaxy," as Jim Thorne had predicted.

One day a strange horse appeared on the crest of a nearby ridge. The chestnut mare saw it first, lifted her head, and moved her trim ears forward. The stallion sent out his belligerent warning, telling the newcomer to stay away, that these mares belonged to him. Such warnings were familiar to Flax, and she paid little attention. The lead mare, however, remained alert, her eyes fixed on the stranger.

This horse did not reply to the stallion's challenge, but began to pick its way down the slope. The stallion, now in a frenzy, repeated his challenge so vehemently that the mares stopped feeding and the colts came slinking to their sides. The chestnut mare turned and started away at a trot.

Flax was about to follow when she noticed there was something different about this strange horse, something that reminded her of Duke and the Middle Creek corrals. Then she saw what it was—a man was on the horse's back. She uttered an eager little whinny of welcome and started forward. But she had taken only a few strides when the bay stallion turned on her, baring his teeth in anger. He charged and bit her painfully on the neck. Surprised and hurt, Flax whirled and fled. One jump behind her, the stallion continued to punish her rump with his yellow teeth until she was at a hard run after the others.

Flax kept going, even after the stallion was no

longer at her heels. Her neck hurt, and there were tooth marks in half a dozen places on her hip. She understood now more clearly than before the stallion's jealousy, but the violence of his temper when aroused was an even greater discovery. She would know better than to whinny at a strange horse again, and in the future she would keep a wary eye on the stallion, especially when he was in one of his jealous tantrums.

At a long trot the old lead mare took them up the slope. On the top she halted. The horse with the man on its back was still headed in their direction, driving the angry stallion in reluctant retreat. It became clear to Flax then that the stallion, strong and fearsome as he was, could not stand his ground, and she knew it was not the horse but the man that he feared. Why? Did the men on their backs make horses stronger and more dangerous?

The old lead mare traveled steadily during the afternoon and Flax, impressed by her recent experience, stayed in her place in the line. She kept one eye on the stallion, who had finally ceased his noisy bluster and now trailed along sullenly a short distance behind.

Flax was relieved when, at dusk, the chestnut mare halted and, after a long look back, began to graze. The band scattered in the brush to feed, but soon, one by one, began to lie down to rest their weary legs.

They were up and eating at the first light in the morning, and the sun was just above the horizon when a horseman came into view. The chestnut saw him immediately, and turned and started. The stallion sent up a challenge, but no one paid any attention to it.

That day was much like the day before, filled with trotting and halting, then trotting some more. On and on they went, the old lead mare instinctively keeping to country she knew. And always back behind somewhere there was a rider, following with a dogged patience. At times he might disappear, but a few minutes of walking was certain to bring him back in sight.

Early the third morning the man appeared again and put them in motion before they had time for more than a few mouthfuls of grass. At a weary jog, they strung out through the brush. The chestnut took them from valley to valley, her route being roughly a big circle over their regular grazing range. Whenever one rider tired, another seemed to be waiting to take up the chase.

Flax's hoofs were worn to the quick by the constant traveling over the coarse gravelly earth, and several of the old mares now limped noticeably. But they all kept going until midday, when a mare with a young colt slowed down and fell behind, before finally coming to a halt. Then the stallion went into a frenzy of anger. He rushed at her and bit her on the neck and rump. She wheeled about lamely in an effort to get away from him, but could run no more. He kept after her until the horseman drew close, then left her and galloped after the others. The runner passed her and the colt with no more than a second glance.

Flax followed the others obediently, afraid to fall behind because of the truculent stallion. The old lead mare was tired too, and slowed to a walk whenever the horseman seemed to be losing ground, but this never lasted long. Mostly it was jog, jog, jog.

They came to a small pond and, hot and thirsty, crowded to the edge to drink. The older mares filled their bellies, but Flax, having to await her turn, had time for only a few swallows before there was a warning snort and a clatter of hoofs. The rider was surprisingly close and coming fast, flailing the air with a long loop of his rope. The popping noise and his cries really frightened Flax for the first time. She whirled and charged into the bunch, and could sense the panic and confusion. The waterlogged mares ran heavily and the stallion now was up among the others, his white-rimmed eyes rolling with concern.

Suddenly there were two more riders, unseen till then. They flogged their horses along the flanks of the bunch at hard gallops, and their hoarse, angry cries added to Flax's fright.

The chestnut mare gained ground, and the others, with more running room, strung out behind her. The shouts and cries mingled with the pounding of hoofs, telling Flax that danger was close. Forgetting her sore feet, she charged wildly through the fogging dust, bumping into slower horses ahead and going around them.

They ran in this panic for some time before, suddenly, the mouth of a small canyon opened before them. Steep rocky walls rose at either side. The cries behind were louder and shriller. At the end of a stride the old lead mare hesitated, her long ears whipping forward as if at the sight of something remembered. Flax bumped into her, but for once the chestnut did not pause to show her displeasure. She bore sharply to the right. Flax followed and behind them the whole line veered.

The shouts on the right were closer, and bitterly determined. A horse on that side charged hard at them, a rope-swinging man on its back.

The old mare boldly held her course, leaping up the short, steep incline. Flax leaped, too, and they dug at the earth, their powerful hip muscles corded clearly under the skin. Two young mares with colts followed close behind. The youngsters scrambled up the slope with the agility of mountain goats. The rider swirled in behind them, swinging the rope. Long and slithering like a snake, it fell on Flax's rump, driving her to even more desperate effort. She leaped high. The rope fell away, and they were at the top. The chestnut lined out through the brush, and the yelling and the pounding of hoofs behind them lessened. After a time it could no longer be heard.

The lead mare turned in a short circle and looked back, her head high and her nostrils blown wide. All that could be seen was a thick cloud of reddish dust above the small canyon. They went on at a weary walk.

They crossed two small ridges and entered a grassy pocket. The chestnut halted again. Flax put her head down and began to eat, too tired and hungry to wonder where the other horses were.

Soon they lay down to rest their numbed muscles and their worn feet. In the morning they were still lame, but fortunately no one came to bother them as they grazed. Even after the sun had swung high into the sky, the other mares and the stallion had not appeared.

The next day the chestnut moved at a slow, limping walk. Near noon they came across a stray mare that Flax had never seen before. She joined the little band readily. A second mare, who had dropped out during the running, showed up late in the afternoon, followed by her thin, sorefooted colt.

Another day passed and no runners appeared. The bunch, six mares and three colts, alternately fed and rested. Flax spent a good deal of time lying down, but the old lead mare stayed on her feet except in the dark of night.

Ten days passed, ten days which saw the horses recover fully from their ordeal. Once again they settled into the range routine, following the lead mare to the grazing areas and the favorite watering places. Then, one afternoon, they saw other horses, a small band at some distance.

The chestnut studied the strangers carefully for a

long time, but finally lowered her head and resumed feeding. The distance between the two bunches narrowed, and after a time the challenging voice of a stallion was faintly heard. A horse left the strange bunch and galloped forward with a high, belligerent stride. The chestnut and her group watched the newcomer with interest but no concern. To them he was just another stallion and his bluster was of little importance.

It wasn't the stallion Flax knew, but a trim red sorrel instead. He entered the bunch warily, sniffed and smelled, and immediately his attitude changed. That there wasn't any stallion with these mares pleased him mightily. He trotted around them, putting them in a tight little group. Then, switching his long tail and backing his ears, he started them through the brush. They went readily, the old chestnut in the lead as usual.

◄•*Eight*•►

*T*he young colts lacked the caution of their elders and went forward to sniff and then to flirt their thick tails and banter with their new acquaintances. The younger mares soon followed and gradually the two bands began to mingle. Some of the introductions ended in ear-backing and tail-swishing, followed by squealing and kicking, but the skirmishes were soon over. There was plenty of room for everyone, and plenty of grass too.

Only a yearling, Flax had no desire to fight and no position to defend. She wandered about freely, indifferent to the little clashes that were taking place. The red sorrel stallion took no notice of them either. Band organization was the mares' problem, not his, and he knew it would soon be worked out. There would be a leader, simply because there had to be. The very nature of horses demanded it. She would be wise and wary, and know instinctively when it was time to go. The others would follow, relying on her courage and wisdom. This was what held them together, what made it a band, giving them the security and protection of numbers. It was a part of the law of survival.

The only real fight took place between the old chestnut mare and a dun, the leader of the new group. Both were accustomed to being the boss, to having their way. They were careful to avoid each other at first, but the day came when their paths crossed. Neither would back down. The dun flattened her ears and the old chestnut, a veteran of many such fights, charged, squealing out her indignation and jealousy. The dun answered in kind and the mares nearby scattered out of the danger area.

Their teeth bared, the two mares tore viciously at each other's necks and shoulders. Then the chestnut wheeled and began to lash out with her hind feet. The dun turned too, presenting her own rump, and they rained blows on each other as fast as they could kick. It was a determined fight, no quarter asked and none given.

After a few moments it became quite clear that the old chestnut was taking the most punishment. The dun was quicker and stronger. Almost as suddenly as it had started it was over. The chestnut fled, leaving the younger mare dust-caked, tired, and bleeding, but the victor.

The dun did not pursue her opponent and run her out of the band, as a victorious stallion would have done. She was content with a simple victory; there was room in the bunch for them both, as long as the chestnut mare remembered her place. She would; battles such as this left no room for doubt.

For Flax, life in the new bunch was much the same as before. The dun led them to new country where the feed was good. When the first of the winter storms came, the horses were plump and their coats thick and woolly.

They wintered in the river breaks. There was little snow and they were able to get rough ground forage most of the time. One mare died of old age and a cougar caught one of the colts. When spring came, they climbed back to the high flat mesas.

Now two years old, Flax was strong and long-legged, Thoroughbred blood showing plainly in her head and shoulders. She had excellent feet, rounded and hardened by the rocks and gritty soil, and she moved with a long, flowing stride. Her eyes were big and bright and her thin, curved ears constantly alert. The world was big and pleasing to her.

Then the runners came again.

It was early summer. Grass was green and the forage succulent.

Early one morning a tall figure under a big hat came riding toward them through the bright sunlight on a lean, easy-stepping horse.

To Flax there came the flashing memory of another horseman, but she lost it in the confusion of the stallion's challenges. The dun turned, and the run was started.

For three days the runner was always somewhere at the rear, near enough to prevent the horses from eating or resting. He was wearing them down, dulling their caution and alertness.

On the fourth afternoon three more horsemen appeared, coming at a swift gallop. They closed in on three sides, and pushed the bunch into a narrow ravine.

Suddenly the dun halted, as high rails appeared before her. Immediately she sensed a trap and whirled around, but it was too late. The men were behind, shouting and swinging ropes. The horses milled about in wild excitement.

Flax dived into the brush—only to be brought up sharply by a half-hidden fence. Backing out, she tried again, but came up against a steep rock wall. The runners had halted and were putting a rail fence across the ravine entrance.

Flax was uncertain whether to be frightened or not. She had seen a dismounted man before and had not been harmed by him. But she was puzzled and excited by the obvious fright of the other horses. Finally they stopped trying to escape and gathered, suspicious and wild-eyed, in a corner of the enclosure.

The men were in no hurry. Beyond them their well-trained horses rested with drooping heads. The barrier rose pole by pole, high and strong. Then one man walked to the center of the enclosure, where he gathered some small, dry limbs, broke them across his knee, and held a match to the pile.

The wild horses shifted uneasily, but the man paid no attention to them, and they soon settled down again. Gray smoke rose from the smoldering sticks. To Flax the smell was familiar, reminding her of the stove fire in the old shack.

A little later two other men mounted and rode toward them, long rope loops dangling from their uplifted hands.

The nervousness of the wild horses turned to panic. They crowded together, wheeling and bumping into each other. Then a young mare, seeing what she thought was a way to safety, broke out, and ran along the back rails. Some of the others dashed after her. The rest stampeded in the opposite direction, into the low brush at the foot of a rock wall.

Flax was in the group that raced after the young mare. One of the horsemen charged them, swirling his rope about his head. A horse in front lunged upward and began to leap and plunge as if it had suddenly lost its senses. It was the red stallion.

Flax slowed, confused, and it was good that she did, for the next instant she hit the tightly stretched section of the lariat. Strung between the wildly plunging stallion and the saddle horn, the rope moved like something alive and deadly strange. The hard strands bit into her chest, slid upward, and burned across her throat. Frantic with pain and fear, she wheeled back and ran in the other direction, not pausing until she was safe among other wide-eyed watching horses.

Out in the open the red stallion continued to buck and lunge, his head down and his open mouth sucking desperately for air. He fought with all his fine strength, but the second rider moved in and sent his loop skimming along the ground. It caught both of the stallion's hind feet and a second later he fell, held helpless by the two taut ropes.

Then a third man hastened from the fire with a long, dark rod in his hand. Small, blue curls of smoke rose as he leaned forward and pressed the end of the rod with its Lazy-Y brand mark against the stallion's hard-muscled hip. The strong acrid smell of burned hair came to Flax's nostrils.

The two riders rounded up the horses back into the corner and Flax watched while another horse was thrown and branded.

The third time, a rope flashed before her eyes and the loop settled about her neck. It snapped tight, jerking her to a sudden, spinning stop. She lunged forward, leaping into a run, but the rope struck her neck again with savage force. Her feet flew up and out, and she landed on her side. Swoosh! The wind rushed from her lungs. She sucked it back, and righted herself with a mighty contortion. Again she ran, but was held to a circle by the rope. A second rope caught her hind feet, and she swayed, off balance and struggling, before falling heavily to the ground. Worse than the sting of the branding iron was the panic of being stretched helplessly between the two ropes.

Then the loop around her neck was eased. Quickly she twisted to her feet and the rope about her hind legs loosened and fell away. She moved cautiously for a moment, then ran to the other horses and pushed in among them.

Again and again the riders came. By the time the branding was finished Flax was weak with fright.

At last the men disappeared and the horses huddled in the corner began to relax. The colts lay down and some of the weary mares slumped. Others nibbled at the trampled grass. Flax felt a dull pain in her hip and bent her neck to nuzzle her burned hair.

A short time later a number of strange horses entered the enclosure. They trotted forward and sniffed curiously. One was a bay with a bell around her neck and the rest were geldings. Each movement of the mare's head made the bell clank, but neither she nor the geldings seemed to hear it.

Gradually the wild horses began to mingle with the

newcomers, and when night came all of them gathered together to sleep. At daybreak they scattered to feed. The bell sounded gently at intervals, but by now the wild horses had become used to it.

The next morning three men rode into the pen and collected the horses in a bunch. Flax and the range mares were wary, but the geldings moved in calmly and waited. When the mare with the bell headed for the barrier, where the rails had been lifted, the horseman waiting there started off. The mare followed him without hesitation and the geldings trailed after her. The wild horses went, too, welcoming this leadership in their anxiety.

Out on the mesa the leaders kept a steady walking gait. The range horses raised their heads and looked about at the familiar country. When the dun mare tried to strike out to the right, and Flax and two others followed, a rider immediately galloped up from behind and drove them back in line. "Hi-hi," he shouted, slapping his leg.

All day long they traveled, mile after mile over the rolling land. Late in the afternoon when the man in front led them to the crest of a rocky ridge, Flax saw a weathered shed and the outlines of several corrals below on the canyon floor. One corral gate was open when they arrived and the bell mare led them inside.

The heavy gate shut behind them. The horses slumped, glad of a chance to rest, and drank the water that ran under one corner of the big pen. Later some hay was thrown over the fence and they immediately gathered around the piles and began to eat.

The next morning cars and trucks chugged down the bumpy road. Men got out and climbed the fence to look at the horses. After a time two of the runners rode into the corral and all the horses with old brands were cut out, and driven into another pen. These were the saddle geldings and the old bell mare, along with several others which, though they had been caught with the wild bunch, belonged to their brand-owners.

The buyers understood this and after the separating was completed one of them said, "I'll take that big sorrel, the one with the stocking-footed colt."

"I'll buy the flaxy filly," another man announced.

The boss runner, whose name was Andrews, shook his head. "No, I'm going to keep her. You can have any of the others."

"I'm a fool for doin' it, but I'll up the price twenty-five dollars," the man said.

The runner continued to shake his head.

"Fifty," the buyer offered.

"No. I've got plans for her."

"Heck, Gus! I thought you brought us out here to take these broomtails off your hands."

"She's no broomtail an' you know it," the runner replied, grinning happily. "Good blood shows all over her."

After a time the riders came back to rope the sold wild horses. One by one, they pulled them through the big gate, until only Flax was left.

There was shouting and calling, and the clatter of hoofs on wooden floors as the nervous horses were loaded into the trucks and trailers. Doors slammed, engines started, and rigs creaked and groaned as they pulled up the twisting rocky road out of the canyon.

When a gate opened into the pen that held the runners' saddle horses Flax dashed through it eagerly. The saddle horses paid her little attention, however, as they rested with their heads lowered and their eyes half closed.

Now a man dropped down into the pen, clucking and clapping his hands. One by one, the saddle horses obediently filed through another gate and up a loading chute into a big truck. Flax paused before the truck's dark door and received a sharp rap on the hip. Soon she was inside with the others, and their sides, pressing against hers, gave her some comfort.

Gradually she became accustomed to the swaying and jerking of the truck, and it did not take her long to learn that there was little danger of falling. No matter which way she was rocked she always came up against another horse.

Day turned to night, and still the big truck rumbled on. Some of the other horses were half asleep, but Flax couldn't get over her nervousness. Then at last, the deep throb of the engine died away and Flax went down a ramp with the others. Her feet on solid ground once more, she raised her head and sent out a long anxious whinny to the other wild horses. There was no reply.

The geldings moved about in the dark familiarly. Flax heard a sound of drinking and went toward it, coming to a long half-filled water trough. She lowered her muzzle thirstily but lifted it at once, for the water was disagreeably stale and warm. There was hay in a long manger along the fence, and Flax pushed in among the geldings to eat.

Morning revealed a strange country, flat and almost treeless, far different from the high basins and the brushy ridges that Flax had known. Again she sent out a call, keen and anxious, but even the geldings about her seemed not to hear it.

Outside the corrals there was a tall windmill, some low flat-roofed sheds, and a weathered bunkhouse. Beyond them, in a grove of tall trees, stood a large white house surrounded by a white picket fence. A big red bull ambled in to drink from an open trough.

Later in the morning a man and a woman came from the big house to the corrals. Flax knew the man. He was the one who had put the hot branding iron against her hip. "That's the flaxy I told you about," he said to the woman. "Isn't she a beauty?"

"Yes, she is," the woman replied. "She's the prettiest horse I ever saw."

◄•*Nine*•►

After several days in the corral, Flax was let out through a gate. Thinking she was free again, she started instinctively in the direction that led back to her old range. But before she had gone far, she found the way blocked by a high barbed-wire fence. Flax hated fences, especially this kind with the sharp points that pricked her skin.

No matter which direction she took she was eventually confronted by more barbed wire. Finally she moved along the fence looking for a gap, but there was no opening anywhere. She knew then that she was not free, but in a pasture like the small one at Middle Creek.

There were other horses in this pasture, and soon

Flax learned that they were mares, several with young colts. At once she felt a little better. The mares were more friendly than the saddle geldings had been, and in a way it was like being with a wild bunch, though there were no cold, clear waterholes or high ridges with cool breezes. Grass was plentiful, though, and when winter came, hay was brought to them daily in a small truck. It wasn't a bad existence, but Flax longed for the freedom of the river breaks. When spring came, with its new grasses and bright long days, she became still more restless and discontented.

One afternoon all the mares and colts were rounded up and driven into one of the corrals. Later, Gus Andrews and a short man with a weatherbeaten face came and looked over the fence. "There's the flaxy," Andrews said. "I want her broken in gently."

"Okay," the other answered.

"I mean *gently*," Gus Andrews repeated emphatically. "That's what I hired you for."

"Sure," the other man agreed. "I've broke a million of them. She'll purr like a kitten when I'm through."

"All right," Andrews said. Then, to two other men, he added, "Turn the rest of them out. Take them to Sagehen Flats."

Andrews and the horsebreaker left and the two men climbed the fence and dropped into the pen. They began maneuvering the mares around. Almost before she knew what was happening, Flax found herself separated from the others, alone in an adjoining corral. This did not worry her much, for the mares were still near and easily visible through the rails.

But soon the two men mounted horses, circled the mares, and drove them out through a gate into the open country. Flax became panicky when she realized that she was to be left behind. She nickered and cried and galloped back and forth along the high fence. She reared and tested the top rails with her strong chest. She wheeled about in small distraught circles, crying out her lonesomeness and sorrow. But her friends, the mares and colts with whom she had spent the long winter, kept going, driven by the two riders, without a single pause to answer or look back. Soon they would be out of sight.

To Flax, who had been with bunches most of her life, this was unbearable. She made a desperate effort to go over the fence. It was too high, but she did succeed in getting her front legs over the top rail. Hanging there, she sent out her wild cries to the others.

At this the horse trainer came running from one of the sheds and began lashing her across the head with a rope. He hit her again and again, viciously, before she could get free. Frightened, hurt, and confused, Flax retreated to the far side of the pen and became silent. The man gave her a sarcastic grin before he went back to the shed.

It was a long while before Flax recovered enough to look for the bunch again, and by then it was out of sight. She felt miserable and alone, and the welts on her face were painful. Men with ropes, she had learned, meant pain and torment.

When the horsebreaker came to the corral again, Flax retreated nervously. The man's lips twisted peevishly and he said, "Gentle, huh! Don't he think I know my business? The way to break a horse is to let it know who's boss."

He carried a heavy, hard-used saddle and, with a sudden frightening movement, threw it up on the top rail. Flax fled to a corner, whirling there to watch as the man climbed up and dropped inside the corral. He eyed her only briefly before shaking out a loop from a coiled rope.

As the man advanced Flax became more frightened.

She escaped from the corner by dashing along the fence. When the rope sailed forward and landed on her back, she kicked out instinctively with both hind feet.

"Yeah," the man growled. "Well, I'll take that out of you, old girl, and I won't be long about it." He yanked the rope back through the dust, recoiled it, and strode toward her again.

Flax was frantic. She knew this man would hit her with the rope. Trying to avoid him, she raced around the pen. The rope came toward her, its loop wide, skimming along the ground. An instant later it jerked tight around her forelegs, pulling them together. She leaped to get free, and the next thing she knew she was falling. The jar knocked the wind out of her lungs and before she had recovered the man seized her head, twisting her nose upward so she could not get to her feet. "How do you like forefootin'?" the rough voice said. "I didn't reckon you would. Now maybe you'll stand still to be caught."

He released her head then and stood back, watching as she got shakily to her feet. She trembled with fear and excitement while he coiled the rope back into his hand. Saying "Whoa" sternly, he started toward her. She knew what he meant, what he wanted, but she ran—she couldn't help it. And again the rope swirled about her legs, sending her into another hard fall.

"Sharp rope work, if I do say so myself," the man said in a pleased voice as he grabbed her head with rough hands. "You ought to know better," he went on harshly. "If you don't, you'll learn."

Flax fought until she was weak. When she stopped struggling the man released her, but, confused and afraid, she made no effort to get up. "Oh, no, you don't," the man cried angrily. "You don't sulk on me." He gave her a hard kick, and swung the doubled rope across her back.

Flax leaped up and ran across the corral to the far fence. She stood there trembling.

"All you have to do is like I tell you," the man said to her, grinning as he came forward. Flax made no move, afraid that her feet would be jerked from under her again. She had a terrifying feeling of helplessness.

The man put forth his hand and she let him touch her neck. "There! We'll get along all right. But don't you go runnin' from me anymore." He turned back to his saddle for the thick-nosed hackamore, a kind of bridle often used in training young horses.

Just then a door opened in one of the nearby

buildings and a man there called loudly to the horse-breaker.

"Okay. Okay, I'm comin'," the man in the corral replied. He walked to another section of the fence, made a quick movement, and a wide opening appeared. It was a gate, one that Flax had not known was there. The man went through it, closed it behind him and strode on, through the building door and out of sight.

Flax stared at the fence. There was a gate, a way to freedom—if she could only get through it. Raising her head she looked for the band of mares; it was out of sight but she was certain she could soon catch up.

She crossed the corral and nudged the strong, thick boards with her muzzle. They gave a little, enough to offer her an instant of hope before they became hard and solid again. Another nudge produced the same results. It was very puzzling. She had seen an opening there and the man had gone through it.

Then, with no help from Flax, the boards before her swung back and an opening appeared. Though narrower than before, it was wide enough for Flax. Eagerly she leaped for it, but suddenly there was the man, his hand raised in an angry gesture.

Flax was desperate. She had glimpsed a way out

and had no intention of stopping. At the last instant the man jumped back, trying to get out of her way. Flax felt her shoulder hit him, and out of the corner of her eye saw him spin away and fall. She was in the open, free after all the long months. She kept running, barely conscious of the outburst of bitter shouting behind her.

◄• Ten •►

Flax was outside the fences at last, with room to run and fling back her heels and feel the wind lift her silky mane. She was elated. Best of all, she was beyond the reach of the man and his rope. At a long gallop she headed toward the low rise over which the other mares had disappeared.

When she reached the crest she found that the wide shallow valley beyond was empty of horses. Only a few white-faced cows grazed there.

Flax hurried on, galloping anxiously and turning her head from side to side. Not so much as a trace of dust was visible. She continued steadily for several miles before she became discouraged and slowed to a walk. The mares were gone, but she would not go back to the corrals. She knew what she should do, and her keen sense of direction told her the way to go. Striking out at a long purposeful walk, she traveled till sundown, then grazed a while before going to sleep for the night.

In the morning she started again, and a short time later heard the steady sound of an automobile engine. Soon a truck came into sight, raising a trail of dust. Flax stopped to watch it, remembering the truck that had brought hay to the pasture during the winter. Would hay be thrown from this one too?

Close to the spot where Flax waited, the truck braked to a sudden halt. The cab doors flew open and two men leaped out and ran to the rear of the truck. Two horses suddenly appeared—horses with men on their backs. And the men had ropes in their hands. That was all Flax needed to see; she whirled and raced away.

For a time the two horses gained ground, but despite the long miles she had traveled the day before, Flax found a reserve of speed. Low to the ground, she ran with all her fine strength. The front rider whipped and spurred his mount, and for a time the horse held his own. Then the space between them gradually widened and Flax knew she wouldn't be caught. Not long after that the two horsemen pulled up and turned back to the truck.

Flax watched them load the horses and drive away. When the truck was out of sight she went on, walking to recover from the hard running.

Two hours later she saw another ribbon of dust and the truck came into view once more. This time Flax didn't wait. She immediately increased her gait to a trot. When she looked back, the two horsemen were following her at a speed that only matched her own. Flax felt quite safe and saw no reason to tire herself more with a faster gait.

The riders made no attempt to catch up, but twice one of them rode wide to one side, forcing Flax to change her direction. She felt that this was not, at the time, very important and it saved hard running. Her foremost thought was to keep a safe distance between herself and the men.

In midafternoon she saw a long line of regularly spaced upright posts directly in front of her. Between those posts, she had learned, would be tight strands of sharp biting wire. She tried to turn aside, but suddenly the manner of the horsemen changed. They whipped forward and pressed her closely on either flank, forcing her toward the fence. She ran, trying now to outdistance them, and learned with some surprise that she couldn't. Their horses were fresher, and had an advantage in position. She kept running, panic growing inside her.

The pound of the horses behind was steady and strong. Flax knew what she had to do and put on a desperate burst of speed. There were only a few feet to spare but she managed to outdistance the horse on her left enough to turn along the fence. Once more the way in front was open.

The men behind kept coming and, helped now by the fence, they could maintain an even closer control over Flax. Wearily, she settled into a long trot and hoped that her pursuers would soon tire. They didn't, but carefully kept their positions, one on the side opposite the fence and the other directly behind. Flax remained alert, watching for any rush that might come from the rear.

Then, suddenly, the way in front was no longer open. A cross fence came from the left and intersected the first. Flax knew only too well what this meant—a corner!

Alarmed, she slowed her gait. In a corner she knew

she wouldn't have any chance to escape. She swung about, head high, dark eyes bright and anxious. The men checked their horses, watched her closely, and called to each other in pleased congratulatory tones. One was the horsebreaker of whom Flax was so desperately afraid.

Letting their puffing horses regain wind for a moment, the two men rode forward, ropes hanging in long loops from their hands. What they intended to do was perfectly clear to Flax. She wheeled to face the fence corner again. The long strands with their sharp cutting barbs could be painful, she knew, but she feared even more the men themselves, with their harsh hands and swishing ropes.

She knew that she had to escape, and there was only one way—over the fence. In her days with the wild bunch she had jumped often over bushes and rocks. A wire fence, her caution told her, was different, and more dangerous. Nevertheless, she measured the distance and picked up speed.

Suddenly realizing what she was going to do, the two men tried to distract her with loud shouts and cries. But she didn't falter, didn't seem even to hear them. Long strides carried her forward and her strong hind legs lifted her into a soaring arc. She cleared the top wire with an inch to spare.

Now the voices behind were filled with bitter frustration and the riders jerked their mounts to disappointed halts.

Flax knew she had won, that she was still free, but she ran on in the growing dusk until she was certain she was no longer being followed. Then she slowed to a weary walk. The long fence still hemmed her in on the right side, but shortly after dark she came to an open gate. She turned through it, toward the distant ridges.

◄•*Eleven*•►

*F*lax paused in the darkness to eat some grass she had found in a creek bottom. She grazed until satisfied, then lay down to sleep. When morning came she began feeding, but before the sun was very high the restless urge sent her on again.

Red cows with white faces grazed on the good grass in small scattered groups. Many of them had young calves, red and white like themselves, with a freshly scrubbed look. Once Flax saw a band of antelope, dark-headed and thick-bodied on pipestem legs, bars of white across their tawny throats. With curious eyes, they watched Flax's progress across a wide hogback, but she returned only a disinterested glance.

The next day she climbed a long gentle rise and saw

horses in the valley beyond. Her neigh was answered and she was soon galloping down the slope. Some of the strange horses started forward to meet her, but were stopped by a barbed-wire fence. There were no men in sight so Flax introduced herself, sniffing over the top strand of the wire.

The grass on Flax's side was sparse but she nibbled away, comforted by the nearness of other horses. She kept an eye out for an opening in the fence so she could join them.

The day passed without disturbance and a new one dawned. Flax spent most of her time eating. At mid-morning, her flanks filled out, she settled down close to the fence for a nap in the warm sun.

Near noon the bunch stirred. Flax opened her eyes to find two horses approaching—with riders on their backs. She got to her feet hurriedly.

The band, led by a big-footed roan, began to run. On her side of the fence Flax ran with them, though she knew now the riders weren't after her.

The men came on swiftly, driving the bunch toward the center of the pasture. The roan leader took the direction readily, and the others streamed after her, leaving a cloud of dust.

Flax at once slowed to a halt and, aware she would be left, gave a keen and anxious neigh. One rider turned his horse toward her. "Get out of here, you Lazy-Y!" he shouted. "Get on back to your own grass! What're you doin' way over here anyhow?"

Flax didn't want to be separated from the other horses. She bounced up and down on her front feet, trying to get up the courage to jump the fence.

"No, you don't!" the man cried. "Don't you break that fence down!" He spurred his horse forward and whirled a rope about his head.

Flax wheeled away. It was the same old story of men and ropes.

"Go on, get out of here!" The man swung the rope again. "Get on back to Lazy-Y. Gus Andrews is a fool to let a mare like you get this far from home."

Flax struck out through the brush. Not even to stay with her new friends would she face a rope again. The man rode after the mares, and soon all of them were out of sight.

Flax traveled the rest of the day and spent the night alone in the brush. The next morning, after brow–sing on tender twig-tips, she started off again, as sure as ever of her direction. That afternoon she began climbing, as the folds in the land became steeper and higher. Ahead lay the rugged outlines of the high mesa, a view that stirred happy memories in her. Despite her weary legs she lengthened her stride and, shortly before dusk, spotted grazing horses.

Scattered across the lower end of a small grassy basin, they were a welcome sight. Flax sent out an eager, confident neigh. These were free horses, her own kind. She knew she was back where she belonged.

The horses raised their heads and almost immediately sounded a strong challenge. This, too, was familiar and welcome. One horse left the others and came galloping across the bottom, his stride proud and prancing. Flax halted as they drew near each other. Quickly the stallion recognized her as a mare and extended his nose for the customary sniff. Flax stood quietly, then flattened her ears slightly, telling him to mind his own business. Calmly she moved past him to sniff and mingle with the others.

The band Flax had joined was a small one of five mares, two yearling fillies, and three suckling colts. The lead mare, when Flax came close, flattened her ears hard against her neck, but Flax understood perfectly and kept her distance. All she asked was to stay with the bunch, and before many days had passed, Flax was completely accepted. The contentment she felt was increased when she mated with the bright bay stallion.

When spring came Flax's belly was big and she no longer had impulses to run and play. Instead she grazed lazily and spent long hours drowsing in the shade with half-closed eyes. One afternoon instinct caused her to leave the other horses and go a short distance up the creek to a grassy opening in the brush. Here, not long after dusk, her first foal was born. Lean and wobbly, it was a little horse colt, red like its father.

The next day Flax rejoined the band. None of the other horses seemed to find anything very unusual about the small, long-legged creature that bobbed at her flank. Nevertheless, Flax proudly made it known that the colt was hers. She rushed at any who came too near and warned them to keep their distance. Even the old lead mare, understanding this mother instinct, ungrudgingly gave ground. In a few days the edge of her anxiety had worn off, but the constant presence of a small, ever hungry muzzle kept Flax fully aware of her new responsibility.

◄• *Twelve* •►

As the long bright days of summer continued, the peace and quiet of the uplands was broken several times by the appearance of men. With the new colt at her side, Flax was even more alert and cautious, and quicker to run. The colt now could keep up easily and often in flight the two were close behind the lead mare.

When the nights became cold again the mare took them back to the river breaks. Young and strong, Flax wintered in good condition, as did her colt. The larger he grew the longer were the trips he made away from her side and the less he depended on her. She, in turn, ceased to worry so much about him, for there was little more that she could do.

Spring came again and the trek back to summer

range began. They moved slowly, for some of the old mares were weakened and the short new grass had little strength. But, day by day, the hours of sunlight increased and rich shades of green spread over the slopes. Food became plentiful, and they followed the trails and paths of years past.

Flax, knowing it was time to wean her son, nipped his round rump whenever he tried to suck. Well able to live on grass, he finally gave milk up, although he continued to stay near his mother.

One day Flax, again heavy with foal, turned aside into a small clump of junipers and stood patiently waiting, with lowered head. The yearling, who sought her out as usual before dark, was surprised the next morning by the presence of a new small creature with a wet, inquisitive nose and big, wondering eyes. At first he was afraid of it and later somewhat jealous, but his mother quickly put him in his place and made it known that the newborn had first priority at her side. This time Flax had given birth to a filly, with a yellow cast to her baby hair. When the three of them went back to the band, the youngest tripped along sturdily on her long, knobby legs. With two offspring at her heels, Flax was now definitely established as a matron with family concerns.

Days and weeks went by, the filly's small form filling out in a manner that would bring joy to any mother. Her older brother reconciled himself to her, and their life together was well ordered and quite complete.

Then the men came again on their strong-legged horses. Flax sighted them first in the distance. She called the filly to her and waited impatiently for the old mare to give the warning.

The runners tried to drive the band into an old trap. The lead mare did not recognize their strategy soon enough, but Flax, at the last instant, split off. Followed by her frightened colts, she evaded the mouth of the canyon just ahead. Her light brown shape flashed up through the boulders and she ran on until the billowing dust, the shouts and cries were well behind her. Less experienced mares might have turned back to search for the others, but Flax wanted to get well away from the mounted men. Besides, with the two frightened colts at her heels, she was not alone.

The leader now by force of circumstances, Flax kept to rough, broken country where they grazed on the sparse grass that grew about the bases of the rocks. She avoided the large waterholes, knowing them to be places of danger. Days passed and nothing more was seen of the mounted men or the other range horses.

One day in their wanderings they came to a place where certain things stirred vague memories in Flax— a weathered cliff, a rock-strewn slope, a little valley below with a thick fringe of green willows along the trickle of a creek. She stood for some time, looking downward, then turned along the broken edge of the rimrock. In the afternoon she came to a well-defined trail and took it without hesitation.

Below the dark, ragged cliffs was a grassy meadow, and here the hungry colts began to snatch at clumps of food. Flax showed no interest in the grass and, nickering softly, continued down over the slope. Later, when she saw a cabin and the whitened outlines of corrals near the willows, she increased her gait to an eager trot.

A horse in one of the corrals whinnied a greeting. Flax replied and began to gallop. The horse in the pen was Duke. Flax rubbed noses with him over the fence, and looked about for two other horses that she vaguely remembered, but they were nowhere to be seen. The suckling colt took advantage of the pause to sidle to her flank, but Flax was too excited to wait for her to nurse.

She went to the saddle shed and poked around with her inquisitive nose. A rope, a leather halter, and some other pieces of equipment lay there, but the racks themselves were bare of saddles and blankets.

The door to the cabin was closed, but Flax, catching the string in her teeth, lifted the latch in an easy, familiar movement. As the door swung open she paused. In the dark interior nothing stirred. There was the table, the bench, and the old stove. There was the wooden bunk, with its rumpled blankets and a man-smell that stirred half-forgotten but pleasant recollections.

Then Flax saw a battered old metal bucket. Eagerly she pushed her muzzle into it, seeking food remembered as the most tasteful and satisfying she had ever eaten. Nothing was there, and Flax struck the bucket impatiently with her forefoot. The two colts waiting nervously at the doorway jumped backward in fright.

Flax joined them outside but could see nothing startling. A little later she led the way to the corrals and stopped to rub noses over the fence with the gelding. Reassured, the filly nudged her flank and Flax waited patiently while it sucked.

Tufts of grass on the slope beckoned to the hungry yearling and he went there to graze. The filly took the last of the milk and then ambled up to join him. Flax made for the haystack, which was now well rounded, but the fence around it had been repaired, and the barbs were sharp. Finally she, too, moved up the slope to the grass.

The three of them had been grazing about an hour when a soft snort of alarm from Flax brought both colts to her side. A horse and rider had appeared down the valley and the rider raised his hand to shade his eyes and peer at them. After the pause the horse increased its gait to a trot. The yearling at Flax's heels fidgeted nervously and looked expectantly at his mother, for this was the familiar pattern of the horse runners.

Vague inner stirrings held Flax to the spot. The rider's horse was now pointed directly at them. Yet Flax was strangely free of fear. Something about this horse and rider was different. She could feel it.

Then a packhorse behind the other broke into a trot, too, and this was more than the wild yearling could stand. Uttering a shrill warning, he whirled and galloped away. The filly followed him a short distance and then looked back at her mother uncertainly. For a moment Flax was held by impulses too deeply buried to take definite shape. But her natural instinct and caution had their way. Remembering the shouting, rope-swinging riders who had pounded hard at their heels, she wheeled and raced up the slope, the two colts at her heels. High on the rim, her creamy white tail and mane lifted by the breeze, she halted for a long last look backward.

◄• *Thirteen* •►

*F*lax watched a lone horse wander along a hogback and sent up a curious whinny. Immediately the stranger replied. She was an old mare, thin and limping on badly worn feet. Flax went a short distance to meet her, and they rubbed noses. The mare, who had dropped out of a bunch a few days earlier during some hard running, was lonely and wanted company.

Three days later a branded gelding and a young mare joined the group. After the preliminary sniffing, Flax accepted them readily.

The strongest and most vigilant, Flax was the undisputed leader of the little group, a duty she had become accustomed to while wandering with her two colts. She accepted the increased responsibility confidently, and the others followed without question or reluctance. For weeks they roamed the rough, broken country, grazing in the pockets and bottoms and drinking at the waterholes Flax knew so well.

Then one afternoon Flax discovered a band larger than her own. From the rear a dark stallion appeared, and came toward them at a high, truculent trot, his threatening cry loud in the still air. Behind Flax, her little band stood silent. She waited calmly, well understanding that she had nothing to fear. His threats were meant for another stallion, not for mares.

The newcomer was black, with a white spot on his forehead. As he drew nearer and no opponent advanced to meet him, his truculence subsided. After a quick inspection, he came to the gelding and bared his teeth. The gelding shied away quickly. The stallion nickered with satisfaction, pleased at having found new mares for his bunch without having to fight for them. Then, as is the way with stallions, he lost interest in them and started grazing.

Flax soon became aware of a thick-necked pinto with heavy shoulders, who moved among the others with a dominant step. Flax kept a wary eye on her, knowing instinctively that this was her rival. The law of survival was quietly at work.

They did not meet in bold and open challenge as

stallions would have. Instead, they studiously ignored each other until their grazing paths converged. Flax held her ground. The pinto backed her ears and gave her tail a warning swish. Flax's filly, knowing that trouble was coming, backed out of the way.

Flax accepted the challenge immediately, flattening her own ears. The pinto whirled on her heavy feet and charged, her mouth open. They came together, their teeth tearing and slashing at each other's neck and shoulders. They were so intent on punishing each other that they did not seem to feel the punishment each in turn was receiving.

Flax was grimly earnest and had an advantage in height and reach. She caught a fold of the pinto's flesh near the top of the neck and wrenched it savagely, tearing hide and muscle. When this hold slipped she brought her open mouth down along the white shoulder and her upper teeth left a long, red gash there.

The pinto was wily and experienced. She wheeled about, presented her thick rump, and began to kick with all her might. A stallion, usually a cooler and more calculating fighter, might have retreated from this barrage to replan his strategy. This was not the way of a vengeful, determined mare, however, and Flax, too, lashed out viciously.

The two kicked with more savageness than aim. Some blows were deflected. But many landed, the hard hoofs ripping hide and thudding against bone. Relentless and unflinching, Flax took blow after blow, while her own heels flew like triphammers. Head low, she grunted and squealed her anger.

At last the pinto, bleeding and limping, gave ground. Flax pursued, her heels catching her rival on the thigh, and again in the flank. She cried out her jealousy and fierce determination. Acknowledging defeat, the pinto broke and fled.

Flax was satisfied. Her own sides were heaving from the angry effort and she had her own painful scrapes and bruises, but that was of little importance. She had proved herself and was the indisputable boss of the bunch, with first choice of the best grasses and first drink at the waterholes. Where she went they would follow, without hesitation, confident of her courage and judgment.

So the two bands became one, with the tall mare whose mane and tail were creamy white as the leader. And one day the black stallion rushed with open jaws at the big yearling. Bewildered and overwhelmed, the young horse turned and fled. The stallion pursued him to the fringes of the band, and stood guard there to prevent his return. The yearling stayed within view for several days before finally going to join other young outcasts like himself, who would roam together until they were mature enough to have bands of their own. Nature saw to it that on the open ranges there was never any lack of stallions.

Flax took no notice of her son's banishment, for he had reached the age of independence and his battles were no longer her concern.

◄• *Fourteen* •►

Several days later a horseman appeared on the crest of a nearby ridge. He halted to watch the wild bunch, paying no attention to the indignant stallion's challenging cries. Flax, as usual, was alert, ready to run, but the rider remained motionless. The indifference of the other horse drove the stallion to such bitter outbursts that finally Flax, though not really alarmed, took the band down the valley. She did not go far, however, before halting.

The strange horse was making its way slowly down the slope.

Once again the black stallion pawed the earth and made the walls echo with his threats. The man ignored him. After a time he cupped his hands to his mouth and a call came faintly through the clear air. "Flax . . . little girl . . . Flaxy."

The words and the voice caused a strangely pleasant response in the tall mare. But she was still wary. She remembered the ropes, choking and merciless about her neck. She remembered the feeling of frantic helplessness when her front feet were suddenly jerked from beneath her. Tossing her head, she turned and led the band away at a long trot.

Their next regular feeding place was in a high basin and Flax did not stop until she reached it. The horseman no longer in sight, they grazed through the evening hours, then climbed a rocky slope and settled down for the night.

The next morning Flax took them back to the basin, where they grazed in the warming sunlight. Some time had passed when Flax flung up her head and snorted in alarm at a strange sight. It was a man without a horse, a man walking upright on his own hind legs.

The black stallion took a few uncertain steps forward, and the mares eddied about restlessly. The man slowly descended the slope. When he saw Flax, motionless at the bottom, he stopped. Flax remained still, watching. Unusual as this was, she had no feeling of danger. For a long time the man and the flaxy mare studied each other.

Reassured by Flax's calmness, the other horses scattered and began to graze. The stallion joined them, his small flurry of excitement past. There seemed little to fear from a creature who moved so slowly and in plain view. Now the man changed in height. He sat down and, while Flax watched, lay back against the rocks, so that he could hardly be seen.

At first this made Flax suspicious. But time went on and nothing happened. Her curiosity increased and she took a few steps forward. Immediately the filly missed her and hurried to her side. Flax carefully picked her way between the low bushes until she was in the creek bottom. Cautiously she moved across the valley floor.

"Flax . . . little girl. . . ." The sound was clear, soft, and reassuring.

Nevertheless, Flax came to an abrupt halt. It was the distrusted voice of a man. She was filled with a new confusion before her sharpened instinct took command, and she turned and galloped up the valley.

Yet as she ran Flax knew she was not frightened. The call had not been the kind of excited, triumphant cry or angry shout that she had heard before. She looked back, but the man was nowhere in sight.

She felt no fear when the same figure appeared again in the afternoon. The man was standing perfectly still, and held a bulky object at his side. The other horses noticed him, too, and stopped grazing. But the man did not stir and in a short time all the horses except Flax returned to the grass.

"Flax . . . Flaxy," the voice came from the distance.

The horses, hearing the noise, waited for Flax to lead them away, but she made no move. There was something assuring and gentle in the sound she had just heard.

The man sat down, and in this position he looked quite harmless. Filled with conflicting impulses, Flax took a few more steps toward him. The other horses watched her, but only the little filly followed.

"Come on, Flax!" the voice said encouragingly.

A long minute passed. Still cautious, the mare crossed the bottom and climbed until she was only twenty yards from him. There she paused again, her big eyes bright and curious, but still uncertain.

"Flaxy, don't you know me? Don't you remember me, little girl?"

Slowly Jim Thorne stood up, holding out the bulky object. It made a creaky noise, and at once recollection flooded Flax's mind. It was the battered old bucket from which she had drunk the warm cow's milk and eaten her first grain. She could never forget the creaky sound she had hurried to eagerly so many times.

Her caution vanished. Uttering a happy little nicker, she thrust her nose deep into the bucket. And, just as she had known it would be, the delicious food she remembered was there—mashed oats softened with milk.

"I've come for you, little girl," Jim Thorne said in the low, soft voice out of Flax's happy past. "I would have been here sooner—I knew it was you when I saw you at the shack—but I had to wait until a fellow came up from the ranch to look after the cattle. And it took a while to find you. . . ."

He rubbed her neck, and he scratched gently behind her ears.

"You've grown into a big fine mare." He slipped his arm around her neck and gave it a squeeze. "You've got a dandy little filly, too. She looks just like you." Then he noticed the brand on her hip and paused, frowning. "How'd you get that? Somebody caught you. . . . Well, it makes no difference." But it was several seconds before the pucker left his brow.

Flax nudged her old friend with pleased recognition and wasn't much concerned when she discovered that a halter had been slipped about her head. It reminded her of the carefree days at the old shack and didn't bite or choke as the long ropes did.

"Don't you worry," Jim Thorne told her earnestly. "I'll take care of you, and you'll have plenty to eat. You won't have to winter on snowballs anymore."

Flax nickered and the filly, which had been hanging back, stepped forward gingerly.

"We're not going to leave your colt," Jim said in his reassuring voice. "No, sir, we wouldn't do that. She'll be a part of our horse ranch, too. It's way back in the hills, where we won't be bothered. We'll raise some dandy horses there."

Flax searched for the last of the grain in the bucket.

"There's more at the shack," Jim said, "and it's time we headed home."

Only when Jim started to lead her away did Flax feel uneasy. The filly followed, puzzled and reluctant, a few steps behind. It was the bunch that Flax didn't want to leave. They were her whole life now. Why didn't they come on? She threw up her head and nick-ered, telling them to follow, that it was all right. Two of the mares started in her direction but halted, afraid of the man. Flax nickered loudly and anxiously, and tugged at the halter rope.

Jim shook his head in sympathy. "Don't worry about them," he told her. "They'll be all right. You'll have another bunch to lead. Come on. I promise it."

Flax tossed her head in protest. The two mares stood a minute longer, undecided, then made their way back to the others. Flax felt suddenly alone and rejected, and her voice became mournful. Jim gave a gentle tug at the rope and she moved after him, as she had in the days long ago when he was in the process of halter-breaking her. As they climbed, she paused once more to make sure that the little filly was following.

Jim patted her on the neck. "There'll be more horses," he said. "You won't be lonesome. I'll get a good stallion, too. It'll be just like it is now, only you'll have a place of your own."

◄•*Fifteen*•►

A strong welcoming neigh rang out in the night, as Flax and Jim, who was riding Duke, reached the cabin at Middle Creek.

"Easy, girl, easy," Jim said, as Flax pushed forward against her halter. "It's just old Nip and Crimpy. You'll see 'em soon enough." He stood in his stirrups and announced in a jubilant voice, "Simmer down, you two. It's just me and Flax and her filly. I'm bringing them home."

He stripped off his saddle and led the horses into the corral. Flax did not hesitate, but her filly hung back at the entrance. Jim left the corral gate open and took Duke and Flax on to the water trough. By the time they finished drinking the filly had come inside.

He threw hay into the manger, and Flax lined up beside Duke to eat. The filly crowded close to her to try the strange food. It was not long before Flax heard the welcome squeak of the bucket bail, as Jim brought her some grain and milk. She went to him.

"Sure," Jim said, keenly pleased. "You're home now, little girl. You're back where you belong."

But when he had left, Flax found that she didn't like being confined in the pen, not even with the filly and old Duke there. Most of the night she walked the fences, whinnied repeatedly, and listened for the wild bunch.

When Jim came to the corrals the next morning, another man was with him. He climbed the fence for a careful look at Flax. "You sure this is her?" he asked presently.

"Dead sure," Jim replied. "She came to that old bucket. She wouldn't have done that if she wasn't Flax."

"What about that Lazy-Y brand?" the other man asked. "How do you account for that?"

Thorne shook his head. "I can't, Sid. But I know she's Flax."

"One of Gus Andrews' runners must have caught

her," Sid said. "It could cause you trouble, boy."

Jim knew the range laws about branded and unbranded horses, and a troubled line appeared between his eyes. "Maybe . . . and maybe not. There's a lot of brands running back there, some of them so old they must be forgotten. You know how some fellows are . . . slap a brand on everything they can catch. Why didn't they take her out, if they wanted her?"

"She could have been just a colt. Maybe they figured on comin' back later."

"Maybe," Jim admitted reluctantly. "But it was a long time back. Anyway, I've got her now." He held out his hand. "Thanks for comin' out and spellin' me, Sid. When you get back to the ranch, tell Ben Drake I won't be working for him this fall."

Sid's eyes widened thoughtfully. "Why? You got something else in mind, boy?"

Jim nodded. "I aim to strike out on my own. Old homestead back in the Breaks belongs to my pop. Good horse country. I figure to raise some real good ones."

The other man said, "I had that dream once. Good luck." He glanced again at Flax and added, "Better keep that mare close. She's got a plumb wild look in her eye." Then he caught a horse out of another corral, saddled, and rode away toward Seven-K headquarters.

The wildness was there all right. Jim had seen it, and if he needed any more evidence it was in Flax's discontented manner, the way she stood for long moments with her head up, gazing at the distant slopes. Jim did not dare let her out, not even to the small pasture. He knew that wire fences wouldn't hold her, and he was not at all sure he would be able to catch her again, even with the old bucket. The love of freedom was in her blood.

He tried to cheer her up by petting and talking to her in the afternoons when he had finished looking after the cattle. "Just you wait," he told her. "You'll have a bunch to boss again, and plenty of country to run in. And I'll build you a three-sided shed to break the wind on cold nights."

The little filly, at the far side of the pen, was still afraid of him. Looking at her, Jim shook his head. "You're a wild little thing, too," he said. "When I get time I'll start workin' to gentle you down. You'll be a fine big mare like your mammy."

* * *

One afternoon while Jim was gone, two men came riding up the valley. When there was no answer at the cabin, they dismounted and led their horses to the corrals, where they unsaddled in a leisurely way.

As they put the horses into an empty pen, and threw them forkfuls of hay, Flax nickered. One of the men glanced at her. A second later he was climbing the corral fence. "Hey, Gus," he called excitedly to his companion. "Come here!"

"What is it, Marty?"

"Take a look at this mare. See if you see what I do."

Gus Andrews stepped up on a fence rail. His eyes opened wide. "That's the *flaxy mare!*" he exclaimed. "That's her sure as shootin'." He was highly pleased.

"It sure is, brand an' all," Marty agreed. "What a piece of luck! I never figgered to find her in a corral. It'll save us a lot of lookin' . . . an' runnin', too."

"Yes, sir! How do you figure a punk cowhand caught her?" Gus asked. "Some of the hardest runners in the business have been after her and missed."

"I don't know, but that's her all right. Good thing we put that brand on her." Then Marty added, "He may not be too happy about givin' her up."

Gus nodded. "I'll slip him a few dollars. That should

take care of it. He probably doesn't know what he's got anyway. That's a plumb nice filly with her, too."

They returned to the shack and soon thin, gray smoke rose from the stovepipe on the roof.

The sun was low in the west when Jim rode down the slope on Duke. At once his sharp eyes took in the two strange horses and the smoke, but he rode to the saddle shed, where he stepped down and started stripping out the cinch latigo.

The two newcomers walked toward him, their boot heels clicking on the hard-packed earth. Jim let down his saddle and waited, his gray eyes sober and alert.

"Hello," the first man said in a friendly voice. "I'm Gus Andrews. This is Marty Hart. He works for me. I guess you're Jimmy Thorne." He extended his hand and Jim took it, but almost as though he were in a trance.

"We stopped by Seven-K," Andrews went on. "Left our truck there. We're on our way back to the Breaks . . . or were."

Jim nodded, his eyes lowered. "Soon as I turn this horse loose and feed him, I'll rustle up some supper."

"No hurry," Gus told him. "We've got a fire goin' already. Figured you'd be ridin' in pretty soon." He and Marty moved to Flax's pen.

Jim turned Duke in with the other geldings and went to the stack for a forkful of hay for them. "Fed your horses yet?" he asked Andrews, though he knew they had.

"Yes, all taken care of," Gus answered. "Say, I'd like to talk to you about this flaxy mare."

Jim did not look around. "What about her?"

"Pretty nice animal," Gus said. "I believe she belongs to me." His voice was calm and easy.

Jim wheeled about then, shaking his head. "I don't figure it that way."

"Why not? She's wearin' my brand."

"That's right," Marty Hart declared. "It's plain as day."

"I caught her," Jim said defiantly. "She was runnin' loose. I caught her out of a wild bunch."

Andrews nodded. "Sure. She got away from me. We've had an eye out for her for more than two years now."

"We knew she was up in this country somewhere," Marty put in. "Had a couple of reports on a good flaxy mare that sounded like her. Greg Tolman gave the band a hard run not too long ago. Caught some, but she was too smart for him. He says she's the wildest he ever took after. Lots of speed, too. You must've got her in a trap somehow."

Jim knew the man's curiosity was nagging him and resented that he should have even that much interest in the mare.

"Of course, I'll be glad to give you something for your trouble, Thorne," Andrews said willingly. "How about a ten-dollar bill? That ought to be fair enough, oughtn't it?"

Jim shook his head firmly, refusing the offer.

"All right, fifteen then. That ought to square it. After all, she's mine anyway."

The young rider raised his head. "I had her before you ever did," he told them. "I found her up there, just a couple of days old. Her mammy had just been killed by a cougar, and she never would have made it. I brought her in, on my saddle horse. I spoon-fed her. She was so weak and thin I didn't see how she could make it . . . but she did." He paused, half choked up. "I fed her and took care of her, and she followed me around all the time like a dog. . . ."

"If you had her," Gus interrupted, as though he doubted it, "what'd you let her go for?"

"I didn't," Jim replied. "Horse fell with me, over on

the big flat. Busted leg. I just made it to Seven-K, out of my head. They took me to the hospital, and when I finally got back she was gone . . . scared off, I guess. She didn't know anyone except me. I figured something had happened . . . she wasn't but about five or six months old. But I had her. I had her first and the way I look at it that makes her mine."

Gus Andrews shrugged unfeelingly. "That's a good story. How come you didn't put a brand on her?"

"I figured to, when she got bigger. I aimed to do it."

"You know the law on range horses. We caught her fair and square—back in the Breaks."

"That's right," Marty declared. "There wasn't no mark on her. She was as slick as the day she was dropped. I'll swear to that."

Jim's shoulders sagged. "I'll buy her from you," he told Gus. "How much do you want? I've got some money saved."

Andrews considered Jim's offer for a moment. Then he shook his head. "I don't want your money, boy. I want the mare. Anyway, I don't think you've got enough money."

"Seven-K owes me wages." Jim was insistent. "How much do you want? Put a price on her, mister."

124

"The filly's mine, too," Gus went on in a businesslike way. "I guess you know the law on that—as long as they're suckin' they belong to the mother's brand, even if they're not marked."

"I'll buy them both," Jim offered quickly.

"Shucks, boy, what's the matter with you! She's just a horse, and I'm offerin' you good money."

"Maybe to you," Jim replied in his slow drawl, "but not to me. She's a little filly that wouldn't quit—that had too much courage to give up and die. Name a price, mister."

"No!" the man cried exasperatedly. "I want to keep her! Can't you understand that?" He paused, got better control of his temper and went on, "Anyway, you don't need mares like that. What a fellow like you needs is good tough geldings that can take this rough country, boy."

An angry light flared in Jim's eyes. In the pen, a few feet away, Flax and her filly noisily munched their hay. Jim's voice hardened. "You claim this Lazy-Y brand, but you haven't shown me any proof—not yet."

"Now, boy, that's stupid and you know it." Gus Andrews' face flushed with annoyance. "Nobody carries proof he owns a brand around with him. Everybody knows I own Lazy-Y. I've owned it for years. You can check at the state brand office in Boise."

"I don't know it," Jim answered stubbornly. "And nobody is takin' that mare away from here till I do."

"I'm not so sure about that," Gus retorted, his voice harsh.

"I am," Jim declared with flat finality.

"You mean you're askin' me to go all the way back to Seven-K and drive to Boise just to get a certificate of brand ownership?"

"I guess I am," Jim replied evenly. "Anybody who takes that mare has got to prove he owns the brand she's wearin' first. That's the law the way I heard it."

"But I'll prove it. I'll leave the proof with Ben Drake. I'm not tryin' to run a windy on you, fellow."

"I said *first*," Jim declared. "Ben Drake don't own her."

Andrews scowled. "Why, you young whipper-snapper! I'll get something else, too. I'll bring the sheriff back with me. I'll show you who Gus Andrews is in this country." He paused to let his words sink in, but Jim's face betrayed no emotion. "The sheriff will have a few questions to ask, such as how you happen to have a horse penned up that don't belong to you. That won't look so good, my young buckeroo. You still want me to go?"

Jim shrugged. "It's up to you."

"Ben's a friend of mine," Gus continued. "After I talk to him, I wouldn't be surprised if you lost your job."

Jim remained silent.

"And don't think you can get away with anything while I'm gone, either," Gus concluded. "Marty'll be right here to keep an eye on you till I get back. Marty—you know what I mean?" His voice was sharp.

"Sure do, Gus. I'll be right here on the job. You don't need to worry none a-tall."

◄•Sixteen•►

Gus Andrews left Middle Creek the next morning, after telling Marty Hart again just what he wanted. "Don't let that mare out of your sight while I'm gone, day or night. Hear? If she's not here when I get back. . . ." He didn't finish, but Marty's thick-skinned face turned slightly paler with the recognition of a grim threat, meant for him as well as for Jim Thorne. Gus Andrews was determined to have the mare.

Sober-faced but without comment, Jim saddled Duke and headed up the rimrock trail. Looking back from a turn, he saw Marty perched atop the corral fence.

It seemed that Andrews' hired man had hardly

changed his position when, in late afternoon, Jim came down the trail, his shoulders hunched and his suntanned brow furrowed with the troubled thinking he had been doing all day.

It hadn't been an entirely easy day for Marty Hart either and, as Jim reined up, he said, "Hi, boy," in a friendlier tone, as if to show that he personally had no hard feelings.

But Jim's nod was brief and unbending. He quickly unsaddled, took Duke to the corral, and came back leading Nip.

Marty frowned. "What now? Let's get some supper. Ain't you had enough for one day?"

"Guess I'll ride to Seven-K," was Jim's short answer.

"Why? What for?" Marty was immediately suspicious.

"Talk to Ben Drake."

"Won't do you no good, boy. There ain't nothin' Ben Drake can do. The law is the law. You know that, don't you?"

Jim's jaw muscles merely hardened and, wrapping Nip's rein about a rail, he went into the old saddle shed.

Marty eyed the saddle on the ground, got down from the fence, and followed the young rider. "What're you doin' with that halter?" he demanded when he saw what was in Jim's hands.

"Fixin' it," came the answer, flat and somewhat defiant.

"What for? You won't be needin' no halter." Marty's voice was brusque.

"I might," Jim replied levelly but, after a final test of the strong rope with his hands, he hung the halter on a peg. Outside, he saddled Nip and stepped up. "Guess you can take care of things while I'm gone," he said.

A small twinkle was in Marty's eyes when he answered, "I aim to. Stay as long as you want. It won't make no difference."

"It might," Jim replied, his jaws firming up again.

Marty shook his head. "No, it won't, friend. I'm goin' to spend the night right here, at this gate, an' I reckon I ought to tell you that I'm spooky about noises in the dark. I'm plumb liable to take a shot at 'em."

Jim's lips twisted sarcastically. "Why don't you take her into the shack with you?" he suggested. "The door's got a good latch."

The grin returned to Marty's eyes. "That's a idea," he said. "Don't you want something to eat? No use goin' off half cocked."

Jim shook his head. "It's a long ride," he said, and reined away.

Marty's smile turned to a knowing smirk. He muttered to himself, "Longer'n you got any idea of makin', bucko. You ain't foolin' nobody."

Flax came to the fence, put her head over the top rail and nickered, but Jim Thorne didn't look back.

Marty ate a cold supper in the shack, leaving the door open so he could watch Flax's pen. "He won't try it till after dark, likely 'long toward mornin'," he told himself. "A couple of bullets zingin' over his head ought to change his mind."

When the sun had set, Marty seated himself on the ground by the corral gate, his back solidly against the rough boards. For two hours he listened intently to the sounds of the night. On the slope above the cabin a coyote sent up its lonesome cry and somewhere down the valley a cow squeezed out a low deep-chested bellow. "Could be him down there," Marty murmured as he heard the disturbed cow.

In the corral there was a fresh stirring of hoofs and Marty sat up attentively. The mare's dark nose pointed to the south slopes. Stiff from the cold, Marty got awkwardly to his feet. He had figured that Jim might come

131

from that direction. After looking intently for a time, he yelled, "Hey, Thorne, why don't you come on in? What's the use playin' games? It's bedtime."

He began to pace back and forth, flinging his arms about, unused to the rapid temperature changes of the high country. "The heck with this," he muttered, and went to the shed for a saddle blanket to drape around his shoulders. Behind him Flax's hoofs thudded softly as she paced the beaten dust along the fence. "What's the matter with you? Can't you settle down?" He looked up at the fence, assuring himself that it was too high for her to jump.

With his back again firmly against the strong gate, Marty pulled a dark revolver from his belt. "Thorne don't know I got this." He grinned to himself as he laid the gun in his lap.

Gradually he became still. His wide-brimmed hat tipped slowly forward. A snore rattled uncomfortably from his cramped throat, and he awoke with a start, grabbing the gun butt. The coyote was howling again . . . but there was no other sound in the blackness.

Throwing the old ragged blanket back, Marty clambered to his feet and strode to the saddle shed again. "No sense in freezin' out here," he grumbled. When he came back he was carrying the strong leather halter with lead rope attached. He climbed the fence and dropped inside the dark corral. "Whoa! Stand still!" he ordered roughly.

The mare retreated to the far side, then came about, facing him. Marty put on the halter, buckled it, and made a second check of its snugness. He wasn't taking any chances.

Flax followed him to the gate, but refused to go on until the filly came too. On the way to the cabin she paused, raised her head, and looked intently into the night. Marty looked and listened, but could hear nothing.

He remembered then that he had left the corral gate open, and grinned to himself. Let Jim Thorne, slipping around in the darkness, figure that out, if he could. Of course, Jim wouldn't dream that Marty had been silly enough to take the mare into the shack. Even if he did, Jim wouldn't know what to do about it. He wouldn't dare come prowling around there. Anyway, Marty would be waiting. He might just put a bullet through the door, up high so nobody'd get hurt. All he wanted was to get warm; Gus Andrews couldn't expect him to stay out there and freeze to death.

At the door he wondered whether the mare would enter the cabin willingly, but she did and, once inside, seemed concerned only about whether her filly would come too. The filly nickered a bit anxiously, then crowded in against her mother's flank.

"That's fine," Marty approved. "Now I don't have to freeze. Thorne can ram around in the night all he wants to. But he'd better not come around here."

He closed the door and made sure that the strong wooden latch was securely down in its notch. His fingers touching the string brought another thought to his mind, and he chuckled happily as he pulled the leather thong back through its worn hole. The outside knot was too big for the opening but he snapped it off with a quick jerk. "Now let Jim Thorne or anyone else open it," he said to himself, gleefully sure that he didn't have anything to worry about.

Wrapping one of the warm blankets about his shoulders, Marty sat down on the bunk in the dark, listening to the regular breathing of the mare and filly. They seemed as relieved as he was to be in out of the cold. Outside everything was quiet, except for the coyotes, and that bold serenading convinced him that no one was moving around nearby. It wouldn't matter, he thought, if he stretched out for a minute or two. . . .

The mare liked being in the old shack better than in the corral, but the man snoring there on the bunk was not the man she knew and trusted. Quietly she moved over the dirt floor, dragging the halter rope. Going around the filly, she nudged the latch up and opened the door as easily and noiselessly as Jim Thorne himself could have done.

Outside she waited until the filly joined her. After a farewell glance toward the corrals, where the other horses were penned, she struck out up the slope, heading for the trail that led through the rimrocks. The filly trotted close behind her, obviously pleased at being in the open again.

Clearing the beaten trail through the rimrocks, Flax turned her nose to the familiar high ridges and settled into a long, steady stride. The rope dragging under her feet was a nuisance until she learned that she could avoid stepping on it most of the time by carrying her head to one side. Still, it irked her freedom-loving spirit.

When day came Flax and her filly were miles from Middle Creek. They left the trail for grass and had not been grazing long before a firm solid pull on her nose stopped Flax. It was the halter rope again. Flax shifted her feet and pushed her nose outward, but the rope didn't give. The knot at the end of it was caught in a narrow crack between two half-buried boulders. Flax turned and twisted, got her legs tangled up and almost fell down, but it did no good. One thing she had never learned to handle was a rope, perhaps because she hated them so much. The filly left her, to nibble at nearby grass.

Discouraged and weary, Flax was resting in the morning sunshine when she saw a rider trotting up the back trail toward her. The filly took quick alarm and ran a short distance, and Flax began to pull and jerk at the rope again.

"Easy, girl, easy. Don't get all tangled up," Jim Thorne said as he halted his horse and dismounted.

At once Flax became calmer and waited for him to approach. The horse was Nip, and Flax gave him a soft little whinny of welcome.

"I didn't go to the ranch, old girl." Jim admitted. "I knew all along it wouldn't do any good, but I figured Marty would freeze out before morning. At daylight, when I saw the gate open and him saddlin' like he'd gone loco, I was pretty sure you'd be up here somewhere, with that big knot I tied in the end of the halter rope caught on something. It didn't take long to find your tracks."

He became thoughtfully silent and looked back down the slope.

"I had an idea that maybe I could hide you out, you and the filly," Jim went on presently. "But it won't work. Marty's already on our trail. Maybe it's best . . . for you anyway. You'd never be happy in a pen."

He lifted his hand to her halter and stroked her sleek neck a minute before working the thick leather strap out of the buckle. Still holding the strap about her neck, he turned for a second look down the slope. A rider, bent forward to see the tracks he followed, was winding his way up through the rocks.

"Yeah, it's best," Jim repeated slowly. Then he released the strap, swung the halter and rope in a high swishing circle that ended across Flax's rump, the first blow he had ever struck her. "Remember that," he cried harshly. "Git, and don't come back! Take that little thing with you!"

More astonished than hurt, Flax raced away across the flat, the filly running easily at her side.

Jim watched them until they were out of sight, then

turned and remounted his horse. "Now let's see Gus Andrews get you, if he can . . . or anybody else," he said, and rode down the trail to meet Marty Hart, whistling happily to himself.

A boy takes a chance on a race horse and learns
to believe in himself in Glenn Balch's
thrill-a-minute adventure

The Midnight Colt

From *The Midnight Colt*

◄• Chapter 7 •►

Going to ride that new horse of yours today, Ben?" It was after a breakfast of sausage and eggs and hotcakes, and all of them, with the exception of Milly, were headed for the barns and corrals. Ben and Dixie wore their familiar ranch clothes, boots and Levis, light shirts, and felt hats. Pop, Steve, and Gaucho had their specific jobs to do, but Ben and Dixie, in view of their recent return from Boise, had no particular assignments. It was Steve who asked the question.

Ride his new horse? But of course. Ben had been eagerly looking forward to getting Peck away from the race stables, the track and fences, the traffic and paved streets. He held back, however, and said, "I think I will.

139

I'd like to give him a little work this morning."

"I got your Inky horse up," Vince said. The little black roping horse, named by Dixie in one of her fanciful moods, was a joy to ride and do work on, as well as Ben's favorite of the ranch horses.

"Dixie can ride him," Ben said.

"I'll take Listo, if it's all right with Gaucho," Dixie said.

"*Por cierto*," Gaucho said. "You will like her, Miss Dixie," he went on, though Dixie had ridden the mare dozens of times and loved her almost as much as Gaucho himself did. Listo, trained and gentled by Gaucho, was truly a horse in a thousand.

"The corrals are full of horses," Vince said, adding pointedly, "good ones."

Ben grinned and said, "There's a good one in the stalls too, Pop."

Gaucho went on around the big barn to the round breaking corral beyond, where he kept and worked his current bunch of colts. Ben, Dixie, Steve, and Vince went to the tack room, got their saddles and bridles, then went to catch their selected horses. Ben found Peck as he had left him the night before, tied securely in one of the barn stalls.

"Good morning, Peck," he said, going in and slipping the bridle on. "You're on a ranch now—a cow ranch, and they don't think much of race horses. There's not a race track in fifty miles. I hope you behave yourself."

He saddled in the stall and pulled the cinch up snug, noticing that Peck's high back carried the stock saddle nicely. He led the horse along the aisle and through the big doorway, and moved him about in a small circle. Vince and Steve and Dixie were coming from the corrals with their horses, Steve already up on Kelly, his leggy gray.

Steve reined up and asked Ben, "Can that horse really travel? I'd like to see him run."

"Don't you worry about that," Dixie said spiritedly.

"How about giving him a spin?" Steve said to Ben, with a daring grin. "I'll match Kelly here against him." Steve was pretty proud of his gray, which was itself half thoroughbred.

Ben shook his head. "Not today. Peck's not ready yet."

"Are you afraid he'll get beat?" Steve asked, still grinning.

"No," Ben said. "He'll outrun Kelly."

"All right," Steve said, "let's see if he can. I'll bet I can beat you to the corner of the upper field." This was a distance of something over a quarter of a mile, which most ranchers considered long enough for a race.

Ben shook his head. He had not mounted yet but was holding Peck's reins. The brown horse had his head up and was showing some signs of nervousness.

"He's a race horse," Dixie told Steve sharply. "Give him time to get acquainted, can't you? You don't handle hot-blooded race horses like you do old cow horses."

"That's right," Ben said, agreeing thankfully.

Vince Darby turned to his own horse and mounted. "It's time we were moving, Steve; we've got work to do," he said. "You two coming with us?" he went on to Ben and Dixie.

"Yes, sir, I am," Dixie said.

Ben wanted to go with them also, but he hesitated, not being quite sure of Peck.

"What're you waiting for?" Steve said to him. "Want me to top him off for you?"

"No," Ben said. "I can ride him."

"Ben has ridden him a lot," Dixie said, from her saddle.

"Okay, let's see it," Steve challenged. "Or let me do it."

This put Ben in a predicament. It had been his intention to warm Peck slowly and mount him in private, not that he was afraid but because that fitted his plans for training the horse. Steve's good-natured taunts, however, caused his indignation to rise. He suddenly turned to Peck, gathered the reins, and stepped into the saddle.

It may have been the strange surroundings or it may have been the other horses, especially the impatience of Steve's mettlesome gray, but something set Peck off. He grabbed the bit in his teeth and bolted. He gave two long neck-stretching lunges, fighting for rein length.

"Yippee!" Steve shouted gleefully and jumped his own horse forward. Having horses buck with him happened so often that he considered this a joke.

"Hold him, Ben!" Vince shouted, concern in his voice. He didn't share Steve's lightheartedness.

But Ben couldn't hold him. Those two desperate lunges had yanked the reins through Ben's fingers and Peck had his head. He knew he was in a race and the fact that the rider on his back was trying to control him meant nothing. Riders always tried to control him, but if he slowed down he got the stick across his tender back. He flashed through the ranch yard, up past the house, and out on the twin-rutted lane that followed the fence around the upper field. He had his nose stretched out and was running with such blind desperation that Ben realized the best thing he could do was try to guide him, to keep him from either hitting the fence or going into the stony ground beside the lane.

"Easy, Peck. Easy," Ben said firmly.

But Peck was beyond reasoning. He was running a race, and through months and months of training it had been drilled into him to win—to win regardless. Later, when he was tiring, would come the bat, as always in the past.

"Yippee!" Steve shouted from behind. "Stay with him, Ben."

Steve was pushing his gray, trying to catch Peck and help Ben, if Ben needed it. And that was just the thing Ben did not want. The pound of hoofs and those of Vince's horse farther back were the things that made it impossible for him to stop Peck. He turned his head and shouted to Steve to pull up, but the wind whipped the words out of his mouth and Steve did not understand. Steve leaned over his gray's neck and urged him to his best speed.

"Pull up! Get back!" Ben shouted.

Back behind Vince, Dixie was coming up fast on the Gaucho's good mare, and she was yelling at them too. Ben knew she was trying to get them halted, but he couldn't watch any longer. He had to turn back to the front, for they were rapidly approaching the corner, where the lane turned at almost a right angle around the fence's big solid corner-post. Peck couldn't make that turn, not at the speed they were traveling. And beyond it, on ahead, there was a stony rising slope, dangerous ground for a bolting race horse.

Ben knew an instant of deep regret of the pride that had caused him to mount the horse, but that was no help now. Now he had either to slow Peck enough to make the abrupt turn or take to the rough ground beyond, an area which he knew well from previous riding. There was a gully out there, not very wide or deep, one which would never cause a good ranch horse an instant's pause, but for Peck, trained on the smooth tracks, it could mean a dangerous fall. Thoughts poured swiftly through Ben's mind. What could he do? Somehow he had to get Peck around that turn—or take his chances with the rocks and gully. If Steve would only pull up, if those hoofs weren't pounding so close behind—

Ben had a sudden thought. Could he do it? With his eye he measured the distance to the corner. It was short, too short—but maybe there was time. He turned for a quick glance behind and saw that Dixie was up with Vince, and Vince, in response to her cries, was slowing down. Steve, however, was still coming, intent on catching Peck and helping Ben.

"Pull up!" Ben shouted, then dared not wait to see whether Steve understood before whirling back to the front.

Then Ben did a strange thing. He loosened the reins, leaned forward above Peck's neck, and shouted in his ears. A new surge of strength flowed through the brown horse and his belly leveled closer to the ground. It seemed to Ben that he had sprouted wings; he fairly flew, his feet seeming not to touch the ground at all. The pound of the gray's hoofs was rapidly left behind. In spite of the circumstances, Ben could not help but thrill to that burst of speed. Still, he could permit it for only an instant. The big corner-post was looming up rapidly. Ben listened to the hoof beats behind, and was pleased that they were much fainter. Then he knew he couldn't wait any longer. He gathered the reins and came back on them with a firm balanced pressure.

"Whoa, Peck. Whoa, boy," he said, keeping his voice even and unexcited. "Whoa, boy. Whoa. Easy, Peck."

The horse's head came up, not much but some.

"Whoa, Peck. Easy, fellow."

Ben put more pressure on the reins. He did not dare saw at them or pull the horse's head to one side, as he might have with a stubborn ranch horse, for such action might cause Peck to fall, and above all things he wanted to keep him on his feet, both for Peck's sake and his own.

"Whoa, boy. Easy."

They were swiftly coming to the corner. Little Inky Inkpot, Ben's trained roping horse, could have stopped dead still in half the distance, but not Peck. Peck had been trained to run, not to stop. He needed room for the springs of his magnificent muscles to run down after the power was turned off.

"Whoa, Peck. Whoa."

The horse's head came up a bit more and Ben felt a shortening of his stride.

"Whoa, Peck. Easy, boy."

Ben put more pressure on the reins, leaned against them. The speed beneath him lessened. Peck's head came up and Ben hoped his eyes were open, hoped he was watching his footing, for now they were at the corner. Now the big post was just beyond Peck's nose. Now was the time.

"Whoa, Peck." Ben hauled back sharply on the reins. This would have set Inky on his haunches, but Peck was trying to stop on his front feet. Now it had to be. Ben laid the right rein heavily against Peck's neck, gripped tightly with his knees and threw his weight to the left, threw it hard and without reservation. Either Peck would come around, or Ben would go off. Ben's shift of weight upset the horse's balance; his inside shoulder dropped low—too low. That was a tense instant for Ben. He hauled back on the reins, to give the horse something to pull against with his head. Peck recovered, and then they were around the corner.

"Good boy, Peck. Good boy," Ben said with deep-felt relief. He loosened the reins enough to steady the horse's stride. Then he became aware that the pounding hoofs were no longer behind him. "Whoa. Whoa, boy," he said, and pulled firmly on the reins.

Peck's head came up. He whistled through his nostrils as he turned his head for a glance behind. There were no pursuing horses back there. The race was over.

Gradually along the grassy lane beside the field fence the big brown horse coasted to a halt.

"Whoa, Peck. Good boy," Ben said and dismounted. And when he was on the ground he found his knees were trembling so badly he could hardly stand.

"Well," said Steve, grinning broadly as he came up. "I'll have to admit he can run. But he got a head start."

Ben felt too weak to argue. Vince and Dixie arrived. They gathered in a little panting group where Ben stood beside the sweat-drenched Peck. Steve was not excited but Vince's face was still a shade grayer than its usual ruddy tan.

"What's the matter with that horse, Ben?" Vince demanded. "Is he loco?"

"No, sir," Ben said. "He just gets excited."

"Well, that's the next thing to being loco, if you ask me," Vince said. "He's dangerous."

"He thought he was running a race," Ben said, "with Steve chasing him. You ought to know better than that, Steve."

"Shucks, I was just trying to help you," Steve said.

"Well," Dixie said, "you made it worse. You didn't have a chance to catch him anyway."

"What I'm concerned about is these crazy streaks,"

Vince said. "Somebody might get hurt."

"No, I won't, Pop," Ben said earnestly. This was what he had been afraid of, and if his father should forbid him to ride the horse all his plans would be ruined. "Honest, he's not mean. He doesn't kick or strike or bite. He's as gentle as he can be. Isn't he, Dix? Dixie and I have been working him for a month in Boise."

"A month?" Vince said. "Well, it doesn't look to me like you've done much."

"Yes, sir, we have," Ben insisted. "He's better now, Pop. Isn't he, Dix? He's getting better. I can bring him out of it; I know I can."

"And what'll you have then?" Vince asked.

"He'll win races," Dixie said positively.

"What good will that do us?" Vince said. "We're not in the race horse business. They're no good for ranch work."

"I guess I'm in the business, in a way, Pop," Ben said. "I own him."

"We own him," Dixie said.

"That's another thing I can't understand; whatever made you buy him?" Vince said. "We've got the best horses in the country, right here on the ranch. What did you want with a race horse?"

"Well," Ben said, "I didn't—not exactly. But I saw him, and he wasn't being handled right. He's a good horse, but he didn't have a chance, not the way he was being handled. Somebody made a mistake with him."

"I'll say they did," Vince said. "I'd just as soon ride a loco burro."

"But I can bring him out of it, Pop," Ben said. "I know I can, if you'll just let me try."

"If you don't get a broken leg first," Vince said. "Is that the reason you bought him, just to see if you could bring him around?"

"No, sir, not exactly," Ben said, struggling with his explanation. "I like him, Pop. I just do. He's a mighty lot of horse. He's big and he's fast and he's honest."

"But," Vince said, "saying he is and saying you can, what'll you do with him? He'll be no earthly good to us here on the ranch. It looks to me like it'll all add up to a waste of time and feed."

"I'll sell him," Ben said seriously. "I figure to get my money back, and more too."

"We will," Dixie said. "We'll sell him."

"How much did he cost you?" Steve asked.

"Enough," Dixie said shortly.

"You're pretty young to start worrying about money, Ben," Vince said thoughtfully.

"I'm not worrying about it," Ben said. "But I thought if I—if we could make some, it would be all right. I know it takes a good bit of money to keep Dixie and me in school at Boise."

"I'll take care of that," Vince said. "I'll keep you in school."

"But what about the note?" Dixie said, her face a mask of perfect innocence.

Ben could have choked her and Vince Darby jumped as if he had been stung by a hornet. "Note?" he asked. "What note?"

"The one Ben and I signed to Uncle Wes, to get the money to buy Peck," Dixie said.

The look on Vince Darby's face was incredulous. "Do you mean, Ben," he said, "do you mean to tell me you borrowed money—borrowed money to buy that—that race horse?"

"Yes, sir," Ben had to say, though the words could barely squeak by the tight place in his throat.

Vince didn't speak for several seconds. "Well," he said. He turned and flicked his horse on the neck with the ends of his bridle reins. "Well—"

"Guess you are in the race horse business," Steve said with a grin. He wouldn't have been disturbed much if the top blew off of old Crystal Mountain.

"I can do it, Pop," Ben said desperately. "I can break this horse and pay Uncle Wes. I know I can, if you'll just give me a chance." He did his best to sound convincing.

Vince held a stirrup and put his foot in it. "It looks like you'll have to," he said slowly. He swung up. "You've made a deal, and it's up to you to keep it. I hope you can do it. But,"—he reined his horse back to add—"watch yourself with that horse. Don't take any fool chances."